Feminism, Defeated

Feminism, Defeated

KATE M. PHELAN

polity

Copyright © Kate M. Phelan, 2025.

The Author hereby asserts her moral right to be identified as author of the Work.

First published by Polity Press in 2025.

Polity Press
65 Bridge Street
Cambridge CB2 1UR, UK

Polity Press
111 River Street
Hoboken, NJ 07030, USA

All rights reserved. Except for the quotation of short passages for the purpose of criticism and review, no part of this publication may be reproduced, stored in a retrieval system or transmitted, in any form or by any means, electronic, mechanical, photocopying, recording or otherwise, without the prior permission of the publisher.

ISBN-13: 978-1-5095-6655-6 – hardback
ISBN-13: 978-1-5095-6656-3 – paperback

A catalogue record for this book is available from the British Library.

Library of Congress Control Number: 2024945652

Typeset in 11 on 14 pt Warnock Pro
by Cheshire Typesetting Ltd, Cuddington, Cheshire
Printed and bound by CPI Group (UK) Ltd, Croydon, CR0 4YY

The publisher has used its best endeavours to ensure that the URLs for external websites referred to in this book are correct and active at the time of going to press. However, the publisher has no responsibility for the websites and can make no guarantee that a site will remain live or that the content is or will remain appropriate.

Every effort has been made to trace all copyright holders, but if any have been overlooked the publisher will be pleased to include any necessary credits in any subsequent reprint or edition.

For further information on Polity, visit our website:
politybooks.com

For Caroline Norma and Holly-Lawford Smith

Contents

Acknowledgements ix

Introduction 1

1 The Sexual Becomes Political 5
2 The Poststructural Turn 29
3 In Search of a Poststructural Feminism 46
4 Feminism, Displaced 60
5 Lies, Betrayal, and Resistance 73
6 Feminism: Political, Not Metaphysical 88
7 The Loss of the Future 113
8 The Emergence of Gender-Critical Feminism 123
9 Choosing Women 145

Conclusion 179

Notes 183
Index 236

Acknowledgements

I am grateful to the following people: Christine Craik and Sonia Martin, who supported me in my hour of need; Angelika Papadopoulos, whose intellectual influence on me has been profound; Rob Watts, who encouraged me to think about the political; Elise Heslinga, a conversation with whom sparked this book; Anita Samardzija, Phoebe Hollins, Andrew Romanin, Emmet O'Dwyer, Will Tuckwell, and Sun Liu for their companionship; James, Sarah, and Chris Phelan, and Chris Lyne, for their love and loyalty; Mum and Dad, who nurtured my love of the life of the mind; finally, the two women for whom I have written this book: Caroline Norma and Holly Lawford-Smith. It is to Caroline that I owe my sense of feminism as a politics (and much else besides). And it is Holly who, in so many ways, made this book possible (and who suggested the title). *Feminism, Defeated* is, among other things, an attempt to express my gratitude to them.

You show me the poems of some woman
my age, or younger
translated from your language

Certain words occur: *enemy*, *oven*, *sorrow*
enough to let me know
she's a woman of my time

obsessed

with Love, our subject:
we've trained it like ivy to our walls
baked it like bread in our ovens
worn it like lead on our ankles
watched it through binoculars as if
it were a helicopter
bringing food to our famine
or the satellite
of a hostile power

I begin to see that woman
doing things: stirring rice
ironing a skirt
typing a manuscript till dawn

trying to make a call
from a phonebook

The phone rings unanswered
in a man's bedroom
she hears him telling someone else
Never mind. She'll get tired –
hears him telling her story to her sister

who becomes her enemy
and will in her own time
light her own way to sorrow

ignorant of the fact this way of grief
is shared, unnecessary
and political

Adrienne Rich, 'Translations'

Introduction

The depoliticization of feminism appears all but complete. To the trans-inclusionary declaration that 'trans women are women', the gender-critical feminist responds, 'woman is adult human female'. Implicit in the trans-inclusionary declaration is a conception of woman as a gendered being; explicit in the gender-critical response is a conception of woman as a sexed being. Gender is a social kind, sex a natural one. On neither view is 'woman' a saliently *political* category.

For a flickering moment, it was. From the late 1960s until the late 1980s, second-wave feminists theorised women as a class. 'The feminist *raison d'être*', Ti-Grace Atkinson wrote, is 'that women are a class, that this class is political in nature, and that this political class is oppressed'.[1] Feminism was then a political movement, a struggle of women against men for their freedom.

By the late 1990s, the emphasis on the political had been displaced by one on the social. Feminists no longer described women in crude Marxist language, as a class; now they described 'woman' in sophisticated poststructural language, as a term producing its referent, and therefore they referred to women as 'women' – a discursive and unstable construct.[2] At the same time, whether as a consequence or a cause of this shift I am not sure, feminism became a theoretical or philosophical movement, concerned more with 'woman' than women, more with deconstruction than liberation. Formerly the name of a politics, 'feminism' became the name of a philosophy, an epistemology, a method. This displacement of the political has gone unnoticed.

In *Politics and Vision*, Sheldon Wolin suggests that the ascendance of the social reduced the political to the status of a resultant of social factors, thereby effacing the distinctively political.[3] Before Wolin, Robert MacIver had lamented the conflation of the political with the social,[4] and so too had Martin Buber.[5] Nowhere is this conflation clearer than in the declaration with which Bertrand Russell opens his book *Power*: 'The fundamental concept in *social* science is Power, in the same sense in which Energy is the fundamental concept in physics.'[6] Buber considered Russell's declaration a typical example of the confusion between the political and the social.[7]

Perhaps, then, the displacement of the political in feminism has gone unnoticed because, the social having usurped the political, the emphasis on the social appears to incorporate an emphasis on the political. In fact it suppresses it.

'Political' and 'social' are notoriously elusive terms, and it is only once we see the difference between the two traditions of feminism that they shape – in the analysis, in the goal, in the lexicon – that we can appreciate the difference between the two. Nevertheless, we can preliminarily say that 'political' is associated with state, government, authority, public, law, rights, class, interests, enmity, conflict, struggle, revolution, liberation, utopianism, vision, while 'social' is associated with community, fellowship, conventions, norms, roles, education (in the sense of socialisation), artificial, science, and that 'political' is antithetical to what is private, personal, harmonious, while 'social' is antithetical to what is natural, uncultivated, individual. When 'social' displaces 'political', association displaces subordination, fellowship displaces domination, and horizontal structure displaces vertical structure.[8] *Hierarchy disappears from view.* This should be of concern to feminists.

'To articulate the past historically does not mean to recognize it "the way it really was" (Ranke).'[9] Rather, Walter Benjamin writes, '[i]t means to seize hold of a memory as it flashes up at a moment of danger'.[10] In a recently emerged strain of feminism, gender-critical, a memory of the second-wave conception of women as a class flashes up at a moment of danger. It flashes up in women's *indignation* at male people's claim to be women. Implicit in this indignation is class consciousness, an awareness that 'woman' names a category marked out by its femaleness for a life of sexual subjection to men, a life of harassment, rape, battery, prostitution. Holly Lawford-Smith therefore locates gender-critical feminism's roots in radical feminism, 'a theory by women, for women, and about women, *understood as a sex caste/class*'.[11]

But this memory is at risk of being extinguished by an emphasis on the biological. While Lawford-Smith says that gender-critical feminism shares with radical feminism a conception of women as a sex class, she places primary emphasis on 'sex' and secondary emphasis on 'class': 'In its insistence upon the importance of *sex*', she writes, 'gender-critical feminism is continuous with radical feminism'.[12] This emphasis reflects its historical moment: because the trans-inclusionary feminism to which gender-critical feminism reacts emphasises the socially constructed nature of women, and because it uses this emphasis to pursue acceptance of male people as women, gender-critical feminism emphasises the biological nature of women. With trans-inclusionary feminism emphasising the socially constructed nature of women and gender-critical feminism the biological, the debate becomes one over whether women are a social or a biological kind. This obscures a third possibility: women are a political kind.

This is a moment of danger. A trans-inclusionary victory will erase women as a class. But a gender-critical victory will, so long as this feminism emphasises the biological, replace the second-wave dream of freedom with safety. It will replace the abolition of sex class with a refuge in which one class – women – can shelter from the other – men.

In this book I seize hold of the memory of the second-wave conception of women as a class in order that gender-critical feminism might become a repoliticised feminism, a feminism that resumes the struggle for women's freedom.

1

The Sexual Becomes Political

I

A conception of women as socially constructed characterises contemporary feminist thought. The archetypal expression of this conception is Simone de Beauvoir's declaration: 'One is not born, but rather becomes, a woman.'[1]

Insofar as it opposes the patriarchal belief that women's natures render them fit only for a life of 'childcare, home care, and husband care',[2] and insofar as this belief plays a role in the origination and persistence of women's oppression, the idea that women are constructed undermines women's oppression. For example, Mary Wollstonecraft's claim that 'women ... are *rendered* weak and wretched by ... a false system of education'[3] and that the 'nature' invoked to deny women a proper education is in fact the consequence of that denial undermined the exclusion of women from education.

I think it is now worth asking: to what extent does a belief about women's natures continue to play a role in the persistence of women's oppression? In other words, is the historical context in which an emphasis on women's social constructedness was politically meaningful *our* context? I am not sure that it is. Due to the feminist movement, women in liberal democratic societies now formally enjoy the rights and freedoms of men. Their condition no longer remains in need of rationalisation. Their nature therefore need not be invoked as a rationale for anything. The current emphasis on women's social constructedness seems, then, somewhat anachronistic, an objection to a claim no longer made, 'a formula that ha[s] outlived itself',[4] a mark of stasis. Put baldly, the natural–social dichotomy now dominates feminist thought to no clear political avail.

Traced to Beauvoir, the current emphasis on the social is considered continuous with second-wave feminist thought. However, if one places contemporary feminist thought alongside second-wave feminist thought, this emphasis contrasts instead with one on the *political*.[5]

Contemporary feminists do not reject this emphasis. Rather, conflating the social with the political, they assume that their conception of women is continuous with that of the second wave. They assume, in other words, that in the shift from political to social nothing has been lost. In fact something has been lost. That something is feminism.

In this chapter I chart the emergence of feminism, a movement that sought the liberation of women *qua* women. I do so with the aim of recovering the second-wave conception of women as a political kind. By 'recover' I mean 'restore to memory what has been forgotten', but I also mean 'salvage from misunderstanding'. For if trans-inclusionary feminists have forgotten this conception, gender-critical feminists too quickly dismiss it, wary as they are of a conception that appears to elide the biological specificity of the class 'woman'.

II

In 1969, Kate Millett wrote: 'sex is a status category with political implications';[6] also in 1969, New York Radical Feminists wrote of 'the oppression of women as a fundamental political oppression wherein women are categorized as an inferior class based upon their sex';[7] in 1970, Shulamith Firestone wrote: 'Sex class is so deep as to be invisible';[8] in 1972, Adrienne Rich wrote: 'this way of grief / is shared, unnecessary / and political';[9] in 1973, Ti-Grace Atkinson wrote: 'Feminism is, of course, a political position. When the term is used in any pure sense, it refers to the view that women form a class and that this class is political in nature';[10] in 1981, Monique Wittig wrote: 'the categories "man" and "woman" . . . are political categories and not natural givens';[11] in 1987, Andrea Dworkin wrote: 'Feminism is a political practice of fighting male supremacy on behalf of women as a class';[12] and, in 1989, Catharine MacKinnon wrote: 'If one defines politics with Harold Lasswell . . . and with Robert Dahl . . . and with Kate Millett . . . the relation between women and men is political.'[13]

These feminists were responding to the failure, and then to the refusal, to consider sexual relations political, in every sense of the term – a refusal that persists. Millett begins her attempt to develop a theory of sexual politics by asking: 'Can the relationship between the sexes be viewed in a political light at all?'[14] It was not so much that the answer to this question had been assumed to be 'no', but rather that the possibility that sexual relations are political, and hence the very question, had been inconceivable. Inconceivable because sexual relations, relations between men *qua* men and women *qua* women, were – *are* – conceived of as paradigmatically non-political.[15] As natural, mutually beneficial, harmonious, erotic, proper to the bedroom expressions of one's innermost self, sexual relations stand in opposition to the political: they are natural, not artificial, harmonious, not antagonistic, private, not public, individual, not common. To claim that sexual relations are political is thus to claim that the paradigmatically non-political is political – indeed, not merely political but paradigmatically so. Millett continues: 'However muted its present appearance may be, sexual dominion obtains nevertheless as perhaps the most pervasive ideology of our culture and provides its *most fundamental concept of power*.'[16]

In claiming that sexual relations are *political*, second-wave feminists intended 'political' to be taken in the expansive sense that Millett assigned to it: 'power-structured relationships, arrangements whereby one group of persons is controlled by another'.[17] They meant that sexual relations were relations of *Herrschaft*, 'of dominance and subordinance'.[18] In claiming that *sexual* relations were political, they obviously intended to refer to relations between the sexes, between men *qua* men and women *qua* women. Perhaps less obviously, they also intended to cover, or at the very least implicated, the sense of 'erotic'.

It is in literary depictions of erotic relations that Millett observes the dominance and subordination that she takes to be characteristic of the relations between the sexes. Examples of the literary passages analysed by Millett include:

'Oh, oh! Don't. Please don't. It hurts!' she yelled.

'Shut up, you bitch you!' I said. 'It hurts does it? You wanted it, didn't you?' I held her tightly, raised myself a little higher to get it into the hilt, and pushed until I thought her womb would give way. Then I came – right into that snail-like mouth which was wide open. She went into a convulsion, delirious with joy and pain. Then her legs slid off my shoulders and fell to the floor with a thud. She lay there like a dead one, completely fucked out.[19]

Their lovemaking is fantastic for a time:

He must subdue her, absorb her, rip her apart and consume her ... And for a half year, almost a year, they have love passages of intense fury, enraged and powerful, which leave him sobbing from exhaustion and frustration . . .

Do you love me, are you mine, love me.

Yes yes.

I'll take you apart, I'll eat you, oh, I'll make you mine . . . you bitch.[20]

She mentioned in her roundabout way that she didn't want any of that business. 'You don't feel in the mood for it, I suppose', says he, and then he adds: 'that's fine because now I'm going to warm you up a bit'. With that he up and ties her to the bedstead, gags her, and then goes for the razor strop. On the way to the bathroom, he grabs a bottle of mustard from the kitchen. He comes back with the razor strop and he belts the piss out of her. And after that he rubs mustard into the raw welts. 'That ought to keep you warm for tonight,' he says. And so saying he makes her bend over and spread her legs apart. 'Now', he says, 'I'm going to pay you as usual,' and taking a bill out of his pocket he crumples it up and shoves it up her quim.[21]

Millett thus, perhaps inadvertently, identifies the sexual in both of its senses – male–female and erotic – as political, and relatedly so. She suggests that the relations between men *qua* men and women *qua* women are essentially erotic and that erotic relations are essentially relations of mastery and subjection. She thereby 'resolves the linguistic duality in the meaning of the term *sex* itself':[22] in having *sex*, a male person masters a female person, consummating a relation of mastery and subjection, thus confirming his membership of the male *sex class* and her membership of the female *sex class*.

One finds suggestions about the political nature of sexuality scattered throughout second-wave writing. Beauvoir observes that '[m]ales' erotic vocabulary is inspired by military vocabulary: the lover has the ardour of a soldier, his sexual organ stiffens like a bow, when he ejaculates, he "discharges", it is a machine gun, a cannon; he speaks of attack, assault, of victory',[23] and, quoting Benda, '[t]he generative act, consisting in the occupation of one being by another, imposes, on the one hand, the idea of a conqueror, on the other of something conquered. Thus when they refer to their most civilised love relationships, they talk of conquest, attack, assault, siege and defence, defeat, and capitulation, clearly copying the idea of love from that of war.'[24] Atkinson refers to sexual intercourse as a 'political institution'[25] and writes: '"Sex" is based on the differences between the sexes. Sexual intercourse is the interrelation between these two classes, and sexual intercourse, unsurprisingly, is not in the interests of women.'[26] Adrienne Rich writes of 'the law of male sex-right to women',[27] a term – 'male sex-right' – that beautifully synthesises the two aspects of the right: a right *of* the sex class of men, and a right *to* having sex with women. Dworkin describes the meaning of intercourse in a man-made world: 'The normal fuck by a normal man is taken to be an act of invasion and ownership undertaken in a mode of predation: colonializing, forceful (manly) or nearly violent; the sexual act that by its nature makes her his.'[28]

But if sexual relations were political, why were they and how did they become so? In other words, what account of sexual dominion did feminists provide?

III

Strongly influenced by Marxism – impressed by it as an account of power relations but dissatisfied with it as a theory of women's oppression (Marxism, like liberalism, had proven incapable of recognising sexual relations as political)[29] – second-wave feminists developed their claim that sexual relations are political as a claim that they are *class* relations.[30]

In adopting the Marxist term 'class', feminists disclosed two particular features of the relations between men and women:

interdependence and antagonism. In Marxism, 'class' refers to a group of people with a particular relationship with the means of production. Under capitalism, two classes exist: the capitalist class, which is the group of people who own the means of production, and the proletariat, which is the group of people who own only their labour power. The relationship of each class with the means of production is necessarily a relationship between the two classes – those who own the means of production must employ those who own only their labour power,[31] and those who own only their labour power must seek employment by those who own the means of production. What it is to be a member of a class is thus what it is to stand in a particular relation to a member of the other class. In the case of a member of the capitalist class, this relation is one of mastery, and in the case of a member of the proletariat, it is one of subjection. In sum, class has two salient general features: interdependence and antagonism. Each class is constituted by its relation to the other and each class opposes the other. In Marx's description of the history of class struggle, these features are especially clear:

> The history of all hitherto existing society is the history of class struggles. Freeman and slave, patrician and plebeian, lord and serf, guild-master and journeyman, in a word, oppressor and oppressed, stood in constant opposition to one another, carried on an uninterrupted, now hidden, now open fight, a fight that each time ended, either in a revolutionary reconstitution of society at large, or in the common ruin of the contending classes.[32]

Freeman and slave, patrician and plebeian, lord and serf, guild master and journeyman, oppressor and oppressed are all pairs of interdependent and antagonistic identities, pairs each of which exists in contradistinction to the other and each of whose interests oppose the other's.

In applying the term 'class' to sex, feminists reconceived the sexes. Under capitalism, to repeat, what it is to be a member of the capitalist class is what it is to stand in a relation of mastery to a member of the proletariat, and what it is to be a member of the proletariat is what it is to stand in a relation of subjection to a member of the capitalist class. So, under male dominance, what it is to be a member of the male sex is what it is to stand in a relation of mastery to a member of the female sex, and what it is to be a member of the female sex is what it is to stand in a relation of subjection to a member of the male sex. Sex is a political category. As Carole Pateman writes, '[s]exual difference is political difference; sexual difference is the difference between freedom and subjection'.[33]

In reality, second-wave feminists proposed two distinct accounts of sex class. On the first, developed by Firestone, sex causes sex class. In *Socialism: Utopian and Scientific*, Engels writes: 'Its [socialism's] task was no longer to manufacture a system of society as perfect as possible, but to examine the historico-economic succession of events from which these classes and their antagonism had of necessity sprung, and to discover in the economic conditions thus created the means of ending the conflict.'[34] Admiring this account of history, but hoping to end instead the conflict between sex classes, Firestone set out to 'develop a materialist view of history based on sex itself'.[35] The resulting view is this. The female reproductive role – carrying, bearing, and rearing children – renders women, for the period in which they perform this role, dependent upon men for physical survival, thus producing a power imbalance between men and women. This power imbalance becomes political – sex becomes sex class – when we acquire the technological means to liberate women from their reproductive role, yet men refuse to make use of these means, preferring their tyranny. Just as the proletariat must seize the means of production in order to liberate itself, so women must seize the means of reproduction in order to liberate themselves.[36]

As an attempt at Marxist method, this is a dismal failure. Marx and Engels insisted upon a dialectical approach to history. In contrast to a metaphysical approach, which comprehends an object in isolation, in repose, in its death, and thus as either one half of an antithesis – cause – or the other – effect, a dialectical approach comprehends an object in its connection to the whole, in motion, in its life, and thus as being one half of an antithesis – the cause – at one stage in a process and the other half – the effect – at another stage.[37] Taking a dialectical approach, Marx and Engels theorise class as both effect and cause of work. Through work, those who own the means of production become the capitalist class and those who own only their labour power become the proletarian class. Once those who own the means of production become the capitalist class, they must employ those who own only their labour power, and once those who own only their labour power become the proletarian class, they must seek employment by those who own the means of production, class thereby setting work in motion. Firestone, however, theorises sex class as given, as existing outside process and in itself. From MacKinnon's perspective, Firestone mistakes the effect of sexuality – sex class – for an eternal category – sex.

Indeed, consider the two 'fundamental – if not immutable – facts'[38] from which Firestone concludes that 'sex class sprang directly from a biological reality':[39]

> The *biological family* – the basic reproductive unit of male/ female/infant, in whatever form of social organisation – is characterized by these fundamental – if not immutable – facts:
>
> 1. That women throughout history before the advent of birth control were at the continual mercy of their biology – menstruation, menopause, and 'female ills', constant painful childbirth, wetnursing and care of infants, all of which made them dependent on males (whether brother,

father, husband, lover, or clan, government, community-at-large) for physical survival.
2. That human infants take an even longer time to grow up than animals, and thus are helpless and, for some short period at least, dependent on adults for physical survival.[40]

At best, these facts show only that, while women carry, bear, and rear children, they are dependent upon men. First, dependence on men does not entail subordination to men. It becomes subordination only if men exploit it. Firestone simply assumes that they do: 'Nature produced the fundamental inequality – half the human race must bear and rear the children of all of them – *which was later consolidated, institutionalized, in the interests of men.*'[41] Indeed, she takes it to be self-evident that men exploit women's dependence and that this dependence is therefore vulnerability – so much so that she does not even explain why or how men exploit women's dependence. Second, on Firestone's own account, men are dependent on women for the reproduction of the species. Why do women not exploit this dependence by threatening to harm the foetus or neglect the infant, either before men exploit their dependence or in resistance to this exploitation? On close examination, the world that Firestone describes – a world in which women are dependent on men while men are independent, men are self-interested while women place their children's interest above their own, men are exploitative while women are not, women passively accept their mistreatment, female dependence is female vulnerability, female biology is a curse, and sexual relations are antagonistic – is *our* world, a world at a particular historical moment, projected back into the state of nature, a world that simply *is*. Notice that we can say this without refuting (or affirming) women's reproductive role or even their temporary dependence.

On the second account, developed by MacKinnon, the relationship between sex and sex class is one of historical accident. Also inspired by Marxism, MacKinnon writes:

> Marxist theory argues that society is fundamentally constructed of the relations people form as they do and make things needed to survive humanly. Work is the social process of shaping and transforming the material and social worlds, creating people as social beings as they create value. It is that activity by which people become who they are. Class is its structure, production its consequence, capital its congealed form, and control its issue.
>
> Implicit in feminist theory is a parallel argument: the molding, direction, and expression of sexuality organizes society into two sexes: women and men. This division underlies the totality of social relations. Sexuality is the social process through which social relations of gender are created, organized, expressed, and directed, creating the social beings we know as women and men, as their relations create society. As work is to marxism, sexuality to feminism is socially constructed yet constructing, universal as activity yet historically specific, jointly comprised of matter and mind. As the organized expropriation of the work of some for the benefit of others defines a class, workers, the organized expropriation of the sexuality of some for the use of others defines the sex, woman. Heterosexuality is its social structure, desire its internal dynamic, gender and family its congealed forms, sex roles its qualities generalized to social persona, reproduction a consequence, and control its issue.[42]

Just as, through work – the process in which material need is fulfilled and created anew – those who own the means of production become the capitalist class and those who own only their labour power become the proletarian class, so, too, through sexuality – the process in which sexual desire is fulfilled and created anew – the members of the male sex, whose sexual desire is fulfilled and renewed as one whose object is dominance, become the members of a sex class and the members of the female sex, whose sexual desire is fulfilled and renewed as one whose object is subordination, become the members of another sex class. On this view, sexuality transforms sex into sex class.

MacKinnon writes her account of the construction of sex class in the present tense. This gives the impression of a process ever recurring, of sexuality ever organising the sexes into sex classes. While the process repeats itself, each repetition strengthens a relationship between sex and sex class, and finally qualitatively transforms the original condition of the sexes. As more and more members of the male sex and more and more members of the female sex engage again and again in sexuality, the male sex and the female sex become established as classes. Maleness and femaleness acquire political significance. From that moment on, a member of a sex is *by birth* a member of a class.

IV

As is perhaps obvious, it is the account of sex class developed by MacKinnon that I wish to recover. On the one hand, this account has been rejected by poststructural feminists, who consider it yet another 'quasi metanarrative',[43] and on the other it is met with suspicion by gender-critical feminists, who worry that it makes the sex of this class disappear. I now want to defend this account, particularly against the latter suspicion (I will address the former in good time).

On MacKinnon's view, I have suggested, sexuality organises the sexes into sex classes. This suggestion is misleading. For in fact MacKinnon says that 'the molding, direction, and expression of sexuality organizes society into two *sexes*: women and men'.[44] What does she mean? With this locution, she assigns to sex in feminism the place of class in Marxism: as work organises people into *classes*, sexuality organises people into *sexes*. She thereby politicises sex. Had she written that sexuality organises the sexes into two *sex classes*, the sexes would have remained the pre-political substratum over which the political stratum of class is then laid. Incidentally, this is the picture that the distinction between sex and gender yields. As I read her, MacKinnon politicises sex because she regards it as referring in fact to sex class. Because the sexes have been organised into sex classes, because male people have been socialised into masculinity, thus becoming men, and female people into femininity, thus becoming women, we know the sexes only as classes – that is, male people only as men and female people only as women. If we know the sexes only as classes, then any reference to the sexes must be a reference to the sexes as classes. In other words, what we picture, upon saying or hearing 'sex', must be 'sex as class'. MacKinnon therefore worries that, were she to write that sexuality organises the *sexes* into *sex classes*, the reader would picture sexuality as organising the *sex classes* into *sex classes*, hence unwittingly accepting as sex, and thus as pre-political, what is in fact sex class, and thus political. MacKinnon would then have failed to achieve what she means to – the recognition of sexual politics.

MacKinnon is writing in a context where feminists have uncovered women's oppression and are attempting to account for it and where these attempts trace women's oppression back to male and female biology, which examination reveals to be male and female biology under male dominance.

Consider Susan Brownmiller's account of rape. She argues that male and female physiology engenders a 'first rape',[45] rape in primitive form:

> Man's structural capacity to rape and woman's corresponding structural vulnerability are as basic to the physiology of both our sexes as the primal act of sex itself. Had it not been for this

accident of biology, an accommodation requiring the locking together of two separate parts, penis into vagina, there would be neither copulation nor rape as we know it ... we cannot work around the fact that in terms of human anatomy the possibility of forcible intercourse incontrovertibly exists. This single factor may have been sufficient to have caused the creation of a male ideology of rape. When men discovered that they could rape, they proceeded to do it.[46]

So natural does it seem to Brownmiller that a male person who *could* force a female person *would* that she takes his superior strength to satisfactorily account for the 'first rape'. She takes *can* to explain *why*: 'What it all boils down to is that the human male can rape.'[47] Only because ours is a context in which male people's sexual assault on female people is normalised, and thus does not truly puzzle us or demand an explanation, does *can* appear a satisfactory explanation of *why*.

Elsewhere Brownmiller speaks of a male person's 'psychologic urge'.[48] An urge to what? To fulfil his sexual desire? To reproduce? Given that he does not need to engage in intercourse in order to fulfil his sexual desire, presumably the latter. Anthropologists have offered an evolutionary story in which rape is a reproductive strategy.[49] In conjunction with this story, *can* would explain *why*. But if the male has an urge to reproduce, must not the female also have one? If she does, why does she resist, so that a man must use force?

More importantly, supposing that this story is plausible, it explains only why men have forcible sexual intercourse with women who are of childbearing age. It does not explain – except as by-products – forcible sexual intercourse with very young girls, forms of sexual assault that are not intercourse – oral, anal, penetration of the vagina through objects other than the penis, and other kinds of sexual violation – leering, upskirting, wolf-whistling, harassment, image-based abuse.

Recognising that rape in primitive society appears to be

different from rape in civilised society, Brownmiller argues that the former engenders the latter:

> if the first rape was an unexpected battle founded on the woman's refusal, the second rape was indubitably planned ... rape became not only a male prerogative, but man's basic weapon of force against woman, the principal agent of his will and her fear. His forcible entry into her body, despite her physical protestations and struggle, became the vehicle of his victorious conquest over her being, the ultimate test of his superior strength, the triumph of his manhood.[50]

In the first rape, a male person uses force in order to satisfy an urge to reproduce. In the second (an evocative description not only of rape but also of sex in our world), a male person engages in conquest in order to realise his manhood. In these two rapes we have two wholly different 'actions' in the Weberian sense: 'human behaviour when and to the extent that the agent or agents see it as subjectively *meaningful*'. Weber also contrasts action with human behaviour that is 'purely reactive'.[51] The first rape has one goal – to satisfy one's urge to reproduce – and thus one meaning, while the second has another goal – to realise one's manhood – and thus another meaning.[52] It is the second action that is *rape*. Only because the first rape coincides in form with the second does it appear to be rape.

How does the first rape become the second? How does forcing a woman to surrender her body in order to satisfy one's urge to reproduce, just as one might force another to surrender food in order to satisfy one's hunger, and doing so because of scarcity of sexual access, which is analogous with scarcity of food – how does all this become conquering a woman in order to realise one's manhood? Brownmiller claims that the first rape revealed to man that 'his genitalia could serve as a weapon to generate fear', and thus presented rape to men as a means of subduing women. But how do men's genitalia disclose themselves to men as a weapon? How does forced reproduction disclose itself to men as 'victorious conquest over her being, the ultimate test of his superior strength, the triumph of his manhood'? How does the *biological* action of the first rape disclose itself to men as the *military* – the *political* – action of the second?[53] It does not. Only because ours is a context in which, as Beauvoir observes, the sexual is described in the vocabulary of the militaristic, in which the association of sex with conquest strikes us as perfectly natural, does the penis seem to lend itself to an association with 'weapon' and forced reproduction to an association with the 'victorious conquest' just described. In sum, the second rape is both conceptually and causally unrelated to the first.

Supposing that male and female physiology engenders the first rape, the first rape does not engender the second rape, so the second rape cannot be traced back to male and female physiology. Put simply, male and female physiology does not account for the second rape, which is the rape we wish to account for.

Only because ours is a context where sex is class, where the physiology of the male and of the female is the physiology of the master and of the subject, where the penis is a weapon for penetration and the vagina is an orifice to be penetrated, where the penetration of the vagina by the penis is the possession of the female by the male,[54] does male and female physiology appear to be conducive to the action of conquest that is rape. This is to say that, when Brownmiller purports to speak of sex, she in fact speaks of sex class; and, when she purports to speak of the first rape, a biological action, she in fact speaks of the second rape, a political action.

It is to such mistaking of the political for the biological that MacKinnon is reacting when, in an attempt to shift the political back where it belongs, she writes that 'sexuality organizes society into two *sexes*'.

V

Can we not disentangle sex from sex class? Not, at least not with full confidence, until we have abolished sex class and can observe sex outside sex class.

Can we not be guided by our knowledge of sex as it was prior to patriarchy, prior to its organisation into sex classes? MacKinnon disputes the existence of such a time, claiming that 'women's inequality has never not existed'.[55] In my view, Sheila Rowbotham provides a better answer: 'The origins of our oppression, like the roots of all domination, are lost long ago. We are completely without any memory of any alternative. Even the myths of tribes and races of strong women, the golden age of matriarchy, are the creations of male culture.'[56] Unlike MacKinnon, Rowbotham does not deny the possibility of a pre-patriarchal society; rather she argues that, if such a society once existed, it is now accessible to us only from the present, that is, it can be seen and studied only from our present vantage point – the vantage point of a patriarchal society. It is therefore less a society that preceded patriarchy than a society that we, who inhabit the patriarchal present, can countenance as having preceded patriarchy.

Can we not be guided by our current knowledge – of human evolution, reproduction, and biology and of non-human evolution, reproduction, and biology? This assumes that our current knowledge will persist into the feminist future, that it is not somehow the product of a patriarchal vantage point. Can we be sure of this? Given the claim that feminism is revolutionary, that it is 'the whole conceptual reevaluation of the social world, its whole reorganization with new concepts',[57] might not the feminist future be a world in which much of what we now know has been cast to the wind? In other words, to describe sex by holding fixed our current knowledge may be to describe sex by holding fixed the patriarchal conditions. Our description of sex may thus be little more than a description of sex class.

Can we not protect ourselves against this by developing a minimal description of sex? Examples of minimal descriptions include the following: the gamete account, according to which males are organisms on a developmental pathway designed to produce small gametes for the purpose of sexual reproduction and females are organisms on a developmental pathway designed to produce larger gametes for the purpose of sexual reproduction;[58] the chromosome account, according to which a male human being is a human being with a Y chromosome and a female human being is a human being without a Y chromosome;[59] and the cluster account, according to which a male human being is one who has sufficiently many important properties of one particular morphological cluster and a female human being is one who has sufficiently many important properties of another particular morphological cluster.[60] As Kathleen Stock writes, these minimal descriptions of sex 'refer only to a few structural and/or physical aspects of the body as defining conditions . . . They don't . . . build in any particular behavioural or psychological traits – active or passive, dominant or oppressed, or otherwise – as essentially connected to maleness and femaleness'[61] and thus do not condemn women to subordination.

But I wonder whether a minimal description of sex would be a description of a *human being*. As Pateman has written,

> The attempt to set out the purely natural attributes of individuals is inevitably doomed to fail; all that is left if the attempt is consistent enough is a merely physiological, biological, or reasoning entity, not a human being. In order to make their natural beings recognizable, social contract theorists smuggle social characteristics into the natural condition, or their readers supply what is missing.[62]

As a description of a biological organism, a minimal description of sex might serve the biologist's purposes, but does not serve the political theorist's.

For instance, when Stock speaks of female people as vulnerable to sexual assault by male people, does she see in her mind's eye nothing more than two biological organisms, one on a given developmental pathway and one on another, one with one pair of chromosomes and one with another, one with one cluster of morphological properties and one with another? In other words, is her image of a sexually vulnerable female person (and, by implication, her image of a sexually predatory male person) the image of a strictly biological organism? It appears to be, as she attributes this vulnerability, in part, to 'typical differences between males and females in strength, size, and direct aggression'.[63] But these differences only allow men who are already inclined to sexually assault women to do so. In the absence of such inclination, these differences do not render female people sexually vulnerable.

MacKinnon provides an alternative account. *Qua* members of the male sex class, male people find in dominance – in pursuing and conquering – sexual pleasure and self-realisation, while female people, *qua* members of the female sex class, find in subordination – in being pursued and conquered – sexual pleasure and self-realisation. Under the gaze of one who eroticises dominance, the female body becomes a thing to be 'penetrated', 'defiled', 'had', a thing to be violated and mastered. On Stock's account, a man's force is a means of achieving the ends of sexual pleasure when the woman is unwilling to submit. On MacKinnon's account, a man experiences the act of forcing a woman itself as sexually pleasurable: 'Force is sex, not just sexualized; force is the desire dynamic, not just a response to the desired object when desire's expression is frustrated.'[64] On Stock's account, men will continue to force women so long as they remain bigger, stronger, and more aggressive. On MacKinnon's account, once sex class has been abolished, men will no longer experience forcing women as sexually pleasurable and hence will no longer force women, regardless of whether they remain bigger, stronger, and more aggressive.

It would seem that, when Stock speaks of female people as vulnerable to sexual assault by male people, she sees with her mind's eye not two biological organisms but two sex classes.

VI

When MacKinnon claims that 'sexuality organizes society into two sexes', 'sexes' means 'sexes *as we know them*',[65] which is 'sexes *as classes*'. She is expressing a view about the referent of 'sex', not about the ontology of sex. Stock, I think, reads MacKinnon as doing the latter. 'According to this so-called "dominance" model of the sexes',[66] she writes, 'it is as if, long ago, there was only a blooming, buzzing confusion of flesh, and perhaps also of sexual parts of different shapes'.[67] I have argued that MacKinnon is best understood as making a claim about our ability to know what existed before patriarchy, not about what really existed before patriarchy (a blooming, buzzing confusion).

For better or worse, however, second-wave feminists had a tendency to slide from the epistemological claim that we cannot yet know sex apart from sex class to the ontological claim that sex is sex class, declaring that the abolition of sex class would be the abolition of sex, that the creation of a feminist society would be the creation of a 'sexless society'.[68] This declaration implies that sex does not exist apart from sex class, or that sex is a cultural construct. With this declaration, feminists exhibit little of the epistemic humility about sex that they have taught us we ought to have. If we cannot yet know sex apart from sex class, then we cannot say with confidence what sex will and, by implication, will not be in the feminist future.

As Millett writes, '[w]hatever the "real" differences between the sexes may be, we are not likely to know them until the sexes are treated differently, that is, alike.'[69]

The prophecy of a sexless society is best understood as the expression of the conviction that a future in which sex class has been abolished would be a future in which the referent of 'sex' is radically different, sharing with the current referent little more than a name. When, for example, MacKinnon says, 'there would be no such thing as what we know as the sex difference – much less would it be the social issue it is or have the social meaning it has – were it not for male dominance',[70] we ought to hear her as saying that, once 'male' is no longer synonymous, via 'man', with 'conqueror' and 'female', via 'woman', with 'conquered', the referents of 'male' will stand in a new relation, of similarity and difference, to the referents of 'female' – and so the features that distinguish each from the other, the features by which each sex is defined, will be different. Once 'male' is no longer synonymous, via 'man', with 'human' and 'female' is no longer antonymous, via 'woman', with 'human', once the referents of both 'male' and 'female' are the referents of 'human', shall we continue to conceive of male and female as *opposites* (the opposite sexes)?[71] If we do not, how will our conception of them change?

When second-wave feminists such as Wittig, MacKinnon, and Delphy write of sex as a product of male dominance, they are responding to a persistent failure among feminists to recognise sexual politics, to locate men and women and their relations squarely in the realm of the political. In a paper titled 'One Is Not Born a Woman', Wittig observes that 'most of the feminists and lesbian-feminists in America and elsewhere still believe that the basis of women's oppression *is biological as well as* historical'.[72] She proceeds to criticise feminist talk of a matriarchal 'prehistory' on the grounds that it naturalises the categories 'men' and 'women' and, with them, 'the social phenomena which express . . . [women's] oppression, making change impossible'.[73] Now, these feminists are regarded as *social constructionists* about sex. On this characterisation, the salient feature of their view of sex is that it is social. But what Wittig, MacKinnon, and Delphy sought to draw attention to was not that sex is social so much as that it is political. Wittig writes: 'The perenniality of the sexes and the perenniality of slaves and masters proceed from the same belief, and, as there are no slaves without masters, there are no women without men.'[74]

Wolin argues that political theorists have often and deliberately injected imagination – 'fancy, exaggeration, even extravagance'[75] – into their theories in order to illuminate things that are not otherwise apparent. They have hoped that this illumination would motivate the political action that would bring about political society 'in its corrected fullness'.[76] When Wittig, MacKinnon, and Delphy liken sex to class, might they not be exaggerating in order that we see things that are not otherwise apparent, namely that the condition of women, like that of the worker, is *wholly* arbitrary, oppressive, and intolerable? Might they not be urging women to suspend belief in the naturalness, rightness, and unchangeableness of *any* aspect of their condition, even heterosexual desire and childbirth, in order that they raise their sights and struggle for more than reform? When Wittig describes childbirth as 'forced production'[77] and women as 'programmed' to give birth,[78] might she not be hoping for a future in which motherhood is not a woman's destiny – rather than for a future in which female people do not give birth or do not alone bear the capacity to do so? Might she not be objecting to 'childbearing as *the* female creative act', as her emphasis implies, rather than to childbearing as the *female* creative act?[79]

On this reading, the feminist attempt to show that sex is a spectrum is misguided. Dworkin, for instance, asserts that human beings are a multisexed species.[80] This idea rests on a misreading of Wittig's political theoretic claim – the claim that 'there is no sex. There is but sex that is oppressed and sex that oppresses. It is oppression that creates sex and not the contrary'[81] – as a scientific claim, and of Wittig's attempt to propel us into the future as an attempt to reveal the present.[82] It is precisely because sex does exist, precisely because sex is binary, that feminists are visionary political theorists and not scientists (or social scientists). Notice, too, that Dworkin's assertion that human beings are a multisexed species is at odds with Wittig's, MacKinnon's, and Delphy's claim that the establishment of sex class is the establishment of sex. On this claim, it is because the class relation is a relation between two – master and subject – that the sexes are two and that these two are opposites. The reality of sex class entails the reality of the sex binary. So one can deny the latter no more than one can deny the former.

Second-wave feminists wrote in a climate in which the idea that sex is a construct was, at worst, benign. In the present climate, this idea is no longer benign. Now, 'men' and 'women' name genders rather than sex classes, connoting roles rather than interests. A male person claiming to be a woman therefore appears to be a victim of the sex–gender system who asks to occupy a role that this system (which arbitrarily assigns the male person the masculine role) forbids him from occupying – rather than as the oppressor demanding recognition as the oppressed.

In this climate, the claim that sex is a construct is susceptible of political use against women. It can be used to deny the need for *female*-only spaces, and thus to redefine *women*-only spaces from women-only in the sense of *female*-only to women-only in the sense of *persons-who-identify-as-women*-only – and thus to legitimise the inclusion of male people into women-only spaces, an inclusion that their full recognition as women requires. Gender-critical feminists are therefore highly suspicious of the claim that sex is a construct. Though this suspicion is understandable, I am suggesting that it is only when men and women have been obscured as *classes*, only when a male person's claim to be a woman appears innocuous, that the claim that sex is a construct becomes pernicious. In other words, a crucial, yet in Stock's account omitted,[83] moment in the displacement of biological sex by gender identity is the disappearance of the notion of sex class.

Now, it seems, women can demand women-only spaces only on (rightist) grounds of biological needs or on (leftist) grounds of gender identity-affirming needs. On the former, 'women-only' assumes the sense of female-only, while on the latter it assumes the sense of persons-who-identify-as-women-only. As gender-critical feminists wish to preserve women-only spaces as women-only in the sense of female-only, they find themselves having to appeal to biological needs or having to assert the mind-independent reality of sex. They thus find themselves in an argument with those second-wave feminists who theorise sex as a construct. But this argument may reflect difference in historical context, and thus difference on the question of what pursuit of women's interest, which is after all a pursuit within a particular historical context, requires more than difference of philosophical view.

VII

Identifying sexuality as the activity by which sex classes are created, MacKinnon unified the feminist critique of sexual relations in the sense of relations between men and women and the feminist critique of sexual relations in the sense of erotic relations. In this moment, feminism exploded the distinction between sex and violence, love and hate, harmony and conflict, freedom and subjection, private and public, individual and common, *non-political and political*.[84] We are yet to reassemble these concepts.

2

The Poststructural Turn

I

Contemporary feminists do not speak of men and women as sex classes. Indeed, until Lawford-Smith revived it in *Gender-Critical Feminism*, the term 'sex class', a term that connotes the political, had vanished from the feminist vocabulary, being replaced by 'gender', which connotes the social. This apparently innocuous shift is in fact politically significant.

For instance, notice that 'sex' and 'sex class' are conceptually entwined, whereas 'sex' and 'gender' are not. In the sex–gender distinction, 'sex' refers to the biological categories of male and female and 'gender' to the social roles of masculine and feminine into which the sexes are cast[1] – the male sex into the masculine role and the female sex into the feminine role. The masculine gender has therefore coincided with the male sex and the feminine gender with the female sex. But, as 'gender' is conceptually distinct from 'sex', it appears possible for a member of the male sex to be a member of the feminine gender and for a member of the female sex to be a member of the masculine gender. As Judith Butler writes, 'if sex and gender are radically distinct, then it does not follow that to be a given sex is to become a given gender; in other words, "woman" need not be the cultural construction of the female body, and "man" need not interpret male bodies'.[2]

First, Butler uses 'woman' for 'feminine being' and 'man' for 'masculine being'. If gender is masculinity and femininity, and if Butler's claim is that a particular sexed body need not assume a particular gender, then she ought to have written that 'feminine' need not be the cultural construction of the female body and 'masculine' need not interpret male bodies. Or, more simply, a female person need not become a member of the feminine gender and a male person need not become a member of the masculine gender. For Beauvoir, a woman is a member of the female sex socialised into the feminine gender.[3] So, even if a male person became a member of the feminine gender, he would not be a *woman*. *Contra* Butler, 'woman' cannot be the cultural construction of the male body. In Butler's use of 'woman' for 'feminine being' and 'man' for 'masculine being', a slide is apparent from gender as roles – *masculine* and *feminine* – to gender as the persons who, through socialisation into these roles, the sexes become – *men* and *women*. Once that slide has occurred, the sex–gender distinction appears to admit the possibility of a male person becoming a woman and a female person becoming a man.

Second, insofar as 'masculine' means 'that which befits a male person' and 'feminine' 'that which befits a female person', a male person who assumes the feminine gender is a male person who assumes that which befits a female person and a female person who assumes the masculine gender is a female person who assumes that which befits a male person. A male person who assumes that which befits a female person is not of the same kind as a female person who assumes that which befits a female person (the former is an effeminate – abnormal – male person, the latter a normal female person), and a female person who assumes that which befits a male person is not of the same kind as a male person who assumes that which befits a male person (the former is a butch – abnormal – female person, the latter a normal male person). If the conceptual distinction between sex and gender permits a male person to assume the feminine gender and a female person to assume the masculine gender, it thereby creates two further categories – effeminate male person and butch female person; *it does not permit male people and female people to occupy the same category*, to share the same name, much less the name 'woman' or 'man'.[4]

Nevertheless, it does seem that sex and gender can come apart in a way sex and sex class cannot. On the view that the sexes are classes, a male person has, as his birthright, membership of the oppressor class and the rights that accompany this membership. Although he may be deemed insufficiently masculine, a poor specimen of his sex, he does not thereby lose membership of the male sex class. His by birth, this membership and the rights attached to it cannot be forfeited. A member of the female sex has no birthright to membership of the oppressor class. Although she may perform masculinity and may even succeed in being taken for a member of the male sex, she cannot overcome this fact. She can perhaps be granted membership of the oppressor class by its members, but she would not thereby become a member in the sense in which a member of the male sex is one, because her membership would be *conditional*. It would not be hers *by right*. Relevant here is Marilyn Frye's discussion of 'the presumption of male citizenship', that is, 'the principle that if, and only if, someone is male, he has a *prima facie* claim to a certain array of rights, such as the rights to ownership and disposition of property, to physical integrity and freedom of movement, to having a wife and to paternity, to access to resources for making a living, and so forth'.[5] When men abridge or deny other men's rights (as in conscription), they must provide a justification for it (the need to raise an army), because the presumption is, as Frye says, on the side of their having these rights.[6] When men abridge other men's rights unjustifiably, the ones at the receiving end experience this abridgement as emasculating, as a denial of their membership of the male sex class.

In short, the shift from sex class to gender has worked to depoliticise sex, with implications that are now becoming clear. In this chapter I explain why this shift occurred.

II

In *The History of Sexuality*, Foucault tells the history of a transformation of power. For a long time, he writes, power was that of a sovereign – originally the father in the Roman family – over his subjects.[7] This power was 'deductive', 'a right of seizure: of things, time, bodies, and ultimately life itself'.[8] In the modern era, power ceases to be that of a sovereign over his subjects and becomes instead biopower. This power is 'productive', 'working to incite, reinforce, control, monitor, optimize, and organize the forces under it'.[9] Where sovereign power repressed the subject, biopower constructs it. Where sovereign power was centralised, biopower is diffuse. Where sovereign power was possessed, biopower is 'exercised'.[10] On this view, the 'juridical' conception of power, according to which power is 'possess[ed] like a commodity',[11] is now anachronistic and must be abandoned for a poststructuralist one, a conception of power as biopower.

The poststructural turn has implications for a feminist analysis. Put simply, power ceases to be that which members of the male sex class wield over members of the female sex class, becoming instead that which produces the sexed–gendered subjects men and women.

'Power', Foucault writes, is that 'which makes individuals subjects'.[12] Here 'subject' has a dual meaning: subject in the sense of 'self' and subject in the sense of 'person under the dominion of'. That is, the process of making individuals subjects is at once their formation as selves and their subjection.[13]

How is it their subjection? It is discourse, with its normative force, that is invested with the power of turning individuals into subjects. For example, the sex–gender discourse sorts people into the categories male and female and compels them to adhere to the norms of the category into which they have been placed – masculinity for the male category, femininity for the female. It thereby turns people into the subjects men and women, who discipline themselves according to – and are thus the subjects of – the sex–gender discourse.

On this theory, it is not men who govern women; it is the sex–gender discourse that governs both women *and men*. Men have been displaced by the sex–gender discourse, men and women as sex classes have been displaced by men and women as sexed–gendered subjects, and men's subjection of women has been displaced by men and women's subjection to the sex–gender discourse.[14] In short, the vertical structure has been displaced by a horizontal one. This is reflected clearly in the following passage from Susan Bordo's *Unbearable Weight*:

> Within a Foucauldian/feminist framework, it is indeed senseless to view men as the enemy: to do so would be to ignore, not only power differences in the racial, class, and sexual situations of men, but the fact that most men, equally with women, find themselves embedded and implicated in institutions that they as individuals did not create and do not control – and that they frequently feel tyrannized by.[15]

Men are not the enemy of women; men and women alike are tyrannised.

III

Almanina Barbour once observed to Atkinson: 'The Women's Movement is the first in history with a war on and no enemy.'[16]

Barbour intended this as a criticism. On reflection, Atkinson realised that, although feminists insist that women are oppressed (notice the passive voice), they take care to avoid the immediate question, 'by whom?', and, when pushed, often say, 'society'.[17]

In her aptly titled paper 'The Main Enemy', Christine Delphy, frustrated with the Marxist dismissal of women's oppression as a mere consequence of capitalism, one whose eradication required no dedicated movement, argued that men are the enemy and urged women to mobilise on the basis of their shared patriarchal oppression.[18] She saw that this mobilisation would demand an attack on 'the problems of false consciousness, that is, class consciousness determined according to membership in capitalist classes rather than in patriarchal classes, and the identification of women under this pretext with the enemy patriarchal class',[19] and a demonstration of 'how this false consciousness serves the interests of patriarchy and detracts from our struggle'.[20]

No sooner have feminists succeeded in theorising the sexes as classes than Bordo tells us that 'it is senseless to view men as the enemy'.[21] Setting aside for a moment the question of whether Foucault is right, it is true that he offered feminists a way of being feminists and remaining respectable.[22] (In fact the cost of becoming respectable was ceasing to be feminist, as will become clear.) For, let us be clear, the claim that men are the enemy is the claim of a lunatic. It is a claim that, in our patriarchal language, is 'senseless'. In this language, relations between men and women are relations of proper heterosexual love, relations that properly complete two complementary creatures, relations of proper desire and fulfilment. The claim that men are the enemy is simply bizarre. This claim begins to sound plausible if and only if it is reinterpreted as a claim that some perverted men are the enemy, or that some men are the enemy in virtue of aspects of their identity that have nothing to do with manhood, or that, as a result of a corrupting form of socialisation, men treat women in ways they mistakenly believe to be appropriate.

The first reinterpretation, favoured by men who are defensive of themselves and by women who are defensive of their boyfriends,[23] is obviously unsatisfactory.

The second and third, however, are widely accepted among feminists. With respect to the second, feminists speak contemptuously of 'straight white men'. Although they include 'men' in this formula, the exemption of men who are not straight or not white (but are nevertheless men) makes it clear that it is 'straight' and 'white' that they identify as the enemy. Indeed, Bordo is at pains to highlight the 'power differences in the racial, class, and sexual situations of men' (by 'sexual' she means 'sexual orientation'), and she takes these differences to invalidate the claim that men are the enemy. But these differences are precisely among men, members of the male sex class. Only one who cannot conceive of men *qua* men as the enemy would, like Bordo, regard power differences among men as invalidating the claim that men are the enemy. (Sex class is, as Firestone says, invisible.)

With respect to the third reinterpretation, feminists advocate re-education for men (e.g. in the form of 'respectful relationships').[24] This is not a political analysis or an analysis of interests, of 'who gets what, when, how'.[25] I cannot imagine Marx theorising capitalist profit-seeking as an unfortunate result of socialisation,[26] lack of Marxist education, exposure to the Marxist equivalent of pornography (perhaps, depictions of happy workers), and so forth. Indeed, I can only imagine Marx ridiculing such a theorisation. In a paper titled 'A Critique of the Sex/Gender Distinction', Moira Gatens observes that the sex–gender distinction implicitly neutralises sexual difference and sexual politics: the sexed body becomes a blank and apolitical slate on which gender is inscribed. As she tells us elsewhere, the solution to the problem of patriarchy is, then, a programme of reinscription, of 'unlearning ... patriarchy's arbitrary and oppressive codes and ... relearning ... politically correct and equitable behaviours and traits which will, in turn, lead to the whole person: the androgyn'.[27] In this solution Gatens perceives the liberal humanism of ostensibly radical politics.[28] This is an astute critique. Unfortunately it has gone unnoticed by feminists, who continue to pursue, perhaps even more fervently, a programme of reinscription. I wish to state explicitly what Gatens all but does: a programme of reinscription is an apolitical solution. According to the ideology of this solution, it is not that men and women have irresolvably conflicting interests – mastery over women and freedom, respectively – so that women must *defeat* men if their interest is to prevail; it is rather that men are ignorant and feminists are enlightened, so that feminists must *enlighten* men too, in order to make them see that 'women's interest' is simply justice, while 'men's interest' is injustice. Men are not the enemy; they are the pupil (or the invalid who suffers from toxic masculinity, curable through a feminist education). In short, these reinterpretations empty the claim 'men are the enemy' of its feminist significance.

IV

Following Foucault, contemporary feminists consider the second-wave view of the sexes as classes to be antiquated.[29] In her review of Pateman's *The Sexual Contract*, Nancy Fraser asserts that 'gender inequality is today being transformed by a shift from dyadic relations of mastery and subjection to more impersonal structural mechanisms that are lived through more fluid cultural forms'.[30] Similarly, Bordo criticises the '"old" feminist model', which 'tended ... to subsume all patriarchal institutions and practices under an oppressor/oppressed model which theorised men as "possessing" and wielding power over women, who are viewed correspondingly as being utterly power-less'.[31] Finally, in the preface to *Gender Trouble*, Butler writes: 'Power seemed to be more than an exchange between subjects or a relation of constant inversion between a subject and an Other';[32] 'I would hope that ... no one will be too quick to reduce power to hierarchy and to refuse its productive political dimensions.'[33]

These feminists achieve the representation of the second-wave view as antiquated by tacitly opposing 'government' to 'domination', 'impersonal structural mechanisms' to 'dyadic relations of mastery and subjection', so that the appearance of the first element in each pair is necessarily the disappearance of the second. But it is not clear that the two are mutually exclusive. Power may produce and thereby establish relations of mastery and subjection. Consider the following example.

A man does not demand, in the fashion of a master, that a woman have sex with him. Yet, though she does not particularly wish to do so, she does. When asked why, she says that it did not occur to her to refuse ('I never would have ever, ever thought of saying no or yes'),[34] or that she felt she could not ('There've been times in my life when I have really felt like ... "what the hell did I go to bed with that man for? Why am I doing this, I must be mad. Why can't I say no?", you know. It's, it's (pause) it's very hard, I find it – I have in the past found it very difficult to say no to a guy who wants to go to bed with me. Very difficult. Practically impossible, in fact. Not to someone I've just met, but to someone that I'm, I've known a while, and been to bed with').[35] When asked why she felt she could not, she offers the following: 'it was really important to me to be seen to be normal';[36] 'Because, you know, that person wanted me, and I was in a *relationship*, we were going out together and, isn't this what everybody does?';[37] 'if ... I couldn't have sex twice a week, you know, I felt guilty, I felt bad about it. I'd, I would make myself sort of want to do it, or, or no I wouldn't want to but, you know, I would feel bad if it didn't happen twice a week';[38] 'And also that feeling of, "well, I've led them on", you know, "I've led them on this far, I've, I've done these things, I've gotten a bit drunk, I've danced in a certain way, I've got in the car, we've come to the park'";[39] 'If you've been to bed with them once, then there's no reason why, that you shouldn't go to bed with them again in their heads. And of course (pause), I mean, you can see that point of view (laughing).').[40]

We have here an instance of productive power, of government, of impersonal structural mechanism: a woman has sex with a man not because he, sovereign over her, exercises his right to have sex with her, but because she has been produced by discourses in which a normal girlfriend attends to her boyfriend's sexual desires, discourses in which a woman who has aroused a man's sexual desire has a duty to fulfil it, discourses in which a woman who has had sex with a man has effectively promised to continue to do so. This productive power produces a woman as one who has a duty to fulfil a man's sexual desire and a man as one who has a right to the fulfilment of his sexual desire by a woman. It produces a woman as the sexual *subject* of a man and a man as the sexual *sovereign* of a woman. But in producing a woman as the sexual subject of a man and a man as the sexual sovereign of a woman, it conceals them as such. Once she has been produced as one who has a duty to fulfil a man's sexual desire, the woman spontaneously attends to the man's sexual desire, so that he need not exercise his sovereign power. It is when she does not that he must exercise his sovereign power – at first by directing her, then by coaxing her, then by emotionally manipulating her,[41] and finally by taking her or, playing the merciful sovereign, by gallantly respecting her wishes.

Foucault is adamant that power 'is never localised here or there, never in anybody's hands, never appropriated as a commodity or piece of wealth'[42] and hence that '[w]e must not look for who has the power in the order of sexuality (men, adults, parents, doctors) and who is deprived of it (women, adolescents, children, patients)'.[43] For him, all individuals stand in the same relation to power: as effect and conduit.[44] But though all individuals may equally be an effect of power, not all are equal as effects: as effects of power, a man is the master of a woman and a woman is the subject of a man. Is it then true that a man does not have power in his hands? Foucault elides this by (a) presenting a dichotomy – either the subject precedes power or the subject is the effect of power; (b) rejecting the former half of the dichotomy; and (c) falsely aligning talk of one individual as the master of another with that half.

As I have shown, an individual can be both an effect of power and the master of another. Indeed, it is in part by examining various discourses (sexual, psychoanalytic, legal, philosophical) that Beauvoir, Millett, Dworkin, MacKinnon, and Pateman arrive at the view that the subject 'man' is the master of the subject 'woman'. These are discourses in which sexual intercourse is a 'penetration', a violation (he 'defiles' her), a possession (he 'has' her), and the act that transforms a boy into a man and a girl into a woman ('he made a woman of her');[45] they are discourses in which virility is both sexual potency and manhood, vaginal orgasm (pleasure in penetration) is the mark of female maturity,[46] and 'sex' refers to both sexual intercourse and male–female. Monique Plaza captures beautifully the trick by which Foucault conjures women's subjection to men as men's subjection: 'from the place of potential rapist to which your status as a man "subjects" you, you can only hide the networks of oppressive power that women are subject to, you can only defend the right of rapists'.[47] By rejecting as structuralist the notion of the subjection of one individual to another and by presenting as poststructuralist the notion of the subjection of all produced individuals, Foucault recasts the subject position of 'man' – that *as which* men are produced, namely sexual proprietor of woman – as subjecting man. He recasts male mastery of women as male subjection.

Incidentally, I now understand better the contemporary feminist reluctance to define 'woman'. Following Foucault, to define 'woman' is to produce the presumed extension of this definition – 'female people' – as the subjects women; and it is this production of the subject that is the site of subjection, the site of 'violence'.[48] In other words, since 'subjection' now means 'production as a subject', it is not that men rape women, but rather that feminists – who define 'woman' – subject and assault women. I can also see more clearly the perversity of this feminist reluctance. If the subject position of 'woman' – that *as which* women are produced – is the position of man's subject, then to refuse (as feminists do) to define 'woman' is to consign women to a position of literal subjection – 'subjection' in the sense of subordination to men – for fear of figuratively subjecting them – 'subjecting' in the sense of producing them as subjects.

V

In adopting Foucault's conception of power, contemporary feminists assume that his observation of a shift from sovereign power to biopower is historically accurate. But I wonder: if Foucault had considered sexual relations paradigmatically political, would he have observed such a shift? The juridical conception construes power on the model of the sovereign. According to this conception, relations between sovereign and subject are political, in contradistinction to relations between man and woman, which are private. In explaining his notion of 'political power', Locke writes that 'the power of a magistrate over a subject may be distinguished from that of a father over his children, a master over his servant, *a husband over his wife*, and a lord over his slave'.[49] While Foucault assumes that the juridical conception was once accurate and seeks only to relegate it to the past, feminists, who consider sexual relations political, seek instead to explode it and thereby to reveal a different history from the one that Foucault reinforces. By relegating the juridical conception to the past, Foucault thwarts the feminist attempt to explode it.

In addition, feminists have long written of male power as productive and of women as thoroughly and distinctively their oppressor's product.[50] For example, in 1792 Mary Wollstonecraft wrote:

> To preserve personal beauty, woman's glory! the limbs and faculties are cramped with worse than Chinese bands, and the sedentary life which they are condemned to live, whilst boys frolic in the open air, weakens the muscles and relaxes the nerves ... The baneful consequences which flow from inattention to health during infancy, and youth, extend further than is supposed – dependence of body naturally produces dependence of mind ... genteel women are, literally speaking, slaves to their bodies, and glory in their subjection ... Women are every where in this deplorable state; for, in order to preserve their innocence, as ignorance is courteously termed, truth is hidden from them, and they are made to assume an artificial character before their faculties have acquired any strength. Taught from their infancy that beauty is woman's sceptre, the mind shapes itself to the body, and, roaming round its gilt cage, only seeks to adorn its prison.[51]

Male power, feminists suggest, has always been productive. Yet sexual relations have been no less relations of mastery and subjection for that. If Foucault had considered sexual relations paradigmatically political, he would not have contrasted the ability to produce with the ability to deduct, he would not have classified power the way he does, and he would not have told the history he does.

Fraser assumes that the history Foucault gives us is accurate with respect to sexual relations. Recall her claim: 'gender inequality is today being transformed by a shift from dyadic relations of mastery and subjection to more impersonal structural mechanisms that are lived through more fluid cultural forms'.[52] She is not alone among feminists in assuming the existence of a past in which sexual relations were formally and overtly relations of mastery and subjection, women were men's property, and male power was purely deductive – a past in relation to which current sexual relations appear not to be *formally*, and thus not to be *really*, relations of mastery and subjection. The slide from 'not formally' to 'not really' occurs via the association of 'informal' with 'cultural' and of 'cultural' with 'symbolic': Fraser contrasts '*institutionalized* power relations' with '*cultural* meanings of sex and gender',[53] and she interchanges 'cultural' with 'symbolic' ('cultural content and symbolic meaning')[54] and 'fantastical' ('[t]his brings me to the sexual contract as a template for cultural meanings. If the master/subject model is not very helpful in analyzing prostitution on the literal level, it does strike a symbolic chord ... In heterosexual prostitution ... what is sold is a male *fantasy* of "male sex-right"').[55]

Pateman has revealed that this past is mythical. She draws our attention to something that talk of women as property obscures, namely the fact that 'women have been presented as always consenting, and their explicit non-consent ... has been reinterpreted as consent'.[56] Even in the era of coverture, when a wife had no legal existence apart from her husband's, the woman was, in marrying, taken to consent to her condition. That condition was thus taken to be continuous with her freedom and personhood. Put simply, sexual relations have never been straightforwardly relations of mastery and subjection.

This alters our perception of the present. For example, because we regard the husband's historical immunity from prosecution for marital rape as reflecting the wife's historical status as property of the husband, we interpret the criminalisation of marital rape as signalling a change in this status, namely the transformation of the wife into an autonomous person. But a husband was immune because, in marrying him, his wife had consented and not because, as his property, her consent was irrelevant: 'But the husband cannot be guilty of rape committed by himself upon his lawful wife, for by their matrimonial consent and contract the wife hath given up herself in this kind to her husband, which she cannot retract.'[57] The criminalisation of marital rape, then, is not the transformation of the wife's status – from property to autonomous person. Rather it represents the alteration of the terms of the marriage contract, the terms of the male sex right:[58] before criminalisation, the terms were such that a wife could be said to have consented to all sexual use by her husband; after criminalisation, the terms were such that a wife could be said not to have consented to certain sexual uses. The criminalisation of marital rape does not constitute the progress that we have taken it to be. The relationship between the past and the present no longer appears definitively one of progress. Between the past (before the criminalisation of marital rape) and the present (after the criminalisation of marital rape), a formal (institutional) difference exists, but it does not have the significance that we, along with Fraser, have attributed to it – the erosion of the status of sexual relations as relations of mastery and subjection at all levels except the cultural ('symbolic' and 'fantastical').

Moreover, because male power produces in women a sense of sexual duty, a husband does not much have to force his wife, and so did not much rely on his immunity for the satisfaction of his sexual desire. The loss of his immunity is thus not much the loss of his ability to secure the satisfaction of his sexual desire, not much the loss of his sex right.

In short, the history that Foucault tells and Fraser repeats is not the history of sexual relations. In this history, power is never quite sovereign power and so sovereign power is never replaced by biopower.

Contemporary feminists believe that a current feminist theory is one that has rejected a structuralist for a poststructuralist analysis. But structuralism is not for feminists the foil that it is for Foucault, a theory of power once but no longer relevant, and so poststructuralism does not for feminists supersede structuralism as a theory of power. For feminists, structuralism is not the antithesis to which poststructuralism is the thesis. Equally, poststructuralism is not the antithesis to which structuralism is the thesis. Perhaps it is the dichotomy of structuralism and poststructuralism that is the antithesis to which *feminism* – 'feminism unmodified'[59] – is the thesis.

VI

No sooner had second-wave feminists succeeded in theorising men and women as sex classes than this theorisation was dismissed, *by other feminists*, as obsolete.

Feminism then appeared to have lost its *raison d'être*: if men do not oppress women, then what need have we for feminism?

You might object to my conflation of second-wave feminism with feminism, insisting that, while we no longer need the former, we continue to need the latter. But second-wave feminism is the culmination of the feminism that came before it.[60] The animating impulse of feminism was 'an unspecific, often unattached, but just barely submerged discontent that in some inchoate way women relate to being female',[61] a sense that 'women are a group'.[62] It was this impulse that drove feminists first from Marxism to Marxist feminism, then from Marxist feminism to socialist feminism (or dual systems theory), and finally, each theory proving unable to recognise the oppression of women *qua* women, from dual systems theory to the search for a theory and a practice – a movement – of their own.[63] This search yielded MacKinnon's *Toward a Feminist Theory of the State*, which remains the fullest account of sex class. The rejection of the concept of sex class was thus a rejection of the belief that had motivated feminism.[64]

What future, then, remained for feminism? One obvious

response to this question was: none at all. If in the era of sovereign power men oppressed women but now, in the era of biopower, they do not, then perhaps we no longer have a need for feminism. Perhaps feminism 'spreads its wings only with the coming of the [patriarchal] dusk'.[65]

Interestingly, feminists who embraced poststructuralism did not come to this conclusion and did not renounce feminism. Instead they attempted to find a role for a poststructural feminism. In the next chapter I examine these attempts and what they made of feminism.

3

In Search of a Poststructural Feminism

I

Although drawn to poststructuralism, some feminists worried that, embraced wholeheartedly, it would undermine feminism. Lesley Stern wrote: 'Whilst it seems to me important at this time for feminists to disengage from a polemic of oppression ... I think there is a danger in too virulent a critique of the notion of oppression. If it is conceptualised out of existence, rendered immaterial, this is to have serious repercussions upon material intervention.'[1]

In response to this problem, some feminists proposed adhering to poststructuralism in theory but contravening it in practice – adopting an anti-universalist and anti-essentialist posture in theory and abandoning it for a strategically universalist and essentialist one in practice.[2] For Marx, theory was to be realised in practice;[3] for poststructuralist feminists, theory was to be set aside when it came to doing practice. In what sense is a theory *feminist* when it is severed from feminism as a practice, as a political movement? What purpose does such a theory serve? To what end do feminists develop a theory intending for it to be inconsequential? It cannot be the end of truth, for the worry that poststructuralism would undermine feminism reveals that feminists did not consider poststructuralist theory true. If Foucauldian theory were true, men would no longer oppress women, feminism would no longer be needed, and Foucauldian theory would undermine feminism rightly rather than problematically or dangerously. So, had feminists considered Foucauldian theory true, they would not have thought that its undermining of feminism is a cause for concern. That they did is, I think, evidence that, for all that they claimed, they felt the second-wave account to be true.[4] (It occurs to me that criticisms of the second-wave account are criticisms of its universalisingness, totalisingness, whiteness, middle-classness, adherence to structuralism, simplisticness, but almost never its *falseness*.)

Why, if they did not believe that poststructuralist theory was true, did feminists commend it? What motivated them to urge that we 'disengage from a polemic of oppression', only to then caution us against such disengagement?[5] It is conflicting desires – the desire for respect from the academy and the desire to remain faithful to women.

At any rate, their bifurcated approach could not be sustained, for the (poststructuralist) theory displaced the second-wave account upon which the (feminist) practice relied. These feminists thus set in motion what they feared: the erasure of women's oppression and the disappearance (or recuperation) of the struggle against it.

Other feminists attempted to find a role for a suitably poststructural feminism. Such a feminism, Nancy Fraser and Linda Nicholson write, would 'be explicitly historical, attuned to the cultural specificity of different societies and periods, and to that of different groups within societies and periods'. It would eschew 'ahistorical, functionalist categories like "reproduction" and "mothering"', opting instead for 'categories ... inflected by temporality, with historically specific institutional categories like "the modern, restricted, male-headed, nuclear family"';

and, where it could not eschew such ahistorical categories, it would 'genealogize' them, thus rendering them 'temporally and culturally specific'. It would be 'non-universalist'. 'When its focus became cross-cultural or trans-epochal, its mode of attention would be comparativist rather than universalisist, attuned to changes and contrasts instead of to "covering laws."' 'It would replace unitary notions of "woman" and "feminine gender identity" with plural and complexly constructed conceptions of social identity, treating gender as one relevant strand among others, attending also to class, race, ethnicity, age and sexual orientation.'[6] It would be, in a word, *micro*, as befits the nature of biopower.[7]

But it seems to me that this ostensibly poststructural feminism is in fact traditional feminism, terribly diminished. In an attempt to remain dedicated to the cause of women without attributing a universal structure to domination,[8] poststructural feminists qualify and pluralise this dedication into oblivion. Concern with the condition of women *qua* women becomes concern with the condition of particular groups of women, who live in particular societies at particular times.[9] But the result is traditional feminism at the level of the micro. This is because a feminism concerned with the condition of particular groups of women, who live in particular societies at particular times, attributes a universal structure to domination at the local (culturally specific) level. From a poststructural perspective, one cannot attribute a universal structure at the local level any more than at the global level. Once power is no longer possessed by the sovereign, once it produces a subject and circulates through it, its effects become indeterminate and unpredictable. Structure becomes structurelessness. Fraser and Nicholson's description of feminism evokes not a poststructural world but a series of small structural worlds.[10]

In fact I think that Fraser and Nicholson's feminism assumes a universal structure to domination also at the global level: why, unless one believed that women across place and time were oppressed, would one propose to study particular groups of women who live in particular societies at particular times, and why, unless one believed that domination had a universal structure, would one think that women across place and time were oppressed?[11] Contemporary feminists dutifully repudiate the view that women's oppression is transcultural. Butler writes,

> The political assumption that there must be a universal basis for feminism, one which must be found in an identity assumed to exist cross-culturally, often accompanies the notion that the oppression of women has some singular form discernible in the universal or hegemonic structure of patriarchy or masculine domination. The notion of a universal patriarchy has been widely criticised in recent years for its failure to account for the workings of gender oppression in the concrete cultural contexts in which it exists.[12]

But if women's oppression is not transcultural, then the fact (which contemporary feminists do not deny) that women in different cultures are oppressed is sheer coincidence, which I find implausible. Butler continues: 'Where those various contexts have been consulted within such theories, it has been to find "examples" or "illustrations" of a universal principle that is assumed from the start.'[13] She is right. For example, adopting Pateman's theory, we notice that prostitution exists across cultures and we interpret this as the exercise of male sex right. We thereby confirm the universality of this right. On reflection, Butler misleads us with the term 'assumed'. We do not assume; we suspect, and then we inquire. What would she have us do? One cannot inquire without a guiding suspicion. Contemporary feminists, too, assume – they assume the non-universality of women's oppression. Why is this assumption preferable? After all, culture is not hermetically sealed. Contemporary feminists are surprisingly uncritical of 'cultural differences'. They rightly criticise second-wave feminists for taking sexual difference for granted, but they – unlike second-wave feminists – take cultural difference for granted. By contrast, consider Alice Walker's portrayal of cultural differences in 'Coming Apart'. On a business trip to New York, a middle-aged Black husband, taking his wife down Forty-Second Street, stops in front of a shop window:

> Four large plastic dolls – one a skinny Farrah Fawcett (or so the doll looks to her) posed for anal inspection; one, an oriental, with her eyes, strangely, closed, but her mouth, a pouting red suction cup, open; an enormous eskimo woman – with fur around her neck and ankles, and vagina; and a Black woman dressed entirely in a leopard skin, complete with tail. The dolls are all life-size, and the efficiency of their rubber genitals is explained in detail on a card visible through the plate glass.[14]

Here 'cultural differences' – white, oriental, eskimo, Black – are variations on the theme of eroticised female degradation. They are patriarchal fabrications. Contemporary feminists will, rightly, object that these 'cultural differences', which are indeed patriarchal fabrications, are also the fabrications of a particular culture – north American – and are thus not genuine cultural differences. But, once they acknowledge that 'cultural differences' are sometimes a cultural construct, how can they talk of them with as little wariness as they do?

An aside, one I make because Fraser and Nicholson charge second-wave feminism with essentialism: it is Fraser and Nicholson's feminism, not second-wave feminism, that essentialises women. For second-wave feminism, women are a sex class. The universal existence of women, which is also the universal existence of men, is just the universal existence of a class (or two classes). The disappearance of these classes will be the disappearance of women and men in the feminist sense.

Second-wave feminism thus attributes to women (and men) no essence. As Wittig might put it, the universal existence of women is the universal existence of a (class) relation, not an essence;[15] it is the universal existence of a political kind, not a metaphysical one.

Fraser and Nicholson believe that women exist universally – if they did not, they would not enjoin feminism to study women across place and time. As they reject the claim that women's oppression is universal, they cannot believe that the universal existence of women is the universal existence of a class. They must, I think, believe that the universal existence of women is the universal existence of the female sex, where femaleness, preceding place, time, and oppression, is an ahistorical essence.

Given that the second-wave view that women are a sex class is not universalist in the sense of being ahistorical or essentialist, and given that, though they will not admit it, Fraser and Nicholson share with second-wave feminists the belief that women are oppressed across place and time, what is it in second-wave feminism that Fraser and Nicholson find objectionable? I think it is not its metaphysics but its ambition – not its structuralism or its modernism but its *epicism*, its willingness to offer a (political) theory fit for the (political) task at hand: 'to reassemble the whole political world'.[16] Indeed, they write:

> Practical imperatives have led some feminists to adopt modes of theorizing which resemble the sorts of philosophical metanarrative rightly criticized by postmodernists. To be sure, the feminist theories we have in mind here are *not 'pure' metanarratives*; they are *not ahistorical* normative theories about the transcultural nature of rationality or justice. Rather, they are *very large social theories*, theories of history, society, culture, and psychology, that claim, for example, to identify causes and/ or constitutive features of sexism that operate cross-culturally.[17]

They object to second-wave theory – the theory of Firestone, Rosaldo, Ferguson, Folbre, Hartsock, and MacKinnon – not because it is universalist, but because it is 'very large'. This is a remarkable criticism. If patriarchy is large, must not feminist theory be correspondingly so? Is it not for those who wish to preserve patriarchy to insist that feminist theory is inappropriately large? Poststructural feminists observe a masculine or patriarchal impulse in feminist epicism.[18] I observe a patriarchal impulse in the admonishment of women theorists who refuse to aspire to smallness.

II

Notice that Fraser and Nicholson evaluate feminist theory according to the criteria of social science. They understand second-wave theories as '*social* theories' that 'purport to be *empirical* rather than philosophical'[19] and criticise them accordingly: 'they are insufficiently attentive to historical and cultural diversity';[20] 'they falsely universalize features of the theorist's own era';[21] they 'falsely generalized to all societies an historically specific conjunction of properties'.[22] In place of such theories, they propose a poststructural feminism, which – recall their description[23] – is superior according to social scientific criteria: a feminism that specifies its sample, refuses to explain in terms of covering laws, generalises cautiously, and produces ever more data that illuminate nothing.[24]

We shall wonder how we ought to evaluate feminist theories, if not according to the criteria of social science. What is feminism, if not a social, empirical theory? This question is itself evidence of the thoroughness with which the social has usurped the political.[25] For the answer is: feminism is a *political theory*. Political theory differs from social science substantively and methodologically: substantively, social science is concerned with social phenomena, while political theory is concerned with political phenomena; methodologically, social science is empirical, while political theory is visionary.[26] Social science describes the presently ordered social world, while political theory envisions and aims to bring about a newly ordered political world. Political theory thus has an imaginative element. Wolin assigns to the imaginative element in political theory a role similar to that which Coleridge assigns to it in poetry: that of an '"esemplastic" power, which "forms all into one graceful intelligent whole"'.[27] This is precisely what MacKinnon seeks to do: to replace 'a rich description of the variables and locales of sexism and several possible explanations for it' with an 'account of male power as an ordered yet deranged whole',[28] in order to reveal the various, apparently unrelated uses and abuses of women as all of a piece and that piece as sexual subjection.[29] While Fraser and Nicholson believe that feminist theory must 'account for the oppression of women in its "endless variety *and* monotonous similarity"',[30] MacKinnon believes that feminist theory must reveal this seemingly endless variety as being in fact monotonous similarity. She hopes to thereby inspire the transformation of the whole, the creation anew of the political order. Social science is successful insofar as it accurately describes the presently ordered social world, while political theory is successful insofar as it brings about the newly ordered political world that it envisions. Thus political theory relies for its success upon action, the action that reconstitutes the political order. Perhaps the rejection of 'large theories' is at bottom an evasion of the demand that those theories place upon us: the demand for correspondingly large action.

Feminism, I am suggesting, is primarily a vision of a newly ordered political world, in which women are free, and, derivatively, a description of the presently ordered one, in which women are subjected to men. MacKinnon suggests as much when she writes: 'Women's situation cannot be truly known for what it is, in the feminist sense, without knowing that it can be other than it is.'[31] Strictly speaking, though, we cannot know that women's situation can be 'other than it is' until it has become 'other than it is'; we can only hope.

In 'On Reading Marx Politically', Wolin argues for a political rather than a scientific reading of Marx, a reading of Marx as a political theorist rather than a scientist. According to Marx's theory, capitalism contains the seed of its destruction and replacement by communism. This prediction has not been borne out. The theory that yields it would appear to be, *qua* scientific theory, a failure. But it ought to be understood, and thus judged, not as a scientific but as a political theory, a 'power-laden'[32] theory, power-laden in the sense of both grasping 'the . . . powers in the world' and 'empower[ing] the theorist in his efforts to change the world'.[33] Marx's theory, Wolin suggests, was scientifically false in order to incite the transformation of the world. It predicted the revolt of the proletariat in order to bring it about. A theory according to which capitalism could and would endlessly adapt, and thereby defuse the crises that it generated, would be impotent, indeed, not merely impotent – incapable of producing action – but disempowering; it would give a reason for actionlessness. The prediction of revolt was a 'means of averting rather than confirming the analysis', 'a way of theory being false to itself in order to be true to action'.[34] The dichotomy between truth – faithfulness to reality – and action – faithfulness to a vision of what reality might become – is, however, misleading. For the prediction of revolt was a way for the theory to be false to itself in order to be true to the action *that would prove the prediction accurate and the theory true*. Might MacKinnon's generalisations – about women and men, about sexual violence, about sexuality – not be similarly understood, as an attempt to produce the unified and dramatic action necessary to make women's situation other than it is? And might not *making* women's situation other than it is allow us to *know* it for what it was – as MacKinnon described it?

In her critique of poststructural scepticism, Bordo associates second-wave feminism with 'the practical' and poststructural feminism with 'the theoretical'. She writes: 'The programmatic appropriation of poststructural insight ... in shifting the focus of crucial feminist concerns about the representation of cultural diversity from practical contexts to questions of adequate theory, is highly problematic';[35] 'This is not to say that the struggle for institutional transformation will be served by univocal, fixed conceptions of social identity and location. Rather, we need to reserve practical spaces for both generalist critique (suitable when gross points need to be made) and attention to complexity and nuance. We need to be pragmatic, not theoretically pure, if we are to struggle effectively with the inclination of institutions to preserve and defend themselves against deep change.'[36] In representing poststructural feminism as theoretically sophisticated but practically useless and second-wave feminism as theoretically crude but practically useful, Bordo grants poststructural feminism too much and second-wave feminism too little. She is right to say that poststructural feminism is practically useless (in Wolin's language, impotent) and that second-wave feminism is practically useful (potent), but she is wrong to dichotomise theory and practice. In the case of visionary political theory, practice actualises and thus verifies theory. 'The question whether objective truth can be attributed to human thinking', Marx wrote, 'is not a question of theory but ... a practical question. *Man must prove the truth, i.e., the reality and power, the this-sidedness of his thinking, in practice.*'[37] Second-wave feminist theory is practically useful, and for being practically useful delivers us to truth.[38]

III

While this iteration of poststructural feminism did not fully cast off traditional feminism, another iteration did. This iteration is Butler's. In Foucauldian fashion, Butler conceives of 'sex' as a 'regulatory ideal'.[39] That is, she conceives of 'sex' less as a descriptive than a normative category, less as what one does have than what one must have. It is normative in that the human body just is the male body or the female body. As Butler writes, 'the moment in which an infant becomes humanized is when the question, "is it a boy or girl?" is answered'.[40] In virtue of this normativity, 'sex' compels bodies to conform to it. It thereby produces the bodies that it purports to describe.[41] As an example, historically, surgeons have operated on intersex infants in order to make them more recognisably male or female.[42] In doing so, Butler would say, they eliminated a threat to the category of sex, which is the category of a binary, thus shoring it up.

As the regulatory ideal of 'sex' designates certain bodies as intelligible, it simultaneously designates others as unintelligible.[43] 'This latter domain', Butler clarifies, 'is not the opposite of the former, for oppositions are, after all, part of intelligibility; the latter is the excluded and illegible domain that haunts the former domain as the spectre of its own impossibility, the very limit to intelligibility, its constitutive outside.'[44] It is these unintelligible bodies that Butler regards as the victims of 'sex'.

Which bodies, specifically, are unintelligible? If '"intelligible" genders are those which in some sense institute and maintain relations of coherence and continuity among sex, gender, sexual practice, and desire',[45] then unintelligible bodies are those that do not: perhaps the intersex body, the trans-sexed body, the homosexual body, the bisexual body, the gender-nonconforming body, the non-binary body, the transgendered body. But recall Butler's distinction between 'opposite' and 'unintelligible'. 'Homosexual' would seem to be the opposite of 'heterosexual' and thus not unintelligible, as would 'transgendered' of 'cisgendered', as, for that matter, would 'woman' of 'man'. But for Butler the extension of 'unintelligible genders' is the queer community, which surely includes homosexual and transgendered bodies. So I must confess that I am not sure quite whom Butler considers to be unintelligible. Moreover, is not our ability to name and, by implication, conceive of the intersex body, the trans-sexed body, the homosexual body, the bisexual body, the gender-nonconforming body, the non-binary body, the transgendered body – is it not proof that they are intelligible? If it is, then the victims of 'sex' are necessarily unnameable. But why, then, is Butler concerned for the queer community? Perhaps her view is that the queer movement has helped to render these hitherto unintelligible bodies intelligible.

We might wonder why, if '[i]t is through *sex* ... that each individual has to pass in order to have access to his own intelligibility',[46] the male body and the female body are not, in virtue of being male or female and regardless of 'coherence and continuity among sex, gender, sexual practice, and desire',[47] intelligible, and, by implication, why the intersex body alone is not, in virtue of being neither male nor female, unintelligible. This is because, Butler (I think) would say, the normative sexed body, the properly sexed body, is not simply male or female. For being gay, a male person is considered effeminate, unmanly, not as he ought to be *qua* male; and, for being a lesbian, a female person is considered masculine, unwomanly, not as she ought to be *qua* female. The normative male body is thus heterosexual and masculine and the normative female body is heterosexual and feminine.

At any rate, on Butler's account, it is the regulatory ideal of 'sex' that is the source of injustice, it is the unintelligibility of those who deviate from this ideal that is the injustice, and it is those who suffer this unintelligibility who are the victims of injustice. Unlike the iteration outlined earlier, Butler's is a truly *poststructuralist* account. It is 'sex' that has power, producing some as properly sexed and thus human and others as abject. Power is that which produces the subject, not that which the sovereign wields.

IV

Second-wave feminists sought to *politicise* the category of sex. They meant to thereby generate among women the class consciousness that, transforming them from a 'class in itself' into a 'class for itself',[48] would set in motion their struggle for liberation. Butler seeks instead to *denaturalise* the category of sex.[49] She means to thereby 'open up the field of possibility for gender'[50] in order that the hitherto unintelligible might gain a name and thus a place in the world. The displacement of the second-wave feminist account by the Butlerian poststructural feminist account was thus the displacement of the goal of *women's liberation* by the goal of *gender inclusion*.

With Butler's account, 'denaturalising "sex"' usurps the place of 'politicising "sex"', with the consequence that the former appears to be the latter. 'The deconstruction of identity', Butler insists, 'is not the deconstruction of politics; rather, it *establishes as political* the very terms through which identity is articulated'.[51] It 'establishes as political' not in the sense in which Millett's analysis of literary discourse or Dworkin's analysis of pornographic discourse does, the sense of revealing sexual relations as relations of mastery and subjection, but in the sense of revealing as *produced*. For, since it is the *production of the subject* that is now *subjection*, to politicise 'sex' is just to reveal the sexed subject as produced. The second-wave feminist project of politicising 'sex' in the sense of representing sexual relations as relations of mastery and subjection thus becomes the poststructural feminist project of denaturalising 'sex', of genealogising and deconstructing 'woman'. The project of saying something hitherto unsayable about women – 'women are a class ... this class is political in nature, and ... this political class is oppressed'[52] – becomes the project of re-saying what others have said about 'woman', ostensibly 'to open up the field of possibility for gender'.[53]

To second-wave ears, the goal of opening up such a field is as nonsensical and perverse as that of opening up the field of possibility for class. The categories of gender cannot be diversified any more than the categories of '[f]reeman and slave, patrician and plebeian, lord and serf, guild-master and journeyman, in a word, oppressor and oppressed'.[54] Perhaps, as proof of this, we have succeeded in opening the following possibilities: transition from one gender to another and identification as neither. No positive gender possibility beyond *man* and *woman* exists as yet.

Moreover, I am not convinced that the denaturalisation of 'sex' does open up possibilities, for I am not convinced that the belief that the sex–gender binary is natural is what precludes other ways of being. I think it is instead our inability to imagine other ways of being that preserves the sex–gender binary. As Richard Rorty writes,

> the most effective way to criticize current descriptions of a given instance of the oppression of the weak as 'a necessary evil' ... is to explain just why it is *not* in fact necessary, by explaining how a specific institutional change would eliminate it. That means sketching an alternative future and a scenario of political action that might take us from the present to that future.[55]

I am, however, anticipating. To summarise: regarding the second-wave account as obsolete, but not wanting to renounce their project, feminists sought to develop a poststructuralist account. Where Fraser and Nicholson failed, Butler succeeded. But her success, I will now argue, was feminism's defeat.

4

Feminism, Displaced

I

As Butler's poststructuralist account was taken to supersede the second-wave account as *the* feminist account, the feminist project radically changed. The second-wave account identifies men's oppression of women as the injustice and the liberation of women as the goal. Butler's account identifies the unintelligibility of those who deviate from the regulatory ideal of 'sex' as the injustice and the intelligibility of these same people – in Butler's words, the 'extension of . . . legitimacy to bodies that have been regarded as false, unreal, and unintelligible'[1] – as the goal. The second-wave account gives rise to a project of sex class abolition or women's liberation. Butler's account gives rise to a project of gender diversification (recall Butler's aim: 'to open up the field of possibility for gender')[2] or gender inclusion. This, of course, is the project under the description of which we know feminism today.

In order to supersede the second-wave account, Butler's must be a superior *feminist* account. So, in addition to being poststructuralist, it must also be feminist. In this chapter I argue that it is not feminist. The feminist project was not radically transformed; it was displaced.

II

Butler's account does not recognise in an obvious way women *qua* women as victims of injustice. Female persons who succeed in conforming to the regulatory ideal of sex – namely by being female, heterosexual, woman-identifying, feminine-presenting persons – would seem to be intelligibly human and thus 'included'. To be sure, female persons *qua* lesbian, man-identifying, or masculine-presenting would seem to be excluded. But the claim that distinguishes feminism from all other social movements is that women qua *women*, women regardless of other aspects of their identity – sexuality, gender identity, or gender presentation – suffer a distinctive injustice. Butler theorises instead the distinctive injustice suffered by those who do not conform to the regulatory ideal of sex.

Butler's claim that the sexed body is the human body elides a longstanding feminist observation: 'female' does not name a human being. As Frye writes,

> The word 'woman' was supposed to mean female of the species, but the name of the species is 'Man'. The term 'female man' has a tension of logical impossibility about it that is absent from parallel terms like 'female cat' and 'female terrier'. It makes one suspect that the concept of the species which is operative here is one according to which there are no females of the species. I think one can begin to get a handle on what this means by seeing how it meshes with another interesting phenomenon, namely the remarkable fact that so many men from so many stations in life have so often declared that women are *unintelligible* to them.[3]

If women *qua* women are not intelligibly human, then perhaps we can add women to the list of the excluded. But those already on the list are excluded by virtue of the equation of the (properly) *sexed body* with the human body, while women are excluded by virtue of the equation of the *male body* with the human body. Each equation has different victims – the former, anyone not (properly) sexed, the latter, anyone not male. So adding women to the list of the excluded would entail (a) changing the source of injustice from the equation of '(properly) sexed' with 'human' to an equation of 'male' with 'human'; (b) changing the victims of injustice from the not (properly) sexed to the not male; and (c) changing the remedy for injustice from gender diversification to the revision of the meaning of 'human', so that this term may no longer be synonymous with 'male'. The account that emerges from these changes would bear no resemblance to Butler's.

Finally, supposing that Butler's account could accommodate the recognition that women *qua* women are excluded, we ought to ask: what is gained and what is lost in redescribing what women suffer as unintelligibility and exclusion, not as subjection, and what they yearn for as intelligibility and inclusion, not as freedom? Wendy Brown observes that the demand for recognition – for inclusion as that on the basis of which one has been excluded ('sexual orientation, trans-sexuality, age, height, weight, personal appearance, physical characteristics, race, colour, creed, religion, national origin, ancestry, disability, marital status, sex or gender')[4] – relies upon the ideal of a universal way of life and that, empirically, this ideal is a white middle-class masculine one: a way of life with marriage, child custody, job security, freedom from harassment, health care, stable housing, a willing taxi driver.[5] The demand for inclusion thus relies upon the very ideal that produces the exclusion.[6] In addition, as a demand for inclusion in a specifically middle-class way of life, it renaturalises capitalism and, with it, class, protecting them from critique.[7] Brown exposes the project of inclusion as empirically and thus contingently a 'strikingly unemancipatory' one.[8] The question is: is the project of inclusion *necessarily* unemancipatory? Or, as she asks, '[t]o what extent do [sic] identity politics require a standard internal to existing society against which to pitch their [sic] claims . . . ?'[9] The demand for inclusion is necessarily an endorsement of a standard internal to existing society, for it is only against an existing standard, a standard according to which one is entitled to inclusion, that one can legitimately demand inclusion. As an endorsement of a standard internal to existing society, the demand for inclusion can be nothing more than a demand for inclusion into the existing order. This can be seen in the case of the demand for the inclusion of trans women. Here the demand is for inclusion into women-only spaces – such as prisons, bathrooms, and sports. It is for inclusion into a sex-segregated world, a world organised around the sex–gender binary. In line with this, the use of trans women as models in advertising campaigns[10] and the creation of sex toys for nonbinary people are celebrated as achievements of inclusion.[11] But inclusion into what? From MacKinnon's perspective, inclusion into a world organised by sexuality, a world of sexual hierarchy.

Second-wave feminists perceived that women *qua* women cannot be included in the existing order. As Pateman shows, the liberal state is premised upon a conception of person as self-proprietor, and the conception of person as self-proprietor is a conception of person as man, where a man is a proprietor of a woman. The liberal state thus implies women's subjection to men.[12] More simply, shaped as it is by a concept of humanity as *man*kind, our current form of life cannot survive the recognition that women *qua* women are human. Second-wave feminists dreamed not of the inclusion of women into the existing order – not of 'a piece of the pie as currently and poisonously baked'[13] – but of the liberation of women – a process understood as necessarily involving the creation of 'something new'.[14] 'Liberation' is the emancipation of the class 'woman' from subjection to the class 'man'; it is not the acquisition, for individual women, of liberalism's freedom.[15] It cannot be, for the emancipation of the class 'woman' will inevitably produce a new conception of freedom.

As the project of inclusion necessarily preserves the existing order, while the project of liberation necessarily creates a new one, the two are incompatible.

Perhaps despite Butler's account being unable to accommodate the recognition of women *qua* women as excluded, the project of gender diversification will nevertheless secure women's liberation, for gender diversification by definition destroys the gender binary.

But, on the second-wave view, gender is a *class* relation – a relation between oppressor and oppressed – not a binary. The categories of gender therefore cannot be diversified any more than the categories of '[f]reeman and slave, patrician and plebian, lord and serf, guild-master and journeyman, in a word, oppressor and oppressed'.[16] 'Diverse' genders, in other words, can be no more than variations on the theme of oppressor and oppressed – consider, for example, the genders 'butch' and 'femme'.

III

Butler represents rendering intelligible as a matter of *expanding*[17] – opening up, extending.[18] She thereby represents the achievement of intelligibility as an achievement of *inclusion*. But if, as she argues,[19] the production of intelligible bodies entails the production of unintelligible bodies, then we cannot render the latter intelligible without rendering the former unintelligible. Rendering intelligible is thus not a matter of simply adding new classes to the existing taxonomy. It is rather a matter of simultaneously adding new classes *and removing or reconstituting old ones*. Talk of 'opening up', 'extending', or 'including' obscures the removal or reconstitution of ways of being that such opening up, extending, or including entails. Consider the following example. In a taxonomy in which the class 'woman' exists in contradistinction to the class 'man', a person with the distinguishing features of a member of the class 'man' is unintelligible as a woman. The revision of the class 'woman' so that it includes this person is the reconstitution of the contradistinction in which the classes 'woman' and 'man' exist, and thus the reconstitution of these classes. While the reconstitution of these classes may render this person intelligible as a woman, it renders members of the former class 'woman' unintelligible. Where these members previously had the identity of an integral human being – woman – they now have the identity of a fragment of a human being – 'people with vaginas', 'uterus havers', 'vulva owners'.[20]

Butler recognises the limits of inclusion: 'radical and inclusive representability is not precisely the goal: to include, to speak as, to bring in every marginal and excluded position within a given discourse is to claim that a singular discourse meets its limits nowhere, that it can and will domesticate all signs of difference'.[21] She proceeds to enjoin us to 'begin, without ending, without mastering, to own – and yet never fully to own – the exclusions by which we proceed'.[22] But, in representing her goal as one of '*opening up* possibilities' and '*extending* legitimacy', she seems to me to deny the exclusions by which she proceeds.

The representation of Butler's project, the project of gender diversification, as one of *inclusion* obscures the conflict of interest between the intelligible, who stand to lose intelligibility, and the unintelligible, who stand to gain it – and, with that, the legitimacy of the interest of the intelligible in refusing intelligibility to the unintelligible. In refusing intelligibility, the intelligible appear, then, to be acting purely out of malice. Take for example the recognition of trans women as women: when trans-inclusionary feminists represent this recognition as an inclusion of trans women, they obscure the conflict of interest between women and trans women, eliding the possibility that gender-critical feminists are motivated by concern for women, so that the only explanation of their refusal to recognise trans women as women can be that they are transphobic. (It is ironic that trans-inclusionary feminists, adherents of Butler, deny 'the exclusions by which [they] proceed', while gender-critical feminists, opponents of Butler, acknowledge them.[23])

IV

Inclusion could be achieved (as in the case of gay and lesbian people, it seems)[24] without liberation being derailed; we could believe that the projects of inclusion and liberation were compatible, indeed, that they were two subprojects of a single overarching project: (the amorphous) social justice. We could believe that the proponents of inclusion and the proponents of liberation shared the same goal, were a 'we': feminists.

Faced with the demand for the inclusion of trans women, the proponents of liberation can no longer entertain such beliefs. For the recognition of trans women as women will efface the very premise of the project of liberation (that women are a sex class), rendering this project incoherent. So proponents of liberation must now oppose inclusion.

Proponents of inclusion, however, can continue to indulge in the pretence that their project is compatible with that of liberation. As inclusion is in the ascendant, liberation poses no threat to it, so proponents of inclusion risk nothing by professing support for liberation. They can claim that gender-critical feminists thwart trans women's inclusion, while denying that they, in turn, thwart women's liberation.

In fact proponents of inclusion *must* continue to indulge in this pretence. As I hope to have shown, the history of feminist theory and practice permits appealing to 'feminism' in order to reject the demand for trans women's inclusion, but not the demand for female people's liberation. As we will see, Butler had to *fabricate* a history (this explains why her engagement with specific feminist texts is so minimal and so cursory);[25] she had to invent[26] a tradition of 'French feminism' against which she positioned her work as superiorly feminist,[27] in order to be able to pursue inclusion in the name of feminism. This paper-thin history became historical record-thick, as the history it papered over was forgotten.[28] This combination of fabrication and amnesia made possible the current situation: the acceptance of inclusion, of *gender affirmation*, as a feminist ideal.

There are limits to the rewriting of history, and one of them is feminists' central and persistent concern with wrongs done to *female* people: prostitution,[29] pornography,[30] foot-binding,[31] witch-burning,[32] suttee,[33] female genital mutilation,[34] marital rape,[35] sexual harassment,[36] beauty practices,[37] domestic labour.[38] This concern opens the possibility of a trans-exclusionary *feminism* and precludes an anti-female liberation *feminism*. So, while proponents of liberation can oppose inclusion on feminist grounds, proponents of inclusion can oppose liberation only at the cost of renouncing feminism. But because they are unwilling to renounce it, they must instead deny that inclusion thwarts liberation.

Delphy criticises feminists for refusing to admit that certain disagreements between them are fundamental and irresolvable – and, by implication, that certain agreements are contingent. She has in mind especially the disagreement between 'difference feminists' and 'equality feminists'.[39] Difference feminists believe that men and women are essentially different, while equality feminists believe that this apparently essential difference is in fact the constructed difference of class: men and women are different in the same way master and subject are different. Attempts to reconcile these beliefs[40] are, Delphy argues, misguided, for they rely upon different conceptual frameworks: difference feminism relies upon an 'additive' framework, while equality feminism relies upon a 'holistic' framework. In the additive framework, the parts precede the whole: men and women precede their hierarchical relation. This means that the parts exist unto themselves, have natures of their own. In the holistic framework, the whole precedes the parts: the class relation between men and women is constitutive of men and women.[41] As attempts to reconcile these beliefs are misguided, so too is the assumption that debate will reveal the superior belief or position. This assumption rests on a further assumption: that equality feminism and difference feminism have a common political goal. The idea that debate will reveal equality feminism to be superior by showing that it can achieve liberation for women (while difference feminism can give them only a curtailed citizenship) takes it for granted that equality and difference feminists share the goal of liberation. In fact they do not. It is only the equality feminists who want liberation, and it is only from their perspective that difference feminism achieves a *curtailed* citizenship. Presumably the difference feminists consider liberation a deluded and destructive goal. (Or, perhaps more neutrally, equality feminists want liberation, where liberation involves the complete transformation of men and women, while difference feminists want liberation, where liberation involves (a) the revalorisation of men and women, such that women are no more different from men than men are from women, and (b) the reorganisation of society, such that women's differences are not disadvantages. From the perspective of equality feminists, the valorisation of women's differences is valorisation of the attributes of a slave,[42] and the reorganisation of society such that women's differences are not disadvantages is a reorganisation of society such that women continue to have the attributes of a slave, but these attributes are no longer unnecessarily disadvantageous. Such liberation may be an improvement, but is not liberation. Equally, from the perspective of difference feminists, the complete transformation of men and women is necessarily a transformation of what is biological – and thus immutable and valuable by virtue of playing a part in the survival of the species. Such liberation is impossible, destructive, and not a liberation.) As each conceptual framework produces its own goal (the additive produces specific rights for women, the holistic produces the liberation of women; or the additive creates the conditions under which women's differences are not disadvantages, the holistic creates the conditions under which women's differences disappear), we lack a shared goal by which to adjudicate between the two beliefs or positions.

Delphy concludes: 'To continue interpreting divergences within feminism as mere misunderstandings, or as different strategies, is to bury one's head in the sand: some divergences are not about different ways of achieving the same goals, *they are about different goals.*'[43]

Delphy's analysis of the relationship between difference feminism and equality feminism applies to trans-inclusionary and gender-critical feminism. The latter two rely upon different conceptual frameworks: trans-inclusionary feminism upon a framework in which man and woman are genders and genders are social kinds; gender-critical feminism upon a framework in which man and woman are classes and classes are political and relational kinds. Katharine Jenkins's attempt to reconcile the concept of gender as identity and the concept of gender as class is therefore fundamentally misguided.[44] The concepts of gender as identity and gender as class belong to different conceptual frameworks: identity – a thing – belongs to the additive or metaphysical, whereas class – a relation – belongs to the holistic or dialectical.[45]

Only by distorting one, or perhaps both, of the concepts can we reconcile them. For example, when we suggest that trans women are members of the class 'woman' because they, too, are 'sexualized as targets for incursion, abuse, and devaluation',[46] we purportedly reveal how gender as identity tracks gender as class, with the consequence that identification as woman becomes only a heuristic for membership of the class 'woman'. Or, when we suggest that trans women are members of the class 'woman' because they, too, are subject to the norms of femininity,[47] we reconceive of what it is to be a member of a sex class as what it is to be subject to a set of social norms, not as what it is to stand in a political relation to a member of the other class; as what it is to be an occupant of a social role, not as what it is to be a member of a class. Or, when we suggest that trans women are members of the class 'woman' because they, too, are subordinate by virtue of certain 'observed or imagined bodily features presumed to be evidence of a female's biological role in reproduction',[48] we reconceive what determines a person's membership of this class as perception – not actuality – of femaleness, with the consequence that male people mistakenly perceived as female become members of this class and female people mistakenly perceived as male cease to be. But male people mistakenly perceived as female are male people mistakenly treated as female. So now both those rightly treated as members of the class 'woman' and those wrongly treated this way are equally members of this class. In addition, as it is only insofar as trans women are perceptible as female that they are members of the class 'woman', gender as identity becomes only contingently linked to gender as class.

Arising from different conceptual frameworks, the concepts of gender as identity and gender as class serve different goals. The conceptual framework upon which the concept of gender as identity relies produces the goal of inclusion, while the conceptual framework upon which the concept of gender as class relies produces the goal of liberation. Debate cannot therefore reveal the superior concept: if measured against the goal of combatting gender injustice or inclusion, gender as identity is superior; if measured against the goal of ending the oppression of women or liberation, gender as class is superior.

Indeed, in order to present her revision – the twin concepts of gender as identity and gender as class – as an improvement upon the previous concept of gender as class, Jenkins must slide from the goal of 'end[ing] the oppression of "women"'[49] to the goal of 'combatting gender injustice'.[50] As I have argued, oppression of women and gender injustice (an opaque term that Jenkins does not define) are two distinct wrongs: the oppression of women by men; and the exclusion of those who do not conform to the regulatory ideal of 'sex'. These wrongs are conceived of by two distinct theoretical traditions – second-wave feminism and poststructuralism – and call for two distinct responses: liberation and inclusion. Having slid from the feminist to the poststructuralist goal, Jenkins criticises the feminist concept of woman for thwarting the 'feminist' (in fact the poststructural) goal, and then revises it so that it better serves this goal. She thereby leaves feminism with a concept of woman that does not serve its goal of ending the oppression of women.

Jenkins presents a trans-exclusionary definition of woman as failing to serve the feminist goal of ending the oppression of women by likening it to definitions of woman that exclude 'women of color and working-class women'.[51] Tellingly, Jenkins provides not a single example of a feminist definition of woman that excludes women of colour and working-class women. The second-wave feminist definition of women as members of the female sex class does not exclude such women. At any rate, trans women are obviously not a subgroup of women, as women of colour and working-class women are.

In sum, feminist philosophers' attempts to reconcile the concepts of gender as identity and gender as class or to prove the superiority of one over the other are futile. These concepts rely upon different frameworks and serve different goals. Delphy writes of coming to see that difference feminists disagreed with equality feminists not, as she had long believed, because they had a 'faulty analysis, which could be sorted out by debate', but because they had a 'different' vision 'of "liberation"'.[52] (Delphy is right to place 'liberation' in scare quotes: though both groups may espouse liberation, they each mean something different by it.) In other words, this disagreement was an irreducibly political one. The situation with respect to trans-inclusionary and gender-critical feminists is a little different. Trans-inclusionary feminists are unwilling to admit that inclusion and liberation are different goals. So, while gender-critical feminists have raised their heads out of the sand, trans-inclusionary feminists continue to keep theirs buried. It then appears that the former are irrationally hostile (phobic) to the latter – irrationally because the latter refuse to admit that they are hostile to them.

5

Lies, Betrayal, and Resistance

I

How, then, did Butler's account succeed in acquiring the status of *feminist*? In part, this happened because Butler herself explicitly classifies it as such. In the preface to *Gender Trouble*, which bears the subtitle *Feminism and the Subversion of Identity*, she writes: 'I understood myself to be in an embattled and oppositional relation to certain forms of feminism, even as I understood the text to be part of feminism itself.'[1] She continues:

> In 1989 I was most concerned to criticise a pervasive heterosexual assumption in feminist literary theory. I sought to counter those views that made presumptions about the limits and propriety of gender and restricted the meaning of gender to received notions of masculinity and femininity. It was and remains my view that any feminist theory that restricts the meaning of gender in the presuppositions of its own practice sets up exclusionary gender norms within feminism, often with homophobic consequences. It seemed to me, and continues to seem, that feminism ought to be careful not to idealize certain

expressions of gender that, in turn, produce new forms of hierarchy and exclusion.[2]

Frustratingly, Butler neither identifies a specific feminist scholar who made the presumptions and restrictions she described here nor provides an exemplary passage to illustrate what she means.

I can think of one way in which feminist scholars might be said to make presumptions about 'the limits and propriety of gender' and to restrict the meaning of 'gender' to 'received notions of masculinity and femininity'. In *The Dialectic of Sex*, Firestone attempts to develop, from the female reproductive role (in conjunction with the male reproductive role), an account of the subordination of women *qua* women to men *qua* men. In doing so, she implicitly takes the heterosexual, childbearing, and child-rearing female person – patriarchy's proper woman – to be a representative of the female sex class. Similarly, the Marxist feminists Mariarosa Dalla Costa and Selma James attempt to develop an account of the exploitation of women *qua* women starting from the housewife.[3] In doing so, they take the wife and mother – again, patriarchy's proper woman – to be representative of the female sex class.

This is methodologically problematic. If only some women become patriarchy's proper woman, and if those who do not are nevertheless members of the female sex class, then those who do are not representative of the female sex class. Attempts to develop from them an account of the oppression of the female sex class *qua* the female sex class must therefore fail.

This is not, however, Butler's criticism. Her criticism is that making the presumptions and restrictions discussed above produces 'new forms of hierarchy and exclusion'.[4] Though Butler does not specify these new forms, they must relate to the exclusion of those who do not conform to received notions of masculinity and femininity – gender-nonconforming people. This criticism presupposes that feminism has a duty to pursue the inclusion of gender-nonconforming people, such that its exclusion of them should be a failure for which it would deserve to be condemned. Butler provides no argument for this presupposition, proceeding as though it were self-evident.

It is not self-evident. From the second-wave perspective, the distinctively feminist goal is the liberation of women *qua* women. Feminism's first and foremost duty is the pursuit of this goal. Only insofar as the liberation of women *qua* women entails the inclusion of gender-nonconforming people, only insofar as feminism's duty to pursue the former entails a duty to pursue the latter, does feminism have the duty that Butler presupposes. She does not explain how the former goal entails the latter. When she asserts that feminism ought not to produce new forms of hierarchy and exclusion, she neither reminds us of a duty that feminism has accepted but failed to fulfil nor makes explicit a duty implicit in feminism. Rather she imposes a duty upon feminism. In short, she represents her work as improving upon existing feminism by addressing its failure to fulfil a duty *that she has imposed, without justification*, upon it.

She maintains this representation by not engaging with much feminist scholarship and by interestedly (mis)reading the little with which she does. In *Gender Trouble*, she places Wittig in dialogue with Foucault:

> For Foucault, the substantive grammar of sex imposes an artificial binary relation between the sexes, as well as an artificial internal coherence within each term of that binary. The binary regulation of sexuality suppresses the subversive multiplicity of a sexuality that disrupts heterosexual, reproductive, and medicojuridical hegemonies.
>
> For Wittig, the binary restriction on sex serves the reproductive aims of a system of compulsory heterosexuality; occasionally she claims that the overthrow of compulsory heterosexuality will inaugurate a true humanism of 'the person' freed from the shackles of sex. In other contexts she suggests

that the profusion and diffusion of a nonphallocentric erotic economy will dispel the illusions of sex, gender, and identity.[5]

In fact the Wittig who authored 'One Is Not Born a Woman' is in dialogue with second-wave feminists – Beauvoir, Firestone, Atkinson, Delphy, Dworkin, Guillaumin. This Wittig regards sex as class. She thus regards the 'system of compulsory heterosexuality', the system by which persons are organised into sexes, as the system by which men become masters and women slaves. Her opposition to a system of compulsory heterosexuality is an opposition to men's subjection of women. By taking away from Wittig the second-wave feminist words 'class', 'men', and 'women' and replacing them with the poststructuralist words 'binary' and 'system of compulsory heterosexuality', Butler presents Wittig, and thus feminism, as opposed not to men's subjection of women but to a system of compulsory heterosexuality, and concerned not for women but for all victims of this system, only some of whom are women.[6] She shifts the constituency of feminism from *women* to *victims of compulsory heterosexuality*.[7] As 'victims of compulsory heterosexuality' is a group that includes gender-nonconforming people, feminism then does have a duty to pursue the amelioration of these people's condition; and this amelioration consists in their inclusion. This shift allows Butler to make the criticism of feminism that she does, and thus to position her work as improving upon existing feminism.

This is a significant moment in the history of feminism. By presenting Wittig and, thus, feminism as opposed to a system of compulsory heterosexuality, Butler reconstitutes feminism as a politics. Carl Schmitt argues that '[t]he specific political distinction to which political actions and motives can be reduced is that between friend and enemy'.[8] Before Butler, feminism identified the enemy as men and the friend as women. After Butler, feminism identifies the enemy as the regulatory ideal of 'sex' and the friend as the victims of this ideal.[9] On the surface,

Butler's reconstitution of feminism appears as a logical expansion and the resulting feminism as a more inclusionary and politically stronger movement.[10] On closer examination, this reconstitution emerges as the displacement of feminism (and, as I will show, of politics).

If women *qua* women are victims of the regulatory ideal of sex, they are not victims the same way others are. Others are victims by virtue of the normativity and binary form of this ideal: because they do not fit in the categories of the binary, they are unintelligible. Women *qua* women are instead victims by virtue of the *content* of the categories of the binary: as the content of the categories 'man' and 'woman' is 'master' and 'subject', women exist in a relation of subjection to men. Because women are victims by virtue of the content of these categories, successful conformity to the category 'woman' does not rescue women from victimisation. It is as members of the female sex class, not as failures to conform to the category 'woman', that women are abused, objectified, harassed, raped, and battered; and membership of the female sex class is secured by one's female body regardless of how feminine or 'womanly' – how 'cis' – one is.[11]

Although differently, both women and the gender-nonconforming are nevertheless victims of the regulatory ideal of sex, we might think. But notice that, in virtue of this difference, each has a different enemy and a different friend. For the gender-nonconforming, the primary enemy is the regulatory ideal of sex or the normative sex binary, for it is this that renders them unintelligible, and the friend is all those who do not conform to the ideal and are therefore unintelligible. For women, the primary enemy is men, for it is to men that they exist in a relation of subjection, and the friend is women, for it is with women that they share this relation of subjection. If the specifically political categories are those of friend and enemy, then feminism and queer theory are two distinct politics. The dissolution of the sex binary via gender diversification is not the dissolution of men, and the dissolution of men is not the diversification of gender but the obliteration of it. As two distinct politics, feminism and queer theory cannot coexist as one politics – feminism. One must displace the other. Tragically, queer theory has displaced feminism.

II

Butler could not have succeeded in presenting her account as superiorly feminist unless feminists had permitted her to. Why did they? Wherein lay the appeal of Butler's account to them?

Butler tells (and thus, as she would surely admit, constructs) a history in which feminism was exclusionary. 'In the 1980s', she writes, 'the feminist "we" rightly came under attack by women of color who claimed that the "we" was invariably white'.[12] Under the description 'exclusion' she runs together this exclusion of *women* – women of colour and working-class women[13] – and the exclusion of sexual minorities, so that the latter appears to be one more instance of the long-running feminist failure to recognise as constituents those who properly are. Feminism then appears to have the duty that Butler imposes upon it, namely the duty to 'include' sexual minorities.

But these are two significantly different exclusions: the former is the exclusion of women, whom feminism claims to serve, while the latter is not. The former is illegitimate, the latter is legitimate.

By citing feminism's past illegitimate exclusions, Butler stokes a feminist fear of illegitimate ones. Then, by failing to distinguish between illegitimate and legitimate exclusions, she exploits this fear when she claims that 'feminism ought to be careful not to ... produce new forms of hierarchy and exclusion'.[14]

Women have pursued their interest and have sacrificed much in doing so. But they have also been reluctant to prioritise their interest as, and because it is, their interest. Even radical feminists, fed up with a left that would support the interests of every oppressed demographic except women, prioritised women's interest on the grounds that sexism was 'the root and paradigm of the various forms of oppression',[15] that the pursuit of this interest was instrumental to the pursuit of all oppressed people's interests. This reluctance is the understandable though nonetheless tragic failure to believe that women's liberation alone, and thus women's liberation itself, is worth fighting for. What other political movement – abolitionist, Marxist, environmental, Zionist, civil rights, anti-apartheid, Black Lives Matter – has defended itself by claiming, pathetically, to be 'for everybody'?

Butler's assertion that feminism ought not to produce new forms of hierarchy and exclusion *legitimises* feminists' reluctance to prioritise women's interest, redescribing their failure as success. A *political failure* in the form of a refusal to assert the worth of women becomes a *moral success* in the form of a more inclusive feminism. Indeed, the language and the tone in which contemporary feminists denigrate second-wave feminists is moralistic: these feminists are white, middle-class, racist, exclusionary, universalising, essentialising, victimising, in a word, *bad*.

For women to prioritise their interest as women is for women to prioritise identification *as* a member of the female sex class, which is also identification *with* members of the female sex class. It is for women to prioritise loyalty ('friendship') to women. Reluctance to prioritise women's interest is thus reluctance to prioritise loyalty to women. In 2000 Dworkin asked:

> Could women 'set a high price on our blood'? Could women set any price on our blood? . . . Could women . . . have a code of honor woman-to-woman that weakens the male-dominant demands of nationalism or race-pride or ethnic pride? Could

women commit treason to the men of their own group: put women first, even the putative enemy women?[16]

Could women put women first?[17] On Butler's account, women *qua* women are not a distinctive class and do not have a distinctive class interest. At best, they, as sexual minorities, are victims of the regulatory ideal of sex, sharing with those minorities an interest in gender diversification and inclusion. If women *qua* women are not a distinctive class, then we need not – we cannot – put women first. Butler's account relieves women of the political imperative to put women first and, thus, of the burden of our failure to do so. It allows Ellen Willis to unironically pinpoint second-wave feminism's demand for 'unity of women across barriers of class, race, cultural values, and sexual orientation' as contributing to its demise.[18] She does not consider the possibility that it contributed to its demise by asking of women what they could neither do nor confront not doing: put women first, the consequence of which was that women had to deny the demand for unity.

Indeed, Butler's account relieves women of the need not merely to put women first but to conceive of them as a political class at all, a category of people who suffer a common subjection, a category or group with a common interest, a public. Second-wave feminism asked women to have the courage to conceive of themselves as unified *politically*. Women were – and remain – conceivable as unified only biologically. 'Women as women, women unmodified by class distinctions and apart from nature, were simply unthinkable to Mill, as to most liberals, and to Luxemburg, as to most Marxists.'[19] And so they remained to Butler, as to most poststructuralists – and perhaps, sadly, to most feminists. So unthinkable are women as women, apart from nature, that poststructural feminists can conceive of them only as an *essence* or a *disunity*. So unintelligible is second wave's 'woman' that, despite the absence of 'explicitly essentialist formulations of what it means to be a woman', Alcoff can 'render' this notion 'coherent' only by 'supplying a missing premise that there is an innate female essence'.[20] Rejecting the conception of woman as an essence, poststructural feminists must, then, embrace a conception of woman as a disunity. It is instructive that they invoke the unity of race and (economic) class in order to claim that women are a disunity: 'Western feminist thought . . . posit[s] an essential "womanness" that all women have and share in common despite the racial, class, religious, ethnic, and cultural differences among us.'[21] Why is it that race, class, religion, ethnicity, and culture are sufficiently unities that disunify women, but sex class is not sufficiently a unity that disunifies race, class, religion, ethnicity, and culture?[22] Why are women *uniquely* a disunity? Is it coincidental that the poststructural feminist doubt 'that the term "women" denotes a common identity'[23] resembles the previous leftist male rejection of women's claim to class status? Did Butler's account appeal to feminists because it released them from the need – and hence absolved them of the failure – to conceive of women as, and to act as, a political unity?

Butler also held out to feminists the promise of respectability. Second-wave feminists spoke with simplicity and directness, on the unscholarly subject of sexual relations, in response to what they saw in the world, to the women around them, in a vocabulary forged in praxis,[24] a vocabulary partly liberal, Marxist, and feminist, of 'men', 'women', 'sex-class', 'oppression', 'liberation', 'sex', 'harassment', 'rape', 'prostitution', 'pornography', 'struggle', 'revolution'. In contrast, Butler wrote evasively, on the scholarly subject of sex and gender, in response to theorists (Lacan, Foucault, Kristeva, Irigaray, and Derrida), in the vocabulary of poststructuralism, of the 'regulatory ideal of sex', the 'sex binary', 'masculinity', 'femininity', 'unintelligibility', 'intelligibility', 'subject', 'abject', 'subversion', 'parody'.[25]

Second-wave feminists offered a feminism that was *inappropriate*: inappropriate in its audacity (it claimed that *women*, those ladies of leisure, are oppressed by men), in its sweeping declarations ('Whatever they may be in public life, whatever their relations with men, in their relations with women, all men are rapists and that's all they are'),[26] in its subject matter (the intimate), in its tone (dramatic, earnest, contemptuous), in its sources (women's stories), and perhaps above all in its ambition (a new world). Butler offered a feminism that was *appropriate*: appropriate in its theoretical sophistication, in its subject matter (gender),[27] in its emphasis on women's differences ('there was also no "she", no singularity, but a sea of differences among US women'),[28] in its refusal to make positive claims ('It is *not* possible to oppose the "normative" forms of gender without at the same time subscribing to a certain normative view of how the gendered world ought to be. I want to suggest, however that the positive normative vision of this text, such as it is, *does not* and *cannot* take the form of a prescription: "subvert gender in the way that I say, and life will be good"'),[29] in its endless qualifications ('"identity" as a point of departure can never hold as the solidifying ground of a feminist political movement ... This is not to say that the term "women" ought not to be used, or that we ought to announce the death of the category'),[30] and in its modest challenge to the status quo ('subversion'). Against this brand of feminism, second-wave feminism appears unsophisticated, immature, 'embarrassing'.[31] Consider the following passage from Fraser and Nicholson's paper 'Social Criticism without Philosophy':

> Since around 1980, many feminist scholars have come to abandon the project of grand social theory. They have stopped looking for *the* causes of sexism and have turned to more concrete inquiry with more limited aims. One reason for this shift is the growing legitimacy of feminist scholarship. The institutionalization of women's studies in the United States has meant a dramatic increase in the size of the community of feminist

inquirers, a much greater division of scholarly labor and a large and growing fund of concrete information. As a result, feminist scholars have come to regard their enterprise more collectively, more like a puzzle whose various pieces are being filled in by many different people than a construction to be completed by a single, grand theoretical stroke. In short, *feminist scholarship has attained its maturity.*[32]

Fraser and Nicholson present 'grand social theory' and 'concrete inquiry with more limited aims' as dichotomous. Without a shared paradigm, feminists cannot do collective puzzle solving. They cannot see the same phenomena, they cannot ask the same questions, they cannot make the same predictions, they cannot generate the same data, they cannot offer the same interpretations, they cannot come to the same conclusions. Their findings therefore cannot accumulate, forming an ever more detailed picture of women's condition. In the absence of a shared paradigm, feminist inquiry has the narrowness of scope of mature scientific inquiry, but it does not achieve the progress that mature scientific inquiry does. Indeed, what do we now know that would indicate that feminism has progressed, that today we have a more comprehensive understanding of women's condition than we did before the rejection of grand social theory? In claiming that 'concrete inquiry with more limited aims' has replaced 'grand social theory', Fraser and Nicholson assume that both serve the same purpose; but they do not. Grand social theory provides the framework within which such an inquiry can be conducted. In short, the two are complementary, not dichotomous.

With MacKinnon's agenda for theory, feminism appeared to be on the cusp of acquiring a shared paradigm, and thereby maturing. But poststructural feminism promptly reframed maturity as the rejection of grand social theory, drove feminism away from its search for such a theory, and proclaimed its maturity. By proclaiming its maturity before it had acquired a shared paradigm, poststructural feminism deprived feminism of the possibility of attaining maturity.

Fraser and Nicholson attribute feminists' abandonment of grand social theorising in favour of conducting concrete inquiries with limited aims to the 'growing legitimacy of feminist scholarship'. I am suggesting the reverse: feminist scholars attained legitimacy by abandoning one in favour of the other.

I am not sure why feminists succumbed to the desire for respectability. For the very reasons why second-wave feminism was not respectable in the academy, it was respectable within the feminist movement; and for the very reasons why poststructural feminism is respectable in the academy, it is not respectable in the feminist community outside the academy.[33] This suggests that the shift from second-wave to poststructural feminism is a shift in community, and thus in accountability. While second-wave feminists were accountable to women in the feminist movement, poststructural feminists are accountable to academics. So, while for second-wave feminists respect was respect acquired from women, for poststructural feminists it is respect acquired from academics.[34]

III

In asking why feminists allowed Butler's account to displace the second-wave account, I have elided those feminists who criticised the shifts that occurred in feminism because they saw these shifts for what they were: not the maturation but the abandonment of feminism, and with it the abandonment of women. In an article of 1982, Nancy Miller warns that the displacement of sex by gender, of the body by the performance – a performance that, once the body has been displaced, becomes theoretically available to a person regardless of their body (i.e. femininity becomes available to male people, masculinity to female people) – will see the re-disappearance of women and of their suffering.[35] In her presciently titled *Feminism without Women*, Tania Modleski suggests that men (aided by women, indeed aided by feminists) have usurped women and appropriated feminism. A shift from 'women' to 'gender' – from women's studies to gender studies, from *Signs: Journal of Women in Culture and Society* to *Gender and Differences*,[36] from an embodied female being to free-floating artifice – and an obsessive 'anti-essentialism' that denigrates the use of the word 'woman' to refer to an embodied female being[37] have allowed men to equate 'woman' with 'feminine' and to claim the name 'woman' for their feminised male selves, or rather, since men have always equated 'woman' with 'feminine', to do so now in the name not of male supremacy but of feminism[38] – one that, having jettisoned women, is in the service of 'gender criticism',[39] which in turn is 'a conduit to the more comprehensive field of gender studies'.[40] Whereas gender studies ought to be subservient to feminism as a political movement, being judged 'according to the contributions it can make to the feminist project and the aid it can give us in illuminating the causes, effects, scope, and limits of male dominance',[41] it is feminism that, being no longer a politics, is subservient to gender studies. In the article mentioned earlier, Teresa de Lauretis questions the charge of 'essentialism'. Observing that most feminists believe 'that women are made, not born, that gender is not an innate feature (as sex may be) but a sociocultural construction (and precisely for that reason it is oppressive to women), that patriarchy is historical (especially so when it is believed to have superseded a previous matriarchal realm)',[42] Lauretis's argues that the essentialism imputed to feminism is an 'outright construction',[43] which 'serves less the purposes of effective criticism in the ongoing elaboration of feminist theory than those of convenience, conceptual simplification, or academic legitimation'.[44] Echoing de Lauretis's point that the charge of essentialism is not made with the aim of developing feminist theory, Modleski suggests that poststructural feminist reminders of differences between women serve the 'theoretical purpose of dissuading feminists from claiming commonalities across class and racial lines'.[45] Besides, these 'reminders' – as though feminists who believe that women have in common membership of the female sex class believe that women have in common everything, that they are not different in many other ways – are never followed by substantive discussion of those differences and are ignored once they have been used to berate feminists. Likewise, Seyla Benhabib sees the 'debunking as essentialist any attempt to formulate a feminist ethic, a feminist politics, a feminist concept of autonomy, and even a feminist aesthetic' as constituting a 'retreat from utopia',[46] a refusal to envision the future in which we wish to live. (She, too, questions the accusation that these attempts 'articulate only the sensitivities of white, middle-class, affluent, first-world, heterosexual women',[47] reinforcing de Lauretis's suggestion that the essentialism that poststructural feminists impute to second-wave feminism is their own fabrication.) The things she warns us about – the elimination of the specificity of feminist theory and the undermining of the emancipatory ideals of the women's movement by postmodernism[48] – have now come to pass. Susan Bordo, in the same 1990 chapter discussed earlier, observes that in the present moment 'feminism stands less in danger of the "totalizing" tendencies of feminists than of an increasingly paralyzing anxiety over falling (from what grace?) into ethnocentrism or "essentialism"'.[49] Somar Brodribb exposes the masculine-ness and misogyny of poststructuralist theory.[50] A few years earlier, Toril Moi had warned feminists that the price of accepting Foucault's theory 'is nothing less than the depoliticisation of feminism'.[51] 'If we capitulate to Foucault's analysis', she wrote, 'we will find ourselves caught up in a sado-masochistic spiral of power and resistance which, circling endlessly in heterogeneous movement, creates a space in which it will be quite impossible convincingly to argue that women under patriarchy constitute an oppressed group, let alone develop a theory of their liberation'.[52] In similar vein, Nancy Hartsock argues that the poststructuralist theory of power does not serve women, since it obscures domination.[53] Sabina Lovibond expresses suspicion of the postmodernist demand that women, whose emancipation remains 'a patchy, hit-and-miss affair', reject 'emancipatory metanarratives'.[54]

These criticisms and cautionings appealed to a commitment to *women*: '"Less essentialist than thou" is as much of a waste of time and is as intellectually bankrupt as "more oppressed than thou" was ten years ago. I thought we were grown up. I thought we were smart. Crucially I thought we actually cared about *women*.'[55] But those at whom these criticisms and cautionings were levelled did not share this commitment. Having been accepted into the academy, they chose to answer to theorists and to theorise as poststructuralism – rather than the reality whose apprehension animated feminism – demanded. These feminists' commitment to women thus became subordinate, a thing to be reconciled with poststructuralism. Reconciliation not being possible, they cheerfully discarded this commitment ... *in the name of commitment to women*.[56] So the criticisms and cautionings appealed impotently to a commitment that had been displaced. They stand now as traces of a feminism and commitment to women that some women refused to forget.

6

Feminism

Political, Not Metaphysical

I

Poststructural feminists read, evaluate, and condemn second-wave feminism as a metaphysical – an outdated structuralist – project. Their own project, then, appears, by definition (i.e. by virtue of being named poststructural), to supersede second-wave feminism. In this chapter I read these projects as political rather than metaphysical projects. On such a reading, poststructural feminism, far from advancing the feminist project, emerges as renouncing it.

Schmitt sets out to provide an account of the nature of the political in a book dedicated to this concept. Typically, he says, 'political' is associated with 'state' and 'state' with 'political': 'The state thus appears as something political, the political as something pertaining to the state – obviously an unsatisfactory circle.'[1] Schmitt proceeds by distinguishing the political from other 'various relatively independent endeavors of human thought and action, particularly the moral, aesthetic, and economic',[2] observing that every such endeavour rests on its own distinction (the moral rests on the distinction between good and evil, the aesthetic, on the distinction between beautiful and ugly, the economic, on the distinction between profitable and unprofitable), and identifying the distinction upon which the political rests: friend and enemy.[3]

Schmitt argues that, just as the distinctions upon which other endeavours rest are irreducible, for instance the distinction between good and evil cannot be reduced to the distinction between beautiful and ugly or between profitable and unprofitable, so too is the distinction upon which the political rests. So the (political) enemy need not be morally evil, aesthetically ugly, or an economic competitor.

Crucially for our purpose, the distinction between friend and enemy is not reducible to other distinctions, as in religion, economic class, or ethnicity. These distinctions may acquire political significance through the identification of who is the friend and who is the enemy, but they are not themselves constitutive of the distinction between them. For instance, the distinction between capitalists and proletariat, between those who own the means of production and those who do not, acquires political significance as the proletariat comes to consciousness, identifying the capitalist class as the enemy and itself as the friend.[4]

I have said that after Butler feminism identifies the enemy as the regulatory ideal of sex. In fact it would have been more accurate to say that poststructural feminism repudiates the very notion of enemy as structuralist.[5] On Schmitt's view, a class unwilling to define the enemy is a class that fails to become a political entity:

> If the political power of a class or of some other group within a state is sufficiently strong to hinder the waging of wars against other states but incapable of assuming or lacking the will to assume the state's power and thereby decide on the friend-and-enemy distinction and, if necessary, make war, then the political entity is destroyed.[6]

As one half of the population, women can surely 'assume the state's power', decide on the friend–enemy distinction, and wage war.

Poststructural feminists will object that they are not unwilling to define the enemy; rather they reject the notion of an enemy. Feminists have persistently exhibited a reluctance to define the enemy.[7] As mentioned earlier, in 1974 Atkinson relayed Barbour's remark that feminists speak of women as oppressed, not of men as oppressing women, and reflected that, when feminists are asked, 'by whom are women oppressed?', they respond, 'by society'.[8] In 1993 Bordo claimed that 'it is indeed senseless to view men as the enemy'.[9] And in 2000 bell hooks declared that 'feminism is for everybody'.[10] A feminism for everybody is a feminism against nobody, a feminism without an enemy. In light of this, the poststructural repudiation of the notion of an enemy appears a little too convenient – political cowardice dressed up as intellectual commitment – all the more as one considers that the poststructural turn has not led Marxists to abjure the belief that capitalists are the enemy, nor has it led others to expect them to do so.

Just as the poststructural repudiation of the notion of an enemy emerges as an unwillingness to define the enemy, so the poststructural wariness of the category 'woman' emerges as an unwillingness to define the friend. In Butler's work I find three reasons for her refusal to define 'woman'.

First, a definition of 'woman' is necessarily normative, and thus exclusionary.[11] A definition of 'woman' provides a standard, a *norm* against which to measure a person's womanhood. A norm is regulatory, bringing those who are judged in accordance with it into conformity to it. In this way a definition constructs the referent that it purports to describe. Those who are judged in accordance with a norm and who do not conform to it are deemed abnormal. In this respect, a norm excludes.[12] For example, according to the second-wave definition of 'woman', one is a woman insofar as one is a member of the female sex class. This definition compels those judged in accordance with it to act as a member of the female sex class would – that is, in the 1970s, to recount their experiences of sexual harassment in consciousness-raising groups; in the 2020s, to announce #MeToo on Twitter. Those who claim to not have been oppressed, to have freely chosen to become, for example, stay-at-home mothers and to find fulfilment in this role, are deemed 'victims of false consciousness', 'brainwashed', suffering a sickness of the mind. The second-wave definition of 'woman' is in this way exclusionary.

But notice what it is that this definition, with its normativity, its regulatoriness, constructs: *the feminist subject*. The process of regulation is the politicisation of the female person, the transformation of female persons from members of a sex class in itself into members of a sex class for itself.

Second-wave feminists had a tendency to talk of women's 'true' and 'false' selves, where the former are their feminist selves and the latter their patriarchal ones. Daly, for example, writes: 'behind the foreground of false selves, of fathers' favorites, there is the deep Background where the Great Hags live and work, hacking off with our Dreadful double axes the Athena-shells designed to stifle our Selves'.[13] Contemporary feminists hear this talk as metaphysical or moral, as the attribution of an essence or a positive reevaluation of femaleness.[14] In fact it is *political*. On the political definition of 'woman', a woman is true to her womanhood insofar as she is a friend, a woman-identified woman, a woman who, with and for women, struggles against men. A woman who is instead loyal to men is false to her womanhood, 'anatomically female ... but ... [with] male-possessed brains/spirits'.[15] The political definition of a group, the identification of it as a friend to which another group is an enemy, ties identity to loyalty:[16] a real member of the group is one who is allegiant to it.

Interestingly, MacKinnon exploits a political definition of 'woman' in order to suggest that trans women are women (and that trans-exclusionary feminists are not):

> We're being told by this group – those of the feminism of female body parts – that they are our team, and the trans women, whose feminism and identification as and with women is often far stronger and more substantive, in my experience anyway, and who really are against violence against women, including prostitution, are not. If anyone wants to exclude some women from the group women, I have a list.[17]

Trans women are women – our team – because their feminism is strong and substantive, while trans-exclusionary feminists are not; they ought to be excluded from the group women because their feminism is weak and unsubstantive. Implicit in this is a definition of 'woman' as 'person loyal to woman'. Such a definition is incoherent, for it effaces the object of loyalty. If 'woman' is 'person loyal to woman', then 'person loyal to *woman*' is 'person loyal to *person loyal to woman*', and 'person loyal to person loyal to *woman*' is 'person loyal to person loyal to *person loyal to woman*', and on it goes. On the second-wave definition of 'woman' as member of the female sex class, a woman, once conscious of her condition, once enlightened, once properly a woman, is loyal to women. 'Woman' is thus related – but not reducible – to 'loyalty to women'. And loyalty to women is not loyalty to feminists, as it is for MacKinnon; it is loyalty to all members of the female sex class, regardless of their own loyalties.[18] For gender-critical feminists, it is loyalty to women regardless of their trans-inclusionary politics, regardless of their betrayal of women.

The second-wave definition of 'woman' is at once descriptive and normative, at once political and politicising – 'an incitement to women to reconsider past choices and past loyalties and to choose to "cast themselves into the world" as free'.[19] But it is unclear to me that this normativity is, as Butler believes, problematic. I admit to finding unpleasant the understanding of non-feminist women as unenlightened. But perhaps I object more to the contempt with which feminist women regard these women, and perhaps contempt need not accompany this understanding.[20] At any rate, I am not sure that a feminist can avoid this understanding. For as a feminist, one must believe in the rightness of the feminist project, and one cannot believe in the rightness of the feminist project without believing in the wrongness of those who contradict it. It therefore seems to me that commitment to women's liberation entails this form of exclusion. Butler's insistence that feminism should not be exclusionary is tantamount to a request that feminism renounce itself.

The second reason for Butler's refusal to define 'woman' is that doing so would mean 'keeping in their place the very premises that have tried to secure our subordination from the start'.[21] This claim rests on the mistaken assumption that the feminist definition of 'woman' reiterates the patriarchal one. She writes:

> There are those who would claim that there is an ontological specificity to women as child-bearers that forms the basis of a specific legal and political interest in representation, and then there are others who understand maternity to be a social relation that is, under current social circumstances, the specific cross-cultural situation of women. And there are those who seek recourse to Gilligan and others to establish a feminine specificity that makes itself clear in women's communities or ways of knowing.[22]

These feminist accounts, which treat 'women' as coextensive with 'childbearers', 'mothers', and 'feminine beings', seem to Butler to reassert the patriarchal definition of 'woman', according to which a normal woman is a childbearer, a mother, a feminine being. This leads her to ask: 'Is the construction of the category of women as a coherent and stable subject an unwitting regulation and reification of gender relations?'[23]

On the one hand, *some* second-wave accounts, such as Firestone's and Dalla Costa and James's, do seem to me to treat patriarchy's normal (proper) woman as representative of women, with the consequence that patriarchy's 'woman' becomes feminism's 'women', patriarchy's ideal feminism's constituency. On the other hand, as accounts of women's oppression, even these accounts presuppose a new definition of 'woman'. On the patriarchal definition, a woman is a female person, where 'female person' is one whose subjection to a male person completes him, as reflected in the pronouncement 'man and wife': as she becomes his wife and subject (she assumes his surname), he becomes a man. The relation between a man and a woman is one of mastery and subjection, and this relation of mastery and subjection is the expression and fulfilment of a man's and a woman's nature. On this definition, the feminist claim that sexual relations – relations between men *qua* men and women *qua* women – are oppressive of women is nonsensical. So either this claim is nonsensical or the definition of 'woman' operative in it is different from the patriarchal one. The anti-feminist infers the former, the feminist the latter. What, then, might this definition be? This is to ask what definition would render intelligible the feminist claim that sexual relations are oppressive. And that would be a definition of 'woman' as a human being, a man's equal. As a man's equal, her subjection to him oppresses rather than fulfils her. In other words, the feminist proposition that women are human beings does not predicate a new property (humanity) of an old subject (women); it introduces a new subject. As Rowbotham, Daly, and Frye help us to see,[24] patriarchal language, in which 'man' and 'human' are synonyms and 'man' and 'woman' antonyms, is a language in which 'woman' cannot designate a human being. A proposition in which 'woman' does designate a human being thus reflects the creation of a language in which 'man' and 'human' are no longer synonyms, 'man' and 'woman' are no longer antonyms, 'the male and the female sex' are no longer 'the *opposite* sexes' – in short, a language in which 'woman', along with 'man' and 'human', has a new meaning.

To the trans-inclusionary slogan 'trans women are women', gender-critical feminists respond 'woman is an adult human female'. They see their use of 'woman' as consistent with established use, in contrast with the trans-inclusionary feminists' use, which is revisionist. However, contextualised within their gender-critical *feminist* politics and within their indignation about the ongoing abuse of women and the trans-inclusionary indifference to this abuse, their use of 'woman' assumes a revisionist significance. Frye distinguishes between two senses of 'human being': member of the species *Homo sapiens*; and full person. A member of the species *Homo sapiens* has certain biological capacities and is worthy of certain treatment – humane treatment, in contrast with the treatment that non-human animals deserve (a member of the species *Homo sapiens* ought not to be penned up, neglected, whipped, starved, taken from its mother, put down). A full person is one who partakes of the 'radical superiority' of the species *Homo sapiens*, one who 'may approach all other creatures with humanist arrogance',[25] one who is worthy of respect.[26] Now stop to reflect on the fact that treatment considered appropriate for women is experienced by men as demeaning.[27] In established (patriarchal) use, 'woman' means 'adult *human* female' in the first sense only (member of the species). In feminist use, 'woman' means 'adult *human* female' in the second sense (full person). Because gender-critical feminists have taken themselves to emphasise the biological nature of women, they have seen themselves as placing emphasis on 'female' ('woman is an adult human *female*'), and hence as meaning only that 'woman' names the adult female of the species *Homo sapiens*. I want to suggest that their emphasis on 'female' reflects an emphasis on 'human'. What motivates their claim 'woman is an adult human female' is an outrage at the mistreatment of female people; and what distinguishes them from all those who prioritise trans women's interests is a belief – implicit in this outrage – in the *humanity*, the full personhood, of female people. Seiya Morita recently brought this emphasis on 'human' to the surface. The epigraph of his 2023 paper juxtaposes two quotations:

> 'A woman is an adult human female.' – gender-critical feminists
> 'Are women human?' – Catharine A. MacKinnon[28]

When MacKinnon asked, 'are women human?',[29] she intended the second sense of 'human': are women full persons? By presenting the gender-critical claim with this question, Morita reveals the hitherto unnoticed political significance of 'human'. Responding to MacKinnon's dismissive characterisation of gender-critical feminist politics as taken 'from the dictionary',[30] Morita writes: 'MacKinnon once understood this: that a dictionary definition can be political. One of her books is titled *Are Women Human?* This is a question posed at the dictionary level, that nevertheless has sufficient political significance in a society where women are not treated as human beings.'[31] Morita is right and wrong: he is right that the significance or meaning of 'woman' in this question is political, but he is wrong that this meaning is taken from the dictionary. The dictionary meaning is *Homo sapiens*; the feminist meaning, which is not yet the dictionary one, is full person.

As the feminist definition of 'woman' recognises her as a human being, it shatters rather than preserves 'the very premises that have tried to secure our subordination from the start' – to repeat Butler's words quoted earlier in this chapter (see p. 93 and n. 22). In addition, it does not reify gender relations; it reconceives them. According to the patriarchal definition of 'woman', the relation between a man and a woman is one of erotic *love*. It is harmonious, intimate, personal, private, and nourishing. According to the feminist definition, it is a relation between friend and enemy, a relation of *hate*. It is antagonistic, cold, shared, public, and destructive.

The third reason for Butler's refusal to define 'woman' is that the attempt to do so necessarily generates factionalisation, thus undermining solidarity.[32] Butler invalidly draws this claim from the empirical observation that every feminist attempt to define 'woman' has been met with resistance within 'the very constituency that is supposed to be unified by the articulation of its common element': 'In the 1980s, the feminist "we" rightly came under attack by women of color who claimed that the "we" was invariably white ... The effort to characterize a feminine specificity through recourse to maternity, whether biological or social, produced a similar factionalization.'[33]

Notice Butler's remark that resistance occurred within 'the very constituency that is supposed to be unified by the articulation of its common element'. Here Butler betrays herself; for how does she recognise those among whom resistance occurred as feminism's *constituency*, if not by recognising them as women? And how does she recognise them as women, if not by accepting a definition of 'woman'? Butler's argument is self-defeating. She considers resistance to the feminist attempt to define 'woman' evidence that this attempt has failed because it is enacted by women, by the referents of 'woman', by those whom the definition of 'woman' must, if it is to be accurate, capture. So, if resistance to the feminist attempt to define 'woman' is evidence that this attempt has failed, then it is also evidence that women are recognisable, which is evidence that women are a unity, which is evidence of the possibility of defining 'woman' without generating factionalisation.

Butler's suggestion that women's differences are such that the feminist attempt to define 'woman' is doomed to be exclusionary and thereby to generate factionalisation is similarly self-defeating. Of the attempt to define 'woman' with reference to maternity, she writes, 'surely all women are not mothers' (as though some feminists believed that they are), 'some cannot be, some are too young or too old to be, some choose not to be, and for some who are mothers, that is not necessarily the rallying point of their politicization in feminism'.[34] The very claim '*all women* are not mothers' presupposes the existence of a distinctive group 'women', some members of which are mothers. The existence of a distinctive group *women* signals the possibility of a definition of 'woman' that does not illegitimately exclude women and hence does not generate factionalisation.

As Schmitt explains, to define the friend is to identify the people with and for whom one will wage war, with and for whom one will sacrifice one's life and take another's, should the need arise.[35] So, by refusing to define woman, poststructural feminists refuse to identify the people to whom they must pledge allegiance, and through this refusal they evade the need to pledge allegiance. When one considers that the poststructural turn in feminism is contemporaneous with the intersectional turn,[36] in which feminism replaces the goal of liberating women *qua* women with that of eradicating all social injustices and turns its allegiance from women *qua* women to all victims of social injustice, one cannot but see the poststructural turn as an attempt to shake the commitment to women *qua* women.

Implicit in Butler's argument that we ought not to define 'woman' because any definition would fail to represent some women is an assumption that feminism has a duty to represent each and every woman. By contrast, on a Schmittian view, each and every woman has a duty to pursue the shared interest of women, even when the cost of doing so is her life. On Butler's view, feminism is a reified movement committed to serving individual women, while on a Schmittian view feminism is the movement of individual women who are committed to the collective of women. These are two very different framings. In the first, individual women ask what feminism can do for them, while in the second individual women ask what they can do for women. In this second framing, individual women who are not mothers do not desert feminism because it focuses on mothers, for they recognise that motherhood is a significant site of the oppression of the collective of women.

II

Poststructural feminists reject the category of woman on the grounds that it falsely essentialises. In response to this rejection, some feminist philosophers, unwilling to jettison this category altogether, have sought to salvage it by delineating it in such a way that it does not essentialise.[37] More recently, gender-critical feminists have dismissed the criticism of essentialism, arguing that 'woman' is coextensive with 'female person', that a female person has an essence, and that having an essence is not something politically problematic to acknowledge.[38] These different groups of feminists are similarly mistaken in their understanding of the category of 'woman'. Poststructural feminists assume that this category is necessarily a metaphysical one, while feminist philosophers and gender-critical feminists alike assume that the category of 'woman' precedes, and therefore can be identified independently of, the friend–enemy, woman–man distinction. All fail to see that, *for feminism*, the category of woman is a *political* category, one half of the friend–enemy distinction, and that, as a political category, it is *irreducible*.

On the second-wave conception of women as a sex class, woman stands to man as subject to master and friend to enemy. Indeed, woman just is one who stands in this relation in such a way that the elimination of the relation is the elimination of woman (and man). As Wittig writes, 'for μs there is no such thing as being-woman or being-man. "Man" and "woman" are political concepts of opposition, and the copula which dialectically unites them is, at the same time, the one which abolishes them.'[39] The definitions of 'woman' that Butler criticises – childbearer, mother, feminine being – are metaphysical definitions, definitions that take a woman to be a thing in itself.[40] On these definitions, women *qua* women share a capacity for childbearing, the role of mother, femininity. But the second-wave conception of women is not a metaphysical one. It is one according to which women *qua* women share not an essence but a relation: a fate of subjection to men.[41]

According to the second-wave conception, 'woman' is coextensive with 'female person' (women form a *sex* class), but the category of female person is political too, and thus irreducible (sex is *class*). This conception defies both the sex–gender binary and the Butlerian challenge to this binary. According to it, women and female people are one, and this 'one' is a political group. The sex–gender (biology–role) binary precludes theorisation of the sexual as political. Only if we redescribe sex as gender, which is to be understood in opposition to sex, only if we claim that what we have assumed to be biology is in fact role, can we theorise sex as political. Of course, the resulting theorisation would be one of gender *as opposed to sex* as political. It would tacitly preserve the patriarchal status of the sexual as the paradigmatically non-political. If the sex–gender binary preserves this status, so too does the Butlerian challenge to it. Butler argues that the construction of gender is simultaneously the construction of sex (as that which precedes gender), so that sex is 'always already gender',[42] and 'the distinction between sex and gender' is 'no distinction at all'.[43] This argument allows us to place femaleness, hitherto in the biological and non-political category of sex, in the social category of gender – and thus, it would seem, to theorise sex as political. But in reality, once again, it allows us to theorise sex as *gender* as political. Recall Butler: sex is 'always already gender'. And, insofar as gender derives its meaning from a relation of opposition to sex, the persistence of gender is implicitly the persistence of sex and the politicisation of gender is implicitly the depoliticisation of sex.

By positing 'woman' as the social category of gender, contemporary feminists theorise the gendered *as opposed to the sexual* as political. The sexual remains private, individual, non-political.[44] They thus preserve the patriarchal dichotomies of private–public, individual–common, non-political–political – that is, the dichotomies that preclude the recognition of the sexual *qua* sexual as political and that second-wave feminists sought to explode.[45]

Perhaps it is not coincidental that contemporary feminism jettisons the second-wave critique of sexuality, including the sex industry. Butler criticises MacKinnon's 'failure to distinguish the presence of coerced domination in sexuality from pleasurable and wanted dynamics of power'.[46] Coerced domination is the proper object of criticism, while desired and pleasurable domination is not, because desire and pleasure belong to the domain of the private, the individual, the non-political.[47] On this logic, the second-wave critique of sexuality is audible only as moral objection.[48]

From the second-wave perspective, gender-critical feminists are right to claim that 'woman' is coextensive with 'female person', but they are wrong to regard 'female person' as a biological category. The human being on a developmental pathway designed to produce larger gametes for the purposes of sexual reproduction, the human being without a Y chromosome, and the human being with sufficiently many important properties of a particular morphological cluster all represent the female person of science, not the female person of feminism.

Consider the female person of Dworkin's writings:

This is nihilism; or this is truth. He has to push in past boundaries. There is the outline of a body, distinct, separate, its integrity an illusion, a tragic deception, because unseen there is a slit between the legs, and he has to push into it. There is never a real privacy of the body that can coexist with intercourse: with being entered. The vagina itself is muscled and the muscles have to be pushed apart. The thrusting is persistent invasion. She is opened up, split down the centre. She is occupied – physically, internally, in her privacy.[49]

In this description, the female body is penetrable, permeable, violable, invadable, occupiable. Gatens criticises this description as essentialising. She reads it as a description of the female body as intrinsically violable and of sexual intercourse as intrinsically a violation of the female body.[50] She assumes that Dworkin is writing of biological femaleness and objects to its representation as violability. But notice that Dworkin's description of the female body is a description of the female body in relation to the male body – 'violable' describes the relation in which the female body stands to the male body, not the female body per se. Notice also, as Gatens does,[51] the militaristic vocabulary in which Dworkin describes this relation – 'invasion', 'occupation', 'colonisation'. This is a political relation, a friend–enemy relation, not a biological one. In short, in Dworkin's writings, the distinguishing feature of femaleness is violability, and violability is political in nature. Having identified the distinguishing feature of femaleness as violability, Dworkin can then write figuratively of a female person being repeatedly *made* female: 'After her heroic escape from being female, she [Joan of Arc] was made twice female: raped and burned ... After death, then, she became female a third time: her naked body, including her genitals, shown to all the people.'[52] If the distinguishing feature of femaleness is violability, then the violation of a female person is a reinforcement of her femaleness. If the female person of Dworkin's writings were, as Gatens assumes, the female person of science, the biological female person, Dworkin's talk of Joan of Arc being repeatedly made female would be incoherent.

Having observed 'the frequency with which they [MacKinnon and Dworkin] employ metaphors of war and invasion: the male body is depicted as a weapon-bearing invader and the female body as invaded or occupied territory',[53] Gatens continues obliquely: 'These are the same body morphologies which have played a distinctive part in the construction of notions of the "ideal" citizen, which in turn have justified the exclusion of certain bodies from citizenship. Women's bodies historically have been seen as unfit for citizenship. Women's bodies are often likened to territories whose borders cannot be defended.'[54] I am unsure what her point is – is she suggesting that these metaphors are problematic because they are historically exclusionary or because they reinforce a patriarchal image of woman? Perhaps the latter, given that she illustrates her claim – that women's bodies are likened to territories whose borders cannot be defended – with a quotation from Queen Elizabeth I: 'I know I have the body of a weak and feeble woman, but I have the heart and stomach of a king, and a king of England too; and think foul scorn that Parma or Spain, or any prince of Europe, should dare invade the borders of my realm.'[55] In the patriarchal image, a naturally weak and feeble woman cannot protect her borders and thus requires a man to do it. Should he fail, that is, should her borders be invaded by another man, it is *his* borders that are invaded, it is he who is wronged. By contrast, in Dworkin's image, men are the invaders not the protectors, this invasion wrongs women not men, and women collectively must defend themselves against men:

> Do women need sovereignty – not only over their own bodies as currently understood in the United States (the right to choose, a happy euphemism for the abortion right); but control of a boundary further away from their bodies, a defended boundary? Do women need land and an army ... or a feminist government in exile, an idea [Phyllis] Chesler has articulated often and provocatively? ... Could women manage self-defence

if not retaliation? Would self-defence be enough? Could women execute men who raped or beat or tortured women? Could a woman execute the man or men who raped or beat or tortured her?[56]

This image could not be further from the patriarchal one.

Another example of a mistaken reading of the political as the metaphysical is Jean Grimshaw's reading of Daly. Daly writes:

Patriarchy is itself the prevailing religion of the entire planet ... All – from Buddhism and Hinduism to Islam, Judaism, Christianity, to secular derivatives such as Freudianism, Jungianism, Marxism, and Maoism – are infrastructures of the edifice of patriarchy. All are erected as parts of the male's shelter against anomie. And the symbolic message of all the sects of the religion which is patriarchy is this: Women are the dreaded anomie. Consequently, women are the objects of male terror, the projected personifications of 'the Enemy', the real objects under attack in all the wars of patriarchy.[57]

Grimshaw criticises Daly for 'postulating a universal and fundamental male need (shelter against anomie) and male fear (of women) ... which ... lead to a universal and basic male motivation, fundamental to all male enterprises, to attack women'.[58] She misreads Daly's political description – 'terror', 'enemy', 'attack', 'wars' – as a metaphysical one. Daly is marking out men as the political enemy of women, as a group whose way of life entails the subjection of women, and she is doing so in order to politicise women, to make conflict with men possible, should the need for it arise.[59]

Gatens objects to Daly's description for this very reason: 'History has shown, and unfortunately continues to show us, where this type of reasoning ends':[60] in war. She takes it as self-evident that feminists ought not to produce descriptions that can end in war. But is this self-evident? If the political relation is the friend–enemy relation, and if enmity's most extreme consequence is war, then the preclusion of the possibility of war is the preclusion of the possibility of politics.[61] Feminists cannot on the one hand claim that the relation between men and women is political and on the other refuse war. Moreover, if one accepts '[t]he accounts of rape, wife beating, forced childbearing, medical butchering, sex-motivated murder, forced prostitution, physical mutilation, sadistic psychological abuse, and other commonplaces of female experience that are excavated from the past or given by contemporary survivors',[62] then is war not perhaps an appropriate response?[63] Indeed, are men not already at war against women?[64] If they are, then for feminists to refuse war is for feminists to accept defeat. Why, then, does the suggestion of war sound excessive and repugnant? Why indeed, if not because feminists do not sincerely believe that the relationship between men and women is political?

Gatens raises a further, similar objection, which is that by placing men in the position of 'the evil other', Daly's description forecloses the possibility of engagement.[65] 'If that group is taken to be fundamentally and essentially evil then one can "justifiably" claim that engagement with them is futile',[66] she writes. Gatens mistakes the attribution of political otherness for moral evilness (recall Schmitt: 'The political enemy need not be morally evil').[67] One can engage with a political other as a political other. Only when the political other becomes an immediate threat to one's way of life must one give up this engagement and wage war.[68] I am not sure what forms of engagement Gatens is afraid of forgoing. At present, feminists engage with men as the enlightened engage with the ignorant, or the teacher with the student.[69] This follows from the contemporary conception of men and women as social kinds: if men treat women as they do as a consequence of their socialisation, then ending men's oppression of women is a matter of resocialising men. Certainly, Daly's description forecloses such engagement. On her description, men and feminists are groups with conflicting ways of life – central to men's way of life is women's subjection, and central to feminists' is women's liberation. The present pedagogical form of engagement therefore rests on a delusion about the nature of the relation between men and women. In other words, from a second-wave perspective, the engagement that is foreclosed is engagement that is thoroughly misguided.[70]

On reflection, engagement with a political other can take a form that the present pedagogical form of engagement suspiciously resembles: conversion. That is, war is one strategy for defeating one's enemy; converting the enemy into one's friend is another. Perhaps, then, what contemporary feminists present as education or consciousness-raising is in fact conversion. If this is so, then it is not about the nature of the relation between men and women but about the nature of their engagement with men that feminists are deluded.

III

In describing the second-wave conception of women as political, I am reminded of Jean Améry's conception of the Jew. If a Jew is one who has a certain cultural heritage or religious ties, then Améry, who does not believe in the God of Israel and knows little about Jewish culture, is not and cannot become a Jew.[71] And yet, he writes, he must be a Jew. Why and in what sense, if not cultural or religious, must he be a Jew? With the enactment of the Nuremberg Laws, to be a Jew became 'to be a dead man on leave, someone to be murdered, who only by chance was not yet where he properly belonged; and so it has remained, in many variations, in various degrees of intensity, until today'.[72] Améry saw, then, that he had a choice: he could deny that he was a Jew ('I could have comforted myself with the thought: no matter what they say about me, it isn't true . . .

I am what I am for myself and in myself, and nothing else');[73] or he could accept his fate in order to revolt against it ('I accepted the judgment of the world, with the decision to overcome it through revolt').[74] While the former could allow him to escape his fate, only the latter could change the fate of the Jew. He concluded that he must do the latter – he must be a Jew. Améry's conception of the Jew is a political one: a Jew is a dead man on leave. This conception necessitates, and thus initiates, resistance; for only by refusing to be put to death, only by hitting back at those who would put him to death does a Jew cease to be someone to be put to death.

I am struck by the contrast between Améry and contemporary feminists. Where Améry considers the Jew 'firmly promised to death',[75] contemporary feminists claim that '"female" no longer appears to be a stable notion, its meaning is as troubled and unfixed as "woman"';[76] where he insists on the need to be a Jew, they ask, 'Am I That Name?';[77] where he acknowledges that Jews who did not live through the Holocaust are not Jews in the sense in which he is, they fear excluding women from the extension of 'woman'; where he emphasises stasis ('little had changed, that [he] was still the man condemned to be murdered in due time, even though the potential executioner now cautiously restrained himself or, at best, even loudly protested his disapproval of what had happened'),[78] they emphasise change;[79] where he sees 'no . . . opportunity to punch the enemy in his face, for he was not so easy to recognise anymore',[80] they deny the existence of an enemy; where he speaks of hitting back,[81] they speak of subverting;[82] where he hopes to recognise reality,[83] they place it in inverted commas.[84] While Améry confronts a political reality, contemporary feminists evade it, using metaphysics to do so.[85]

Schmitt writes, rather intriguingly: 'Only the actual participants can correctly recognize, understand, and judge the concrete situation and settle the extreme case of conflict.'[86]

In other words, no neutral standpoint exists from which one can determine whether the enemy intends to negate one's way of life, and hence whether one must repulse or attack the enemy in order to preserve one's way of life.[87] This suggests that the debate between trans-inclusionary and gender-critical feminists over the meaning of 'woman' is misguided and futile. This debate assumes that a political question – what is at stake, for one's way of life, in the acceptance (or rejection) of trans women as women? – is reducible to a prior semantic one – what is the meaning of 'woman'? It assumes that we can determine the correct political position by answering a prior semantic question. But no neutral standpoint exists from which the political question can be answered. Within the poststructural feminist way of life, trans women are a subversive gender minority, whose acceptance as women upholds the primary value – 'inclusion' – of this way of life. Within the second-wave feminist way of life, trans women are members of the male sex class, whose acceptance as women is the acceptance of the enemy as the friend; and this is defeat.

Just as in Améry's political conception of Jews a Jew is someone fated to die, so in second-wave feminism's political conception of women a woman is one fated to be sexually violated.[88] Trans-inclusionary feminists therefore often cite the rape and prostitution of trans women as evidence of their membership of the female sex class. MacKinnon, for example, writes: 'puzzlingly, they [gender-critical feminists] fail to identify with trans women who have also been sexually assaulted by the same instrument [the penis], which at least on my observation, again to be honest, is virtually all of them at one time or another'.[89] But though trans women may be raped, they are not, as women are, *fated* to be raped. Under patriarchy, it is the female body that is rapable, that is to be raped, whose rape is pleasurable and fulfilling.[90] The male body instead has integrity, is inviolable, is not to be raped.[91] So, insofar as trans women have male bodies, they are not fated to be raped. Moreover, if the female body is violable and the male body inviolable, the rape of the male body cannot have the same meaning, cannot be the same action, as the rape of the female body.[92] The rape of the male body is an abuse, a perversion of the natural order, a wrong. The rape of the female body is instead the correct use of it, natural, pleasurable. Compare the remark 'women will get raped in changing rooms anyway'[93] – given in response to the concern that opening up female bathrooms to trans women will leave women vulnerable to rape – to the prolific commentary on trans women's vulnerability in male bathrooms.[94] Finally, the meaning of the rape of the male body depends upon the meanings of the male body and of the female body: only because the proper target of rape is the female body does the rape of the male body signal treatment of a male person as a female person, and only because the male person is a full human being and the female person a partial one is the treatment of a male person as a female person demeaning. The identification of male victims of rape as members of the female sex class relies upon the idea that the condition of the female sex class is a condition of rapability. But we can identify male victims of rape as members of the female sex class only by redefining 'female sex class' from containing those who are female to containing those who are *treated as* female. Thus the identification of male victims of rape as members of the female sex class simultaneously relies upon and linguistically displaces the female sex class. Because it relies upon the female sex class it entails the persistence of it, but because it linguistically displaces the female sex class it leaves this class unable to struggle for its freedom.

Trans-inclusionary feminists will represent my claim that only the female body is rapable as a perverse cherishing of rapability. MacKinnon does something of this sort when she writes: 'Honestly, seeing "women" as a turf to be defended, as opposed to a set of imperatives and limitations to be criticized, challenged, changed, or transcended, has been pretty startling.'[95] Such a representation misleads. The insistence that only the female body is rapable is an expression of class consciousness. Class consciousness is precisely the awareness that MacKinnon suggests gender-critical feminists lack, an awareness of '"women" as a set of imperatives and limitations to be criticized, challenged, changed, or transcended'. (It would be more accurate, though, to describe gender-critical feminists as having an awareness that men oppress women rather than an awareness that women are 'a set of imperatives'.) If a group of workers insisted that capitalists were not members of their class and denied them entry to their meetings, would MacKinnon see them as reactionary, as attempting to preserve the worker identity? Or would she see them as expressing their class consciousness and as organising? Améry addresses a similar objection in formulating his conception of the Jew:

> Only those who have lived through a fate like mine, and no one else, can refer their lives to the years 1933–45. By no means do I say this with pride. It would be ridiculous enough to boast of something that one did not do but only underwent. Rather it is with a certain shame that I assert my sad privilege and suggest that while the Holocaust is truly the existential reference point for all Jews, only we, the sacrificed, are able to spiritually relive the catastrophic event as it was or fully picture it as it could be again.[96]

Why can gender-critical feminists not be heard as asserting their sad privilege, their lonely burden?

Of this I am sure: MacKinnon believes that accepting trans women as women does not undermine the friend group. Perhaps this is finally the difference between trans-inclusionary feminists and gender-critical feminists: the former judge that the acceptance of trans women as women does not undermine the friend group, while the latter judge that it does. If Schmitt is right, as I think he is, then we cannot neutrally determine whether the acceptance of trans women as women will or will not undermine the friend group, and hence whether gender-critical feminists or trans-inclusionary feminists are right. Both must exercise their judgement and accept responsibility for what comes of doing so.

IV

I have argued that the second-wave description of women's condition is a political one. Consider the second-wave lexicon:[97] 'war',[98] 'enemy',[99] 'invasion',[100] 'possession',[101] 'occupation',[102] 'sister',[103] 'revolution',[104] 'liberation'.[105] Poststructural feminists misrepresent this description as a metaphysical one, and then reject it on metaphysical grounds. They thereby evade confrontation with the reality of women's subjection to men.[106] MacKinnon captures this evasion: 'Few people claimed that women were not violated in the ways we had found or did not occupy a second-class status in society. Not many openly disputed that what we had uncovered did, in fact, exist. What was said instead was that in society, nothing really exists.'[107] A political claim – men violate women – is met not with a political counter-claim but with a metaphysical claim: nothing really exists. The political claim is thus not refuted but displaced, not surpassed but suppressed.

Having misrepresented the second-wave description as a metaphysical one, contemporary feminists can then cast the difference between second-wave and contemporary feminism as a difference in metaphysics:[108] the former is structuralist, the latter poststructural – a difference according to which second-wave feminism is inferior to contemporary feminism (the former is essentialist and universalist, the latter anti-essentialist and anti-universalist). In fact the difference is in endeavour – second-wave feminism is political, concerned with women as a class, while contemporary feminism is metaphysical, concerned with the category 'woman'.

This difference is a difference in accountability – for what and to whom: second-wave feminism is accountable for the liberation of women as a class and to women as a class, while contemporary feminism is accountable for its adherence to poststructural theory and to poststructural theorists. This difference shows up in Kate Ellis's criticism of MacKinnon. MacKinnon says: 'Politically, I call it rape whenever a woman has sex and feels violated.'[109] Women evaluate what they have suffered from the perspective embodied in the law, namely the male perspective. From this perspective, what they have suffered is not rape. They therefore dismiss it as not rape, not a violation, not a wrong, not something to be protested. MacKinnon treats a woman's sense of violation as violation in fact, a woman's perspective as a reliable perspective on reality, in the hope that women might protest what they have suffered, because doing so is to assert that they are not men's to use.[110] It is, adapting Améry, to force the world to revise its judgement of women.[111] Ellis criticises MacKinnon's explicitly political definition on metaphysical grounds: 'This means that truth is not endlessly deferred, as Derrida would have it.'[112] MacKinnon's definition of 'rape' is an attempt to transform women's violability into inviolability. Ellis's rejection of it is an attempt to adhere to Derridean theory.

No sooner had feminism cut itself loose from Marxism and expressed its animating political impulse – that men *qua* men oppress women *qua* women – than poststructuralist feminism emerged to sublimate it.

7

The Loss of the Future

I have argued that poststructural feminism displaced feminism. In this chapter, I consider what this displacement was ultimately a displacement *of*.

On the second-wave feminist view, according to which men *qua* men oppress women *qua* women, feminism's goal is to liberate women *qua* women. This is the goal of a society in which sex is not class, in which 'man' and 'woman' do not name a human being (Mr *x*) and his subject (Miss *y*, Mrs *y*, or Ms *y*) respectively. In this society prostitution, pornography, marriage, and heterosexual relations do not exist, either in the sense that the terms 'prostitution', 'pornography', 'marriage', and 'heterosexual relations' do not refer or in the sense that their referents bear no resemblance to the current ones. This society will be radically different from our present society.

On the poststructural feminist view, according to which the regulatory ideal of sex excludes those who do not conform to it, feminism's goal is to include sexual minorities. This goal is the goal of a (bureaucratic) society whose administrative forms contain, for the question 'what is your gender?', responses other than 'male' and 'female'. In this society prostitution, pornography, marriage, and heterosexual relations continue to exist as practices in which all can participate (all are included). This society will be our present society, reformed.[1] In short, second-wave feminism envisions something new, while poststructural feminism envisions the same old thing, updated.[2]

We assume that it is an account of the present that gives rise to a vision of the future: because second-wave feminism sees a present in which men *qua* men oppress women *qua* women, it dreams of a future in which women *qua* women are liberated; and because poststructural feminism sees a present in which the regulatory ideal of sex excludes sexual minorities, it dreams of a future in which sexual minorities are included. I want to suggest that, in the case of second-wave feminism, it is instead a vision of the future that gives rise to an account of the present.

MacKinnon criticises the dominant history of sexuality, that told by Freud and Foucault. In this history sexuality has changed:

> this sexuality, to have a history, must change. It must come in periods: how desire is defined, how pleasure is got, who does what to whom, how pleasure is restrained, how these restraints are dangerously and heroically broken. Sexuality must behave in this way or history is not had, at least not in the genealogical sense.[3]

That is, only if sexuality exhibits change over time can we trace its history, for only once it changes can we see both what it had been and what it became, via the contrast between them.

MacKinnon argues that, if the history of sexuality is measured against the standard of sexual equality, sexuality appears relatively hierarchical and relatively unchanging:

> while ideologies about sex and sexuality may ebb and flow, and the ways they attach themselves to gender and to women's status may alter . . . the actual practices of sex may look rela-

tively flat. In particular, the sexualization of aggression or the eroticization of power and the fusion of that with gender such that the one who is the target or object of sexuality is the subordinate, is a female, effeminized if a man, is relatively constant.[4]

Before the existence of feminism, the history of sexuality made the standard of sexual equality inconceivable in order that this history might be measured against this standard. A history in which sexual relations are relations of mastery and subjection is a history in which sexual relations are inconceivable as relations of freedom. (Is this why explicitly asking for a woman's consent is considered a detumescent act? Because, once a woman explicitly consents, once she gives herself, sex can no longer be an act of conquest and possession? Because, once sex can no longer be an act of conquest and possession, it can no longer be sexual?) A history in which sexual relations are inconceivable as relations of freedom is a history in which sexual relations are imperceptible as relations of mastery and subjection. For only in contrast to relations of freedom do relations of mastery and subjection appear relations of mastery and subjection. This explains how the description of sexuality can be an obvious description of conquest, and yet we cannot see that sexuality is conquest (in a normative, objectionable sense). Only by becoming perceptible as not-sexual do relations become perceptible as relations of mastery and subjection: only by ceasing to be about sex does rape come to be about power.

But how, then, have second-wave feminists perceived sexual relations as relations of mastery and subjection? How have they written the history that they have? MacKinnon suggests that they have done so by listening to and believing women. But what prompted them to ask women about their experiences of sexuality, how did those women have experiences of sexuality as hierarchy, and how did second-wave feminists interpret those experiences as experiences of sexuality as such, rather than corruptions of it? The question of how second-wave feminists have perceived sexual relations as relations of mastery and subjection is the question of how they have done so, *given that history yields no vantage point from which to do so.*

Herein lies the answer to this question: they have perceived them like this from a vantage point yielded not by history but by a vision of the future. Second-wave feminism envisions a future in which 'woman' is the 'name of a way of being human'.[5] Against this future, the past and the present take a new shape, the past emerging as a time in which 'woman' did not name a way of being human and the present as a time continuous with the past. That marriage is consummated by the act of sexual intercourse, that sexual intercourse is an act of penetration and possession,[6] that sexual intercourse and marriage are milestones in the maturation of a woman, that under coverture a wife had no legal existence apart from her husband's, that women continue to take their husband's surname,[7] that the title for a woman is Miss *y*, Mrs *y*, or Ms *y*, that men continue to expect sex from women and women continue to consider it their duty to give men sex,[8] that marital rape remains practically inconceivable, that the rape of a man's girlfriend or wife continues to outrage *him*,[9] that soldiers humiliate enemy men by forcing them to watch as they rape their wives[10] – all these facts emerge as evidence that 'man' and 'woman' have named and continue to name respectively a human being and his subject, or that sexual relations have been and continue to be relations of mastery and subjection.

An era must have ended, must 'have edges like a field',[11] in order to be history. The era of sexual relations as relations of mastery and subjection has not yet ended, does not yet have an edge, is not yet history. But once 'woman' names a way of being human, this era will have ended. The second-wave vision is thus one of a future *beyond* history.

The poststructural vision is instead one of a future that is *continuous* with history. This difference in the vision of the future provides an explanation for the difference in the account of the present: where second-wave feminism sees power as concentrated in men's hands, poststructural feminism sees it as diffuse; where second-wave feminism sees women as victims, poststructural feminism sees them as agents; where second-wave feminism sees women as a group, poststructural feminism sees them as individuals; where second-wave feminism sees meaning as determinate, poststructural feminism sees it as indeterminate; where second-wave feminism sees the enactment and reproduction of sexual hierarchy, poststructural feminism sees the parody and subversion of gender. For where, against a future of freedom, monotony appears, against a future of inclusion variety appears. As an example, consider 'butch' and 'femme'. Against a future in which sexual relations are relations of freedom, butch and femme are relatively similar to masculine (master) and feminine (subject), and relatively different from the identities that will exist in the future. They are, relatively, an enactment and a reproduction of a (hetero)sexual hierarchy. They are relatively conformist. Against a future in which sexual minorities are included, butch and femme are 'phallic relations of power that replay and redistribute the possibilities of that phallicism'.[12] They are identities that afford women *inclusion* in the male position of master. They are thus progressive. One who, like MacKinnon, imagines a future in which the possibilities of phallicism have been replaced by altogether new possibilities will find the 'redistribution' of the former tedious and unsatisfying. One who, like Butler, imagines a future in which the possibilities of phallicism are accessible to all will see their redistribution as a step towards the future.

In Butler's defence, she suggests that the repetition (butch and femme) of heterosexual constructs (masculine and feminine) can 'displace' those constructs.[13] Insofar as it displaces those constructs, it cannot afford inclusion in them. If the poststructural feminist vision of the future is one in which phallicism's possibilities have been displaced rather than made accessible to all, then this vision is more radical than I have portrayed it. Indeed, it converges with the second-wave vision. But I do not see how the repetition of heterosexual constructs can displace them. Butler treats drag as the hyperbolic or dissonant repetition of gender. She also argues that this repetition[14] can reveal the performative and thus constructed nature of gender, thereby denaturalising it.[15] But the performance of a gender reveals its performative nature only when that performance looks unnatural in a man. Drag reveals the performative nature of femininity only because femininity looks unnatural in a man. The performance of a gender reveals its performative nature, then, only by ultimately *re-naturalising* it. This resolves an apparent paradox of the contemporary moment: gender is increasingly self-consciously, hyperbolically, and dissonantly performed, and yet it is increasingly and regressively fixed in place. For example, male people increasingly perform femininity (e.g. *qua* trans women), and yet femininity is increasingly fixed in place as the gender of a female person, so that female people who are not feminine increasingly question whether they are female. As the performance of a gender reveals its performative nature only when the performance looks unnatural, this is unsurprising: a male person's performance of femininity reveals the performative nature of femininity for a male person, thus re-naturalising femininity as the gender of a female person. Perhaps this is why, reading Butler, one has a sense of a future that never escapes the present, a future in which we parodically repeat gender, troubling and subverting it, never finally transcending it.[16] Indeed, Butler explicitly rejects the possibility of transcending it: 'in my view, the normative focus for gay and lesbian practice ought to be on the subversive and parodic redeployment of power rather than on the impossible fantasy of its full-scale transcendence'.[17] (One cannot but begin 'to wonder, in a mood of despair, if there is not a deep and unacknowledged desire not to change anything at work behind the intellectual haze'.[18])

Moreover, supposing that the repetition of gender can denaturalise it, denaturalising gender does not necessarily displace it. Gender is displaced by an alternative. Repetition and denaturalisation cannot generate alternatives, and Butler explicitly refuses to offer any.[19] This, too, is unsurprising: to offer alternatives is implicitly to make a normative judgement, a judgement about a better way of being than masculine or feminine, and Butler is wary of the normative, which she sees as regulatory and exclusionary. But, as Fraser writes, '[f]eminists do need to make normative judgements and to offer emancipatory alternatives. We are not for "anything goes"'. She continues, obliquely yet presciently:

> it is arguable that the current proliferation of identity-dereifying, fungible, commodified images and significations constitutes as great a threat to women's liberation as do fixed, fundamentalist identities. In fact, dereifying processes and reifying processes are two sides of the same postfordist coin. They demand a two-sided response. Feminists need both deconstruction *and* reconstruction, destabilization of meaning *and* projection of utopian hope.[20]

The second-wave equivalent of the parodic repetition of gender was political lesbianism. A political lesbian is a woman-identified woman,[21] a woman committed to women. Such a woman necessarily refuses to be a woman in the patriarchal sense – that is, woman as man's sexual subject, woman as sexually for man, woman as sexually accessible to man. She is thus an 'escapee' from her class 'in the same way as the American runaway slaves were when escaping slavery and becoming free'.[22]

Butler rejects political lesbianism as 'a cultural impossibility and a politically impracticable dream',[23] on the grounds that it originates 'before', 'outside', or 'beyond' power.[24] It is true that second-wave feminists tended to represent a political lesbian as the original female self that, lying buried beneath the patriarchally constructed, man-identified, false self, women need only 're-member'.[25] Rejecting the possibility of a sexuality outside power, Butler rejects the possibility of repudiating patriarchal sexuality from outside it, claiming that one can resist patriarchal sexuality only by 'acknowledging' and 'doing' the construction one is invariably in.[26] She thereby replaces political lesbianism with a parodic repetition of gender as the strategy for resistance.

First, notice that Butler rejects political lesbianism as an impossibility in the face of its actuality. Poststructuralism denies an outside to power. Yet political lesbianism exists. Butler does not entertain the inference, drawn from the latter, that poststructuralism is false. Nor does she wonder how political lesbianism exists. Instead she theorises it away.

Second, political lesbianism does not originate outside power. It originates in the vision of a future in which 'woman' names a human being, one who is free, one whose subjection to a man is an affront. A political lesbian, a woman whose loyalty is to women, who refuses to be a man's subject, is a woman who acts in the name not of a woman's authentic self but of her *future* self. The second-wave description of this future self as authentic is a description not in the metaphysical but in the normative register. In *Gyn/Ecology*, Daly depicts 'the journey of women becoming'[27] as both a discovery and an invention: 'She dis-covers and creates the Otherworld',[28] 'we re-member / invent Female Friendship',[29] 'women are ... transforming / re-calling meanings of old worlds'.[30] 'Discovery' implies that 'the journey of women becoming' is a journey of women recovering their original selves (their 'genuine Self');[31] 'invention' implies that it is a journey of women creating new selves. Gatens argues:

The True Self is not Daly's way of naming an achieved status – as in the existentialist use of 'authenticity' or Nietzsche's understanding of the 'overman' – it is an assumed, pre-given essence. It is the kernel at the heart of (at least, female) being that is revealed once the layers of the 'false self', which 'encase' the True Self, are 'pared away'.[32]

This reading elides the language of invention. I want to suggest that 'the journey of women becoming' is the journey of women creating new selves, and that Daly describes the creation of a new self as the recovery of an original self in order to normativise and thus necessitate becoming this self.

Butler might object that the vision of a future in which 'woman' names a human being originates outside power. It does not. It causally originates in the patriarchal vocabulary: the claim that 'woman' names a human being uses, or rather *mis*uses,[33] terms in the patriarchal vocabulary ('woman' and 'human being'), thereby transforming their meanings and generating a new – feminist – vocabulary. *Mis*uses because in the patriarchal vocabulary 'woman' designates the subject of a human being, not a human being.

In short, what poststructural feminism displaces is not an untenable metaphysical–structuralist account of the present but a vision of a radically different future.

Butler is right: this vision *is* a 'politically impracticable dream'.[34] It is the vision of a future that, from within the present, *is* unrealisable. It is not that second-wave feminists did not understand this; they did. They simply did not take the impracticability of the dream to be a reason to abandon it. To have done so would have been to take the patriarchal present for granted. The charge of 'impracticability' is a strange one to level at feminism. A feminism that strives for less than the impracticable is a feminism that strives for less than radical change, radical change being by definition change that the existing order cannot permit, and a feminism that strives for less than radical change is a feminism that accommodates itself to the patriarchal order. A feminism with a practicable dream is feminism, defeated – in this case, by itself. It is neither men nor anti-feminist women who charge it with impracticability; it is feminists. I am reminded of Ailbhe Smyth:

> It's dead
> If it's not dead,
> It's dying,
> So to be on the safe side
> Let's kill it anyway,
> In case there's any life left in it.[35]

A poststructural feminism keeps feminism alive in name by killing it in substance. Little wonder that young women are now so willing to identify as feminists: such identification means nothing threatening, if it means anything at all.[36]

8

The Emergence of Gender-Critical Feminism

I

The recent emergence of a new feminism – gender-critical – presents an opportunity for the reclamation of feminism as a movement for the liberation of women *qua* women. But this moment of opportunity is also one of danger – at present, gender-critical feminism opens the possibility of the continued depoliticisation of sexual relations as much as that of their repoliticisation, the possibility of a movement for which women are biology as much as that of a movement for which women are a class. What follows is an intervention made in the hope that we might realise the latter possibility.

Gender-critical feminism emerged in response to a particular historical phenomenon: the demand for the recognition of certain male people, trans women, as women and all that this entails, or, perhaps more accurately, the demand for the recognition of certain male people as women *in the name of feminism* – contemporary, poststructural, trans-inclusionary feminism. In the eyes of gender-critical feminists, this phenomenon is the definitive proof that contemporary feminism is a betrayal rather than a progression of the feminist project and that, if this project is to be completed, a new feminism is required.

Because the contemporary feminism to which gender-critical feminism reacts emphasises the socially constructed nature of women, and because it uses this emphasis to pursue the recognition of male people as women, gender-critical feminism emphasises the biological nature of women.[1] Its slogan is: 'woman . . . adult human female'.

This emphasis on the biological shapes gender-critical feminism's view of what is at stake for women: in changing rooms, prisons, and women's shelters, safety; in sport, competitiveness; in research, knowledge of the female person; in medicine, female-appropriate care.

At first glance, this view appears to follow directly from a conception of women as a biological kind. Gender-critical feminism thus appears to reduce to science; indignation at trans-inclusionary demands appears to reduce to respect for scientific truth.

On reflection, a conception of women as a biological kind cannot alone produce a concern for safety in spaces such as changing rooms and prisons, which is the concern that the inclusion of male people in these spaces will make women vulnerable to sexual violence. Even supposing that women are biologically physically weaker than men, physical weakness implies vulnerability to sexual violence only if men are disposed to sexual violence. Evidently, then, this concern arises against the background of a history of men's sexual violence against women. Similarly, concerns about competitiveness in sport, knowledge of the female person, and appropriateness of health care arise against the background of a history in which women have been considered unathletic,[2] in which research has taken the male body to stand for the human body,[3] and in which women have therefore not received appropriate health care.[4] In short, gender-critical concerns are the product of a conception of women as a biological kind in conjunction with a consciousness of history.

One might wonder, then, whether trans-inclusionary and gender-critical feminism are simply different views of where we are in history: perhaps a history that is in the present for gender-critical feminism is in the past for trans-inclusionary feminism, perhaps the background that persists for the former has receded for the latter. In other words, perhaps gender-critical feminists believe that we have not yet corrected the consequences of history and that justice therefore requires a sex-based distinction in changing rooms, prisons, women's shelters, sport, research, and health care, while trans-inclusionary feminists believe that we have corrected these consequences and that justice therefore does not require such a distinction. MacKinnon appears to believe this with respect to sport.[5] If it were the case that trans-inclusionary and gender-critical feminism are simply different views of where we are in history (in the present vs in the past), we would expect gender-critical feminists to argue for the preservation of a sex-based distinction and trans-inclusionary feminists to argue for the abandonment of this distinction. While gender-critical feminists do argue as we would expect, trans-inclusionary feminists, by and large, do not – they argue for the reconceiving of the sex-based distinction as a sex-identifying distinction, that is, for the reconceiving of male versus female as male-identifying versus female-identifying. Moreover, the reason for the trans-inclusionary dismissal of the need for sex-segregated changing rooms – 'women will get raped in changing rooms anyway'[6] – suggests the belief that one particular injustice, rape, far from being consigned to the past, is outside history, eternal, natural, not an injustice.

What exactly is the gender-critical consciousness of history? As refuge for women, sex-segregated changing rooms, prisons, and shelters serve the interests of women while they are persecuted by men. These spaces have no place in a post-liberation feminist future. In this future women are not persecuted by men, and so do not need refuge. They enjoy the world, not refuge, freedom, not momentary relief from oppression.

A gender-critical feminism that sees these spaces as more than interim measures, as accomplishments that endure in the feminist future, mistakes a patriarchal world for a feminist one and respite from hostility – *and thus hostility* – for freedom. Kathleen Stock's suggestion that the fact that men are overwhelmingly the perpetrators of sexual violence and women the victims is 'at least partly explicable in terms of typical differences between males and females in strength, size, and direct aggression'[7] would seem to commit her to a view of sex-segregated spaces as forever necessary. Nevertheless, she continues, '[t]hat's not to say that developmental and other environmental factors don't play a role too; it is just to acknowledge that things wouldn't be as they are if males were systematically smaller, weaker, and less testosterone-fuelled than females',[8] perhaps allowing that the biological differences between men and women that make women vulnerable in a patriarchal environment would not do so in a feminist one, and hence that the sex segregation needed to make women safe in a patriarchal environment would not be needed in a feminist one.

On the one hand, it has seemed to me that, in their celebration of sex segregation (or sex separation)[9] as a now threatened feminist accomplishment, gender-critical feminists do mistake refuge for world.

On the other hand, I think that gender-critical rage is the rage of a category of people who have patiently awaited the world only to be evicted from refuge, who have suffered injury only to be insulted. It is the rage of a category of people who finally understand their situation: in the eyes of the world, we women are not rightful claimants of it. We will never be granted it, and what little of it we are granted may be taken away.

Now, facing a choice not between refuge and world but between refuge and no refuge, we must fight for refuge. But we must not forget that refuge is not the world, and that the world in which we had refuge was the world that would have taken it from us.

Underlying the equation of a patriarchal world with refuge for women with a feminist world is a liberal conception of women, a conception of women as a subspecies of men: *qua* men, women are citizens of the patriarchal world, *qua* women, they are a minority in need of protection within this world. Only on this conception is a patriarchal world with a refuge for women a world in which women are free. On this conception, women are a *minority group* in need of *protection*, not a *class* in need of *liberation*.[10]

Insofar as gender-critical feminism regards what it struggles to preserve as more than interim measures, it displays a liberal consciousness of history in which women are a minority group whose protection has largely been achieved, not a radical and feminist consciousness of history in which women are a class yet to be liberated.

The second-wave feminists who established rape crisis centres and women's shelters were motivated by a vision of liberation. They saw refuge as a necessary first step to the world, women's shelters as making it possible for individual women to leave abusive men and for women – victims and workers, together – to develop an understanding of their condition as a class and to organise; their intervention would 'alter the power system which creates the foundation of battering behaviour'.[11] In order to secure funding, however, these feminists had to appeal to patriarchal values.[12] They had to present battered women as individual women in temporary need of shelter, fleeing individual and deviant men, perhaps with their children, rather than as representatives of a class that would not be safe until it was free. They had to suppress the political aspect of refuge.[13]

This makes me wonder whether the gender-critical invocation of 'safety' might not be similarly strategic, an appeal to a public that believes that women are entitled to safety and that (some) men pose a threat to their safety, whether for feminist or gender-traditionalist reasons. Perhaps, then, my worry ought to be that, as gender-critical feminists continue to talk of safety, they will come to forget that they originally did so for pragmatic reasons. Or perhaps it ought to be that, in talking of safety, we are failing to heed the lessons of second-wave efforts to strategise.[14] For might we not be where we now are in part because of these efforts? The more we talked of safety, the more we acted as though women were a minority group in need of protection, the less we acted as though women were a class in need of liberation, and the further the conception of women as a class receded.

II

Gender-critical feminism emphasises the biological nature of women because it assumes that a conception of women as a social kind *as* opposed to a biological kind is what has made it possible for male people to claim to be women. In fact, as I hope to have shown, it is a conception of women as a social kind as opposed to a political kind that has made this possible. As the poststructural notion of sex binary displaces the second-wave notion of sex class, male people's demand for recognition as women becomes audible as the excluded's demand for inclusion and inaudible as the oppressor's demand for recognition as the oppressed. The excluded's demand for inclusion is a demand whose acceptance harms no one, including women, who share with trans women victimisation through the sex–gender binary, and thus an interest in subverting it. Stock argues that the sex–gender distinction, in conjunction with the representation of 'woman' as a gendered rather than sexed being – as a person who has been constructed (as Beauvoir might say) or performs (as Butler might say) as the feminine being – has created the conceptual space in which a male person can intelligibly claim to be a woman.[15] Stock may be right. But I am not convinced that the mere existence of this conceptual space accounts for the acceptance of this claim. In other words, I do not think that this claim is accepted simply, if at all, because it is now plausible.

The use of 'woman' as the name of a gendered being appears to follow from Beauvoir's claim that one is not born but made a woman: if one is not born but made a woman, then 'woman' names not the sexed being but the gendered being into which the sexed being is made. Is the claim 'made not born' true of Indigenous Australians as it is of women? If it is, if 'Indigenous Australian' no less than 'woman' names a product of social treatment, then we have an equivalent distinction between biological being and racial being. Race no less than gender is a 'free-floating artifice'.[16] We have the conceptual space in which a person can claim to be an Indigenous Australian regardless of their biological features. Yet we would (and do) baulk at claims to indigeneity made by people who lack the appropriate ancestry. This suggests that the conceptual space in which a claim is plausible does not suffice to render it acceptable. Empirically, what seems to have rendered a male person's claim to be a woman acceptable is the assumption that this claim benefits the person in question without harming anyone else, and that its acceptance is therefore benevolent. Indeed, it is this assumption that has motivated philosophers to attempt to 'engineer' the conceptual space so that the claim is plausible. In short, male people's claim to be women has been accepted because a conception of women as a social kind as opposed to a political kind has created the conceptual space in which this acceptance is benevolent. If this is so, then what gender-critical feminists must emphasise is not the biological nature of women but their political nature.

Feminists have worried that to accept men and women as biological kinds would be to preserve the justification for women's subordination to men or to take for granted the consequence of oppression, and thus to take for granted oppression itself. From this worry they have slid into the belief that exposing men and women as social kinds would undermine the justification for women's subordination and thereby set in motion women's liberation. This belief reduces the political project of liberating women to the philosophical (deconstructionist) project of exposing men and women as social kinds. As is now painfully clear, this belief is misguided. It is now widely accepted that men and women as gendered beings – and, increasingly, as sexed beings – are social kinds, and yet it is equally widely forgotten that women must be liberated.

The belief that exposing men and women as social kinds would set in motion women's liberation is misguided for two reasons. First, in the absence of an alternative political order, women's subordination will persist, regardless of whether we consider men and women social kinds. Second, exposing men and women as social kinds, as products of socialisation whose relations are reformable through resocialisation, has obscured the fact that men and women are political classes with oppositional interests, and hence that the revolutionization of their relations into relations of freedom requires political struggle. Exposing men and women as social kinds has thus obscured the need for the political struggle through which women will be liberated. Contemporary feminists criticise Firestone for essentialising and thus inhibiting women, but it is Firestone who sees that men and women are classes and that women must struggle for their liberation, and who envisions a post-sex class future and charts a path from the present to that future. Insofar as the charge of essentialism is never accompanied by even the barest attempt to chart a path from subordination to liberation, the claim that it is made in the name of women's liberation appears to be a pretence.

This is to say that gender-critical feminists are right to challenge the contemporary feminist conception of men and women as social kinds – but not for the reasons they invoke. They object to this conception on the grounds that it denies that men and women are biological kinds. Their response to contemporary feminism is, then, to assert that men and women are biological kinds. I am suggesting that this conception is problematic *for feminists* primarily because it obscures that men and women are political kinds. For biologists or medical doctors, whose concern is with men and women as biological kinds, it may be problematic primarily because it denies that they are such kinds, but for feminists, whose concern is with men and women as political kinds, it is problematic primarily because it obscures that they are such kinds. Gender-critical feminists ought, then, to respond to contemporary feminism by reasserting the second-wave conception of women as a political kind – a sex class.

III

Gender-critical feminists might worry that responding to contemporary feminism by reasserting the second-wave conception of women as a political kind is an evasion of the problem immediately facing women: the denial of the sexual specificity of this political kind.

I admit that the conception of women as a political kind is useful only against a background understanding that this kind is a sexually specific group – female people. For, once this understanding disappears, the conception of women as a political kind becomes a conception of a sexually non-specific group as a political kind. Such a conception does not serve the sex class 'woman'. But gender-critical feminists have revived this background. The conception of women as a political kind therefore *is* useful. I ought not to criticise them, then, for their emphasis on the biological but rather I should thank them and encourage them to see that this emphasis has now done its work and can, in fact must, be replaced by an emphasis on the political. With a renewed consciousness of women as a sex, we can and must pursue the theorisation of this sex as a class.

Moreover, a conception of women as a political kind is not a conception that makes the sexual specificity of this kind disappear. Indeed, the account that generates it, the account of the creation of the sex classes 'man' and 'woman', is an account on which male people are the constituency of the sex class 'man' and female people are the constituency of the sex class 'woman'. The conception of women as a political kind is thus necessarily a conception of female people as a political kind.

Gender-critical feminists might remain doubtful, on the grounds that conceiving of women as a political kind nevertheless makes classifying male people as women possible, whereas conceiving of women as a biological kind does not. Analytically, this is true: the meanings of 'male person' and 'woman', where 'male' names a biological kind and 'woman' a political kind, are such that the claim 'a male person is a woman' is intelligible, whereas the meanings of the same terms, where 'male' names a biological kind and 'woman' the biological kind 'female', are such that the claim 'a male person is a woman' is unintelligible.

However, history constrains the conditions under which the possibility of the latter's being intelligible can be actualised. It is members of the female sex who, in virtue of their femaleness, have been designated members of the kind 'woman' and members of the male sex who, in virtue of their maleness, have been designated members of the kind 'man'. One who designated a male person as a member of the kind 'woman' would have either mistaken the male person for a female person or misused the term 'woman'.

Suppose that, incorrect though this designation was, it was accepted. Perhaps, as in the case of Lili Elbe, a doctor diagnosed a male person as a female person beneath a male exterior, and this diagnosis gained acceptance from the male person;[17] or perhaps, as is frequent nowadays, a doctor diagnoses a male person as transgender – a person with a female gender identity 'born in the wrong body' or 'assigned male at birth' – and this diagnosis gains the acceptance and approval of that person's family and friends. Genuine acceptance consists not merely in referring to this male person as 'she' or 'her', but also in acting as the belief that this person is female commits one to act. I want to ask gender-critical feminists: if this designation gained genuine acceptance, if we acted towards a particular male person as we do towards a female person, if he therefore were, to all political intents and purposes, a member of the kind 'woman', would it be wrong to classify him as a woman? If it would, why? Why, that is, on specifically feminist grounds? I am not certain that it would be. Gender-critical feminists will baulk at this question, but notice that the classification of this particular male person as a woman is not equivalent to the classification of a trans woman as a woman. For it is conditional on the genuine acceptance of the designation 'woman' for this particular person. Such an acceptance strikes me as a theoretical possibility only.

Gender-critical feminists might then object that, as the conception of women as a political kind does not preclude the claim that this political kind is sexually specific, the conception of women as a biological kind does not preclude the claim that this biological kind has political significance either; so it is unclear why the former is preferable. This is a reasonable objection, prompting the question: what exactly is the difference between a conception of women as a sex that is classed and a conception of women as a class that is sexed?

One who conceives of women as a sex that is classed sees class through the prism of sex, while one who conceives of women as a class that is sexed sees sex through the prism of class. As an example of the former, Brownmiller considers the systematic rape of women in light of male and female biology – of men having a penis and women a vagina, and of men having the strength to overcome women.[18] As an example of the latter, MacKinnon considers a woman's distinguishing features in light of her being a member of the sex class that is rapable, revealing them as constituents of rapability: vulnerability emerges as 'the appearance/reality of easy sexual access'; softness as 'pregnability by something hard'; incompetence as 'seek[ing] help as vulnerability seeks shelter ... trading exclusive access for protection'; domesticity as 'nurtur[ing] the consequent progeny, proof of potency'; masochism as a 'pleasure in violation' that 'becomes her sensuality'.[19] MacKinnon allows us to wonder whether, *contra* Brownmiller, it is not women's physical weakness that gives rise to their rapability but their rapability that gives rise to their physical weakness. If the latter is true, then to organise life around the fact of women's physical weakness is to organise life around the effect of sex class, and thus to preserve sex class in effect. As another example, Brownmiller theorises rape in light of sex, which she takes to express a biological act – the reproductive[20] – whereas MacKinnon sees sex as 'the prime moment of politics'[21] and wonders whether 'sex' names the reproductive act because this act 'is considered an act of forcible violation and defilement of the female distinctively as such, not because it "is" sex a priori'.[22] One who sees that sex might be related only coincidentally to reproduction will not consider sex natural or unchangeable and will not trace sexual abuses back to nature, as Brownmiller does.

The difference between the conception of women as a biological kind and the conception of women as a political kind is a difference in that to which each gives analytical primacy: in sex for the former, in class for the latter. And the difference in that to which each gives analytical primacy is a difference in what it sees. One who sees sex through the prism of class is one who sees that our understanding of sex might be different once sex class has been abolished. Such a person is not sure that our understanding will change or how it will do so, but she is less sure that it will not change than one who sees class through the prism of sex would be.[23] In other words, she worries that the 'eternal hills' on which Mary Harrington hunts 'sacred shades' are not eternal.[24] This gender-critical feminist is alive, as Harrington is not, to the possibility that respecting the immutable reality of sex may be respecting the mutable reality of sex class, and so she is willing to throw caution to the wind, to go in search of other hills.

Harrington's *Feminism against Progress* serves as an illustration of the perils of the conception of women as a biological kind (as opposed to one of women as a political kind). Matt, a former soldier, tells Harrington how the inclusion of women in the military undermined cohesion. First, '[a]lmost always the female would have a sexual relationship with someone in the group, and then move onto another, and another'.[25] Second, the presence of female soldiers aroused jealousy and suspicion in the soldiers' wives. 'Matt's account', Harrington writes, 'parallels the gender-critical case for sex realism in some settings: accounts are already emerging of the explosive consequences of introducing heterosexual desire into women's prisons: harassment, reported rapes, pregnancies, and even heterosexual marriages between inmates'.[26] Harrington's acceptance of Matt's account, and her understanding of what he describes as the work of heterosexual desire, are startling. Why does Matt place the woman in the active role and the men in the passive? Why does he say that *she* would have the relationship, that *she* would move on, as though the men were her helpless victims? Might it not have been the case that the men circulated her? The radical feminist in me cannot but see a resemblance to prostitution: each man takes his turn. Whatever took place, are we sure that it is the expression of a desire that belongs to sex, a desire for the opposite sex? Might it not be the expression of a desire that belongs to sex class, a desire for male mastery and female subjection? And surely the jealousy and suspicion felt by the soldiers' wives are the response of women as members of the female sex class, who must compete with other women for male attention. Finally, it is difficult to reconcile Harrington's understanding of harassment and rape as the consequence of heterosexual desire with her vision of an alternative way of life, in which marriage is central. The 'sex realism' that Harrington advocates emerges to no small degree as sex class realism.

Gender-critical feminists are right to react to contemporary (poststructural, intersectional, trans-inclusionary) feminism by remembering what this feminism has forgotten: the reality of sex. But, as *feminists*, they must remember it not because it is eternal or sacred (though it may prove to be), but because it has been and remains the reality of class, and they must remember the reality of class in order to surpass it. It is not coincidental that contemporary feminism has forgotten the reality of sex *and* the reality of sex class: only because it had already forgotten the latter did it find forgetting the former so terribly easy. Gender-critical feminists must remember the reality of sex, then, *insofar as doing so serves the abolition of class.*

It seems to me that a gender-critical feminism that conceives of women as a political kind, a class that is sexed, does just this. It seeks the abolition of class, remembering and demanding respect for the reality of sex *to that end*. Here 'respect' means conditional acknowledgement of the reality of sex – conditional, that is, on such an acknowledgement's serving the aim of abolition of class. By contrast, a gender-critical feminism that conceives of women as a biological kind, a sex that is classed, remembers the reality of sex as eternal, and demands respect for it as such. Here 'respect' means (unconditional) submission to, even reverence for ('*sacred* shades'), this reality. The difference between the two forms of respect will become fully apparent only in the course of time. At present, those who conceive of women as a biological kind and those who conceive of women as a political kind are united in their struggle against an immediate threat: the denial of the sexual specificity of women. Once they have quelled this threat, once they have settled the question 'are women female?', they will face these questions: What, in women and female people, pertains to sex class and what pertains to sex? What must we conditionally acknowledge and what must we submit to? Those who conceive of women as a biological kind might argue that women's vulnerability is related to sex,[27] and so demand the organisation of life to be made around this fact. Those who conceive of women as a political kind might instead suspect that women's vulnerability is related to sex class, that women are vulnerable because they must be, if it is to be plausible that they agree to be governed by men in exchange for protection from them, that their subjection to men is advantageous and consensual. For them, the moment in which our memory of the possibly contingent reality of female vulnerability begins to engulf us, so that we find ourselves unable to even try to overcome it, the moment in which this memory begins to thwart the struggle for a new, feminist way of life, is the moment in which we must either forget or invent new memories.[28]

As another example, those who conceive of women as a biological kind, who view class through the prism of sex, might see women's reproductive capacities as inherently useful – and hence the control of these capacities as inherently desirable – to men.[29] If they do, they will see women as being forever in need of protection against male appropriation of these capacities. Those who conceive of women as a political kind might instead suspect that the male control of women's reproductive capacities is entailed by the male need for 'progeny' as 'proof of potency',[30] as proof of manhood. On this view, it is only when the sexes are classes, when virility is the measure of manhood, when progeny, as proof of virility, is proof of manhood, that the control of women's reproductive capacities becomes necessary for men. Those who see women's reproductive capacities as inherently useful to men mistake what these capacities are under male dominance for what they inherently are; they mistake features of a sex class for features of sex. On this view, men's control of women's reproductive capacities is derivative of male mastery and female subjection. So, what women primarily require is not control over their reproductive capacities: so long as men are the masters of women, such control will not mean female autonomy, it will mean control over the consequences of female subjection and, as a subject can have only what control her master permits, control over the consequences of female subjection is the power to do only as men permit, which is the illusion of control. What women primarily require is instead sovereignty over their sexed being. Once women have this, once men are no longer the masters of women, virility will no longer be the measure of manhood, so men will no longer have reason to control women's reproductive capacities and women will no longer require protection against male appropriation of these capacities.

On this view, women require control of their reproductive capacities only insofar as this control serves the goal of obtaining sovereignty over their sexed being. If, as Louise Perry and Mary Harrington suggest, such control leaves women more powerless in the face of men's demands for sex,[31] more compliant as sexual subjects, we have reason to reject this control. Perry and Harrington argue that, when sex became unaccompanied by the real risk of pregnancy, women lost the grounds on which to refuse men. Harrington concludes that we must 'rewild' sex, recouple it with the possibility of pregnancy by rejecting the contraceptive pill.[32] Perry and Harrington do not ask why women cannot refuse men's sexual demands without an excuse. Women cannot refuse because, as sexual subjects of men, they lack the authority to do so.[33] They must, then, cast their refusal as counterfactual consent: 'I would, were it not for the possibility of becoming pregnant.' If reproductive control has left women less able to refuse, it has done so by depriving them of an excuse more convincing than others – 'I have a headache', or 'I'm tired'.[34] So long as women are sexual subjects of men, relinquishing control over their reproductive capacities will afford them nothing more than the aberrational evasion of a systematically obligatory submission. Any begrudging refusal ('I would, were it not for...') has only a temporary life – in the sense that, used too many times, it gives itself away as a refusal in disguise, but also in the sense that it sends us in search of a solution: 'I would, were it not for the possibility of becoming pregnant' sends us in search of a solution to the problem of the possibility of pregnancy. 'Wilded' sex may have begotten the problem – the contraceptive pill – to which Harrington considers it to be the solution. Perry and Harrington take women's sexual subjection to men – sex class – for granted. If liberal feminists assume that the existence of female sovereignty necessary for reproductive control means more than conditional control over the consequences of sex class, Perry and Harrington assume the impossibility of female sovereignty. Both assumptions prevent us from achieving female sovereignty.

Perry and Harrington think that our mistake has been to conceive of men and women as social, as opposed to biological, kinds. Consequently they look for the solution in the affirmation of biology and for the problem in the denial of it. In doing so, they mistake the political – male sexual desire – for the biological – men and women as sex classes, as people who demand sex and people who, in the absence of an excuse, submit to this demand for men and women as sexes. And, because they think this way about our mistake, a past in which we affirmed biology seems to them preferable to a present in which we deny it. In truth, that past was a society of sex class no less than the present is. It may have been preferable to the present in the sense that a past where work was secure is preferable to a present where it is precarious. It was a preferable incarnation of an oppressive system – preferable by the yardstick of an oppressive system.

Nietzsche argues that a historical sense is necessary because, and only insofar as, it serves living. 'We need history, certainly', he says,

> but we need it for reasons different from those for which the idler in the garden of knowledge needs it, even though he may look nobly down on our rough and charmless needs and requirements. We need it, that is to say, for the sake of life and action, not so as to turn comfortably away from life and action.[35]

If an historical sense is to serve living, it must be accompanied by an appropriately unhistorical sense:[36] if we do not at all remember the past, we cannot supersede it, but if we only remember it, we collapse under its weight. Having forgotten the past, contemporary feminists cannot supersede it. Remembering the past, gender-critical feminists can. I am worried, however, that, just as contemporary feminists forgot too much – they forgot whom they exist to serve (the sex class 'woman, female person') and why (because they are oppressed by the sex class 'man, male person') – gender-critical feminists risk remembering too much, remembering all that has been true of sex (male strength, female weakness, male aggression, female vulnerability), so that it seems to them that these things must always be true of sex. Consider Harrington. Suggesting that the loss of male-only spaces has been detrimental to men, she cites the evolutionary biologist Joyce Benenson, who argues that, for reasons of survival, men and women have evolved to socialise in distinct ways: male humans cooperate with peers and compete with outgroups, while female humans exclude other female humans in their search for mates, then enlist peers and elders to help with the care of dependents.[37] I cannot but find the resemblance between male humans and female humans on the one hand, men and women as patriarchy would have them, on the other, to be suspicious. In male humans cooperating with peers I see the brotherhood protecting each man's sex right; in female humans excluding other female humans I see women whose existence is validated by male desire. Unsurprisingly, the future that Harrington envisages – a life with marriage, motherhood, and a vegetable patch at its centre – is the past. A gender-critical feminism that remembers too much must look for the future in the past, as Harrington does. But the past is patriarchal.[38] This past makes many futures possible, but not the truly feminist future, the future in which 'woman' names a way of being human. This future is an impossible one, as are all futures that require revolution rather than reform. A gender-critical feminism that looks for the future in the past can deliver women only to a reformed patriarchy – a patriarchy in which women are shielded from the excesses of male sexuality, in which men govern women paternalistically rather than brutally, in which women's activity – care – is valued, though only in the sense of being recognised as a valuable pursuit for a woman. This reformed patriarchy may be preferable to the current incarnation of patriarchy, it may even be the best of all possible patriarchal worlds. But the best of all possible patriarchal worlds is the best of all worlds in which women are the subjects of men. If the patriarchal past does not make the feminist future possible, then gender-critical feminism must *forget*, if it is to deliver women to this future. It must give up some of its 'realism' for the vision characteristic of its second-wave ancestors. It must deny some of 'the reality of sex', in the hope that it will prove to be the patriarchal reality of sex, unworthy of feminist respect. Gender-critical feminists have reacted with 'realism' to the contemporary effort to forget sex. Realism may be preferable to contemporary anti-realism in that it could restore an incarnation of patriarchy that is less hostile to women, an incarnation of patriarchy in which women have refuge. But realism is not the solution to the present problem, which is another form of the problem of patriarchy. To that problem, the solution is a vision of an alternative way of life.[39]

IV

If gender-critical feminism were to do as I am encouraging it to do, how would this movement change? What would it seek? How would it understand this historical moment? What would it see as being at stake for women in this moment? How would it respond to this moment? A gender-critical feminism that conceived of women as a sex class would seek their *freedom* rather than their *safety*. It would understand that it is only through political struggle, taken up by women and directed against men, that women will achieve freedom. It would regard male people's claim to be women as a threat to the consciousness that men and women are classes, and hence to the struggle for women's freedom, and hence to the realisation of women's freedom. In Schmittian terms, it would regard this claim as a threat to the realisation of the feminist way of life. It would therefore object to the acceptance of trans women as women, even apart from the implications of this acceptance for inclusion in all that is 'women-only'.

It would not do this with malice. It would not do this because it holds beliefs about trans women *qua* trans women. It would do this because it sees trans women, *qua* male, as members of the male sex class, because it sees their male bodies as their fate, as it sees women's female bodies as theirs, because it sees this fate, however unwanted, as inescapable under patriarchy. MacKinnon writes: 'no woman escapes the meaning of being a woman within a gendered social system'.[40] She is right. But nor does a man. What is sadly true for women is as sadly true for men. As it sees trans women as members of the male sex class, gender-critical feminism cannot accept them as women, or rather cannot accept them as women without jettisoning the belief that men and women are sex classes; and, since it is far from convinced that this belief is false, it cannot in good faith do this. Were it to do this, it would be doing so neither because it has come to see the belief as false nor because it has come to see trans women as women, but because it has lost the will to continue to pursue women's interest. It would be surrendering.

Once upon a time, gender-critical feminism might have been willing to believe that trans women's need was more pressing, or that the pursuit of their interests would inevitably serve women's. But experience has made it wiser. Time and again, women have devoted themselves to the pursuit of others' interests, and time and again they have found themselves where they have always been. Gender-critical feminists are women out of patience. Where trans-inclusionary feminists see a vulnerable group asking only for acceptance, gender-critical feminists see men demanding *one more time* that women sacrifice their interests; and they find this one more time one too many.

Dworkin observes: 'Politically committed women often ask the question, "How can we as women support the struggles of other people?"'[41] No one else, she continues, 'is so entirely captured, so entirely conquered, so destitute of any memory of freedom, so dreadfully robbed of identity and culture, so absolutely slandered as a group, so demeaned and humiliated as a function of daily life. And yet, we go on, blind, and we ask over and over again, "What can we do for them?"'[42] It is time we asked a different question. For Dworkin, this question is: 'What must *they* do now for us?'[43] But one cannot read Dworkin's writing and retain the belief that men will do anything for women. The question is therefore not 'what must they do now for us?', but 'what must *we* do now for *ourselves*?' Dworkin provides an answer: value our lives, as fully and resolutely as we have valued those of others.[44] Women who value their lives in this way are women who audaciously arrogate the right to weight their interest as others weight their own – that is, the right to pursue their interest *even when doing so comes at the expense of others'*, the right to refuse trans women's demand for recognition as women even when doing so comes at the cost of their exclusion. What is the test of self-respect if not, *just once*, insisting on one's own interest? Are women who do this met with contempt because women are not entitled to such self-respect?[45]

9

Choosing Women

I

If gender-critical feminism is to become a repoliticised feminism, it must follow radical feminism in conceiving of women as a sex class. But it must also depart from radical feminism in one crucial way: it must, as in fact it does, prioritise women's interest as women's interest, and precisely for the reason that it is women's interest.

Radical feminism distinguished itself from Marxist and socialist feminism by theorising women *qua* women as a class, a demographic with a shared and distinctive interest, namely in liberation, the fulfilment of which required a dedicated movement. But radical feminism also claimed, as Marx did of the exploitation of the proletariat, that the oppression of women is the primary oppression, the injustice from which all injustices derive, whose eradication is necessarily the eradication of all injustices. Dworkin, for example, writes: 'the feminist project is to end male domination . . . We also want to end those forms of social injustice which derive from the patriarchal model of male dominance – that is, imperialism, colonialism, racism, war, poverty, violence in every form.'[1] The claim that the oppression of women is the primary oppression gave with one hand what it took back with the other. It prioritised women's interest but prioritised it, rather conveniently, as the *shared* interest of all downtrodden peoples – conveniently because we can then pursue the interest of women on the grounds that it is the interest of all, or at the very least with the assurance that it will not cost others. We can avoid putting a high price on women's blood. Having (rightly) criticised women for the lack of pride apparent in their devotion to causes other than their own, Daly urges them to devote themselves to their own cause, 'refusing to see this as an illegitimate rival to other causes'.[2] For, she continues, '[i]t is not a rival to any truly revolutionary movement, but goes to the root of the evils such movements are trying to eradicate'.[3] Thus women must devote themselves to their own cause not because their cause alone is worthy but because their cause represents all legitimate causes. Ultimately, then, Daly fails to display female pride and to demand it of women.

Radical feminism promised at once too much – the eradication of all social injustices – and too little – the liberation of women *so long as it came at no cost* – or at no cost other than that to the oppressor, which, being the dispossession of what one never rightfully possessed, is not a genuine cost. For all its talk of commitment to women, radical feminism ultimately hedged its bets, hoping that a situation in which the interest of women conflicts with the interest of another downtrodden people would not arise; for, if it did, radical feminism would have to make a choice.

This situation has arisen: women's interest in liberation conflicts with trans women's interest in inclusion.

So feminists must now choose. Gender-critical feminists have chosen women. Unwilling to choose women but also unwilling to admit it, trans-inclusionary feminists have instead denied that they must choose, insisting that women's interest converges with trans women's. It is uncoincidental, as

Lawford-Smith intuits,[4] that contemporary, trans-inclusionary feminism is intersectional. A feminism that is intersectional is one that, believing that all systems of oppression interlock, refuses to countenance having to choose women, and a trans-inclusionary feminism is one that has failed to choose women.

Choosing women requires much, perhaps too much, of women. First, it requires that they prioritise a liberation that they cannot be sure they need. In the patriarchal way of life, relations between men *qua* men and women *qua* women are at once relations of mastery and subjection and relations of heterosexual love. Only when the relations of mastery and subjection become excessively so – for instance, when they involve an adult and a child, or when they are egregiously brutal – do they cease to be relations of heterosexual love and become instead abusive; only then do they cease to be sex and become violence. Relations of *excessive* mastery and subjection are necessarily exceptional. Moreover, they are relations not between men *qua* men and women *qua* women but between men *qua* deviant men and women *qua* persons. As relations of heterosexual love, the relations between men *qua* men and women *qua* women are not relations of mastery and subjection in the normative, objectionable sense. They are not oppressive, they are not relations from which women must be liberated. The second-wave claim that women are oppressed and must be liberated is, first and foremost, a vision of a future in which relations between men *qua* men and women *qua* women are not relations of mastery and subjection and relations of mastery and subjection are not relations of heterosexual love, in which the literary passages that Millett analyses horrify rather than arouse, in which it is unthinkable that we should accept prostitution. It is a vision of a future the possibility of which history denies. To ask that women prioritise their liberation is to ask that they place their faith in this vision.

Some feminists, perhaps above all MacKinnon, have perceived this. MacKinnon writes that 'male dominance is perhaps the most pervasive and tenacious system of power in history' and 'is metaphysically nearly perfect. Its point of view is the standard for point-of-viewlessness, its particularity the meaning of universality. Its force is exercised as consent, its authority as participation, its supremacy as the paradigm of order, its control as the definition of legitimacy.'[5] Its sexual hierarchy is its sexual love. Consequently, 'the reality of women's oppression is, finally, neither demonstrable nor refutable empirically'.[6] But, if MacKinnon is right, if 'male power produces the world',[7] if women do eroticise their subordination,[8] if sexual conquest is sexual realisation, then what can 'the reality of women's oppression' mean? That is, in what sense is this reality a *reality*? In the sense that the future will reveal it as such. Which, of course, MacKinnon cannot be sure of. In the preface to *Toward a Feminist Theory of the State*, she recalls a passing quip of her former teacher's, Leo Weinstein – '"really" is the feminine expletive'[9] – to which she attributes the crystallisation of her sense that 'method has something to do with women'.[10] She understands women's 'really' as descriptive, as referring to a reality buried beneath patriarchal appearances whose apprehension requires a distinctive method. I am suggesting that it is prophetic; it is about a reality that the future will reveal. Curiously, it seems not to have occurred to feminists, including MacKinnon and those who take her claims seriously, that they, too, may be unable to see 'the reality of women's condition'. They proceed as though the question is 'how have they discovered this reality?', or 'how can we expose this reality to others?', which presupposes that they have in fact discovered it. It does not occur to them that maybe they have not, that what they see could be the tip rather than the iceberg, the abuse rather than the use, rape rather than sex, that they could be 'fighting / for what my lack of freedom keeps me from glimpsing'.[11] To take MacKinnon seriously is not to wonder how we feminists have succeeded in discovering the 'reality of women's oppression', it is to realise that we have not; and to realise that we have not is to understand, at least in part, why we have failed to choose women. Like Marxists, we, too, do not believe that women *qua* women are oppressed, not *really*, not in a way that justifies prioritising our cause above that of another group, one that is *really* oppressed.

Second, choosing women *is* an act of disloyalty. Under patriarchy, a woman is the subject of a man and *qua* subject owes him allegiance. As Rich has written, women's honour consists in their fidelity to men, and their fidelity to men consists in sexual fidelity: to their fathers, by preserving virginity until marriage; to their husbands, by not having extramarital sexual relations. A woman can pursue women's interest only so long as it converges with men's: the interest of male workers (exploited by capitalists), the interest of men in racially downtrodden groups (emasculated), the interest of husbands ('Would men but generously snap our chains . . . they would find us . . . more faithful wives'),[12] the interest of fathers (beneficiaries of family-friendly work practices), the interest of sons ('Women should receive a higher education, not in order to become doctors, lawyers, or professors, but in order to rear their offspring to be valuable human beings'),[13] the interest of trans women (victims of the regulatory ideal of 'sex'), the interest of *all men* (oppressed by masculine norms, e.g. teased for crying). Which is to say, women can choose women only insofar as choosing women is compatible with choosing men. Should women's interest in sexual sovereignty conflict with disabled men's interest in sexual access to women, women must abandon the pursuit of their interest – in the name of justice, of course. A woman who shifts her allegiance to women, a woman who chooses women *over men* – a feminist (Wittig wrote that '"feminist" . . . means: someone who fights for women'[14] – perhaps she ought to have added, 'unconditionally') – is unfaithful and dishonourable, or perhaps even *a-faithful*, that is, not merely unfaithful to a particular man, not merely failing by the patriarchal standard of faithfulness, but unfaithful to that standard, a woman with no sense of faithfulness. This explains the outrage at gender-critical feminists, women who unabashedly choose women over men, indeed (*does their cruelty know no limits?*) over vulnerable men, men whose sex right is already underrespected, men most in need of dutiful female submission.

In order to be faithful to men, Rich writes, we women have lied – to men, to other women, and to ourselves:[15] we have plucked our eyebrows, shaved our legs, feigned our sexual pleasure, affected our fulfilment, denied our suffering. In order to act honourably to men, we have acted dishonourably to women. The first lie appears innocuous. But it commits us to more lies. Slowly but surely, the possibility of telling the truth recedes. We have told too many lies. We have staked our reputations on these lies. We cannot admit to ourselves that we have lied so easily, so persistently. We cannot go back. There is nothing for it but to carry on. This may describe how we have come to be where we now are.

But the multiplying lies become a burden. So, when one woman – Caroline Norma, Germaine Greer, Kathleen Stock, Holly Lawford-Smith, Victoria Smith – dares to tell the truth, some of us feel a sense of relief.[16] Thus is this woman 'creating the possibility for more truth around her'.[17] In telling the truth, this woman acts honourably to her foremothers and her sisters and dishonourably to men. In 1987, Dworkin wrote of sexual intercourse as a 'loyalty test'.[18] She meant a test of our loyalty to men: a woman who submits, who is found unspoiled, and who takes pleasure in her violation thereby proves at once her loyalty to men and her womanhood. But it is also a test of loyalty to women: since, when it comes to intercourse, we must say only what flatters men, when women began telling the truth about it to other women, as they did in the consciousness-raising groups of the 1960s and 1970s,[19] they betrayed men for women. Gender-critical feminists are resuming this work, with a not insignificant difference: where women in the 1960s spoke in the privacy of consciousness-raising groups, gender-critical feminists speak in public, on the steps of parliament, no less.[20]

II

Feminists have criticised the expectation that women choose women, on the grounds that such an expectation requires women who also belong to other downtrodden groups to forsake those groups. In 1977 the Combahee River Collective wrote:

> Although we are feminists and lesbians, we feel solidarity with progressive black men and do not advocate the fractionalization that white women who are separatists demand. Our situation as black people necessitates that we have solidarity around the fact of race, which white women of course do not need to have with white men, unless it is their negative solidarity as racial oppressors. We struggle together with black men against racism, while we also struggle with black men about sexism.[21]

First, the demand that women choose women is not a demand that they do so exclusively. Just as it is reasonable for feminists to ask of women that, as *women*, they struggle against the distinctive wrongs done to women, so it is reasonable for Marxism, for example, to ask of workers, including female workers, that, as *workers*, they struggle against the distinctive wrongs done to workers. Feminism's and Marxism's demands for commitment need not pull women in conflicting directions. As women, women can join the feminist struggle to end prostitution; as workers, they can join the union's struggle for improved working conditions. The Combahee River Collective is right that *separatism* is in effect the demand that women exclusively choose women, but as a woman can choose women without becoming a separatist, this problem (insofar as it is such) with separatism is not one with the demand that women choose women.

Second, it must be asked: in what sense are women members of other downtrodden groups? For the criticism that choosing women requires women to forsake other downtrodden groups of which they are members assumes that women are members of these groups just as men are, so that, by forsaking these groups, women are betraying their own kind. I want to subject this assumption to critique. I shall do so by considering two examples. In what sense are women members of the group 'workers'? And in what sense are Black women members of the group 'Black people'?

Feminists have observed that 'work' is 'men's activity'.[22] 'Women's activity' (husband care, homecare, and childcare, as MacKinnon puts it)[23] is non-work (in the sense of not being wage labour). Consistently with this, historically, a worker's wage was a family wage, a wage that supported the wife (and children) whom a worker, *qua* worker, necessarily had and whom he had to support because she, *qua* wife, was not a worker.[24] A man who does not 'win the bread' is less of a man, and a woman who does, either for herself or for her family, is more of a man and less of a woman. As this suggests, it is not that women cannot be workers, but that they cannot be workers *qua* women. Put another way, as workers, women are 'pale reflections of men'.[25] So the struggle for *workers'* rights is a struggle for *men's* rights. Of this struggle women are not the intended beneficiaries, though they may, *qua* 'pale reflections of men', incidentally benefit.

Angela Davis's discussion of the condition of enslaved Black women illustrates the worker–woman dichotomy. In the middle of the nineteenth century, enslaved Black women were predominantly fieldworkers, in spite of the stereotype of the cook, maid, or mammy.[26] As fieldworkers, they were treated 'as if they were men'[27] (they were assigned the tasks that men were assigned, and they were whipped as men were whipped), but, as women, they were treated distinctively (they were raped and they were used as 'breeders').[28] Notice that Davis classifies their rape under their treatment *qua women*, which she distinguishes from their treatment *qua fieldworkers*, which she describes as their treatment *qua men*. The *physical* assault of whipping is a work-related abuse, the *sexual* assault of rape is a woman-related and, as such, a non-work-related abuse. Davis's classification of rape accurately reflects the implicit masculinity of 'worker'.

In contradiction to this, Davis elsewhere attempts to classify enslaved Black women's rape as their treatment *qua workers*. She writes, for example: 'Rape ... was an uncamouflaged expression of the slaveholder's economic mastery and the overseer's control over Black women as workers.'[29] On this view, rape becomes equivalent to whipping – 'an essential ingredient of the strategy of terror which guaranteed the over-exploitation of black labour'.[30] In other words, rape serves the capitalist purpose of generating profit.

First, this raises the question of why men rape women when they have no economic incentive to do so – women from whose labour they do not gain. For instance, why did slaveholders rape their wives? Why did enslaved Black men rape enslaved Black women? Why do male workers rape women? A response to the first question appears in the form of the supposition that, once white men became aware that they could rape Black women with impunity, 'their conduct toward women of their own race could not have remained unscarred'.[31] This supposition is empirically and logically flawed: empirically because it rather astonishingly implies that white men did not rape white women before slavery, and logically because impunity is not itself a reason for action, that is, not unless a man desires to rape a woman would impunity incentivise him to rape her. Davis criticises Brownmiller for naturalising rape,[32] and yet she errs in this very way. So natural does it seem to her that a man who *could* freely rape a woman *would* rape her that she takes impunity to account for his doing so. As for the second question – why did enslaved Black men rape enslaved Black women? – Davis writes as though no such phenomenon existed.[33] Davis's response to the third question – why do male workers rape women? – resembles her response to the first: because they believe that their maleness accords them the right to do it.[34] But, as I said for impunity, a right is not a reason for action. Davis observes that, when working-class men rape, they are 'accepting a bribe, an illusory compensation for powerlessness'.[35] I am struck by this. According to her, when working-class men exercise their sex right – their right, as men, to use women sexually – they exercise only an illusion of power (I am reminded of Fraser: 'what is sold is a *male fantasy* of "male sex-right"'[36]), which serves to blind them to the actuality of their powerlessness. Power and powerlessness based on class are real, power and powerlessness based on sex are illusory. Class hierarchy is a reality, male dominance an idea. As an idea, it can be thought away. This accounts for the 'optimism of the intellect'[37] (as opposed to the Gramscian 'pessimism of the intellect and optimism of the will')[38] that Kathy Miriam observes in poststructural feminism.

Second, as a man who rapes a woman for sexual pleasure rapes her *qua* female-bodied person but a worker is a male-bodied person, Davis must de-sexualise rape in order to classify Black women's rape as their treatment *qua* workers, as of a piece with whipping. She must claim that '[i]t would be a mistake to regard the institutionalized pattern of rape during slavery as an expression of white men's sexual urges, otherwise stifled by the specter of white womanhood's chastity',[39] that '[e]xcessive sex urges ... had nothing to do with this virtual institutionalization of rape',[40] that rape served the same purpose as the whip: to subdue and thereby secure labour.[41] This raises the following questions: why did white slaveholders and overseers rape rather than whip Black women? If rape were a means of subduing, why did they not equally systematically rape Black men? Why was rape a means of subduing? Perhaps rape is a means of subduing women because it is a sex act, and the sex act is an act in which a man conquers a woman; perhaps rape is a means of 'demoraliz[ing] their men'[42] because it is a sex act, and the sex act is an act in which a man possesses a woman – in this case, another man's woman, thereby reminding him that, as a Black man, he has no rightful claim to a woman. In other words, perhaps rape becomes 'a weapon of domination, a weapon of repression'[43] because it is sex. If this is so, then for white slaveholders and overseers the subjugation of Black women and sexual pleasure were not, as Davis assumes, mutually exclusive ends. As penetration, rape was the subjugation of Black women and was sexually pleasurable *as such*.

At one level, I admire Davis's attempt to reconceive rape as work-related abuse.[44] Ultimately, however, it assimilates men *qua* men's oppression of women *qua* women to capitalists *qua* capitalists' exploitation of workers *qua* workers, thus obscuring rather than illuminating this oppression. It theorises rape as political by theorising it as non-sex, and it theorises relations between men and women as political by theorising them as relations between capitalists and workers, one group of men and another. The sexual remains the non-political.

Marxist feminism was an attempt to remedy this situation, to extend the qualification 'worker' to 'housewife' by arguing that the housewife cares for the worker (her husband) and the next generation of workers (her sons), thus *producing* present (her husband's) and future (her sons') labour power.[45] If housewives were workers, their activity – the care of husband, home, and child – would be labour, as opposed to 'a labour of love':[46] 'labour' is that which one does for pay, whereas 'labour of love' is that which one does for pleasure. The relation of husband to wife would be a relation of boss to worker, an impersonal relation, not the personal relation that a relation of love is. The domestic sphere would be in the public, not the private domain. To extend 'worker' to 'housewife' would be, I am suggesting, to obliterate the distinctions, or rather antitheses – productive–antiproductive, labour–leisure, pay–pleasure, impersonal–personal, public–private – upon which 'worker' relies for its meaning. It would not be to extend 'worker'; it would be to radically alter its meaning.

At one level, the Marxist feminist Sylvia Federici understood this. Federici demanded wages for housework; one response was that a wage would make little difference to housewives' lives. Federici replied that this view mistakenly assumes that a wage would be an addition to a life that otherwise remained as it had been: mistakenly, because a wage would be the recognition of housework as work – a recognition that would *revolutionise* 'all our family and social relations'.[47]

At another level, she failed to fully appreciate how this recognition would revolutionise those relations. She assumed that the recognition of housework as work would merely expand the extension of 'work' – teacher, carpenter, police officer, doctor, housewife. But 'housework' is the antithesis of 'work'. It is that in contradistinction to which 'work' is defined. The recognition of housework as work would reconstitute the distinction between 'work' and 'non-work', radically altering the extensions and the meanings of each. Housework therefore cannot be recognised as work, in the sense that its recognition as work would mean the redefinition of 'work'.

One need only read the brilliant epigraph of Federici's *Wages against Housework* to grasp this: 'They say it is love. We say it is unwaged work. / They call it frigidity. We call it absenteeism. / Every miscarriage is a work accident. / . . . Neuroses, suicides, desexualisation: occupational diseases of the housewife'.[48] The reclassification of housework as work is the reclassification of love as unwaged work, of frigidity as absenteeism, of miscarriage as a workplace accident, and of neuroses, suicides, and desexualisation as occupational diseases. This reclassification would drastically alter the meanings of 'unwaged work', 'absenteeism', 'workplace accident', 'occupational disease', along with 'love', frigidity', 'miscarriage', 'neuroses, suicides, desexualisation'. This epigraph allows us to see how a struggle for workers' rights that took as 'work' 'women's activity' and thus as 'workers' women *qua* women would differ from the struggle for workers' rights as we know it: its paradigmatic issues would be unwaged housework, unremunerated sexual service, miscarriage, neuroses, suicides, and desexualisation. In short, 'work' cannot be extended to 'women's activity'. The struggle for workers' rights cannot therefore become anything other than a struggle for men's rights.

I said earlier that some women – those who can more or less perform men's activities, those who can more or less be 'pale reflections of men' – incidentally benefit from this struggle. Does this provide a reason for women to choose workers? It does not, not because only some women benefit, but because some women benefit at the class of women's cost. As I have said, 'work' exists in a relation of antithesis to 'women's activity'. To use Pateman's words, '[t]he attributes and activities of the "worker" are constructed together with, and as the other side of, those of his feminine counterpart, the "housewife".' Carrying tools, wearing overalls, and having lunch prepared by another – the attributes of a husband – will be, by contradistinction, the attributes of a *worker* only as long as carrying an iron, wearing a dress, and preparing lunch for another – the attributes of a *housewife* – are the attributes of a not-worker. Only as long as husband care, homecare, and childcare are the duties of a housewife are they the non-duties of workers ('non-promotable' work).[49] Only as long as performing husband care, homecare, and childcare ennobles a housewife does it demean a worker (including a female worker). If 'work' exists in a relation of antithesis to 'women's activity' (husband care, homecare, and childcare), then the struggle for the rights of workers necessarily preserves the role of woman *qua* woman as servant to man. The same applies to the struggle for the rights of female workers. For sexualised dress, sexual harassment, and office housework are improperly expected of the female worker and are injuries and insults to her only when attractiveness, sexual accessibility, and housework are properly expected of the housewife. The effort to eliminate these injuries and insults, to improve the lot of the female worker *qua* worker, necessarily keeps the lot of the housewife *qua* woman unchanged. So, if some women can be workers, this is possible only as long as women *qua* women, women as a class, remain subservient to men *qua* men, men as a class.

Previously I have been critical of the Marxist feminist conflation of 'housewife' with 'woman', a conflation through which Marxist feminism attempts to obtain the theoretical status of oppressed for women *qua* women: 'housewife' is coextensive with 'woman'; the housewife is exploited; therefore women are exploited. While I maintain that this account of women's oppression *qua* women is wrong, I am now more sympathetic to the emphasis on the housewife. For it is the fate of members of the female sex class to occupy the role of housewife. That some women (perhaps I am one) manage to partially escape this fate or are partially spared it makes it no less their fate. (I said 'partially' because, even as workers, women are not free of the expectation to care for 'husband' (the boss), 'home' (the office), and 'children' (the employees) – to organise an employee's farewell card, to bring the morning tea, to clean up; and I said 'spared' because women who escape their fate do so only at the whim of men.) In this sense, all women are housewives. For women who are not housewives to insist that 'not *all* women are housewives' (I hear Butler: 'surely all women are not mothers')[50] is for them to disavow their class. Federici is right: 'We want and have to say that we are all housewives . . . because as long as we think we are something better, something different than a housewife, we accept the logic of the master, which is a logic of division, and for us the logic of slavery.'[51] Once we recognise that we are all, but for the grace of patriarchy, housewives, we can no longer regard the struggle for workers' rights as a struggle from which women benefit, and so we can no longer choose workers.

I turn now to the second example. The Combahee River Collective, a group of Black feminists, believes that '[o]ur situation as black people necessitates that we have solidarity around the fact of race'.[52] This assumes that Black women and Black men are equally members of the group Black people and thus equal beneficiaries of a struggle against racism. But are they? As 'people' and 'men' are synonyms and 'men' and 'women' antonyms, 'Black people' has one extension – Black men – and 'Black women' another – Black women. Black men and Black women appear to be subgroups of the group Black people. In fact, Black men are the group 'Black people'[53] and Black women are the group 'Black people's–men's sexual inferiors', just as white men are the group 'white people' and white women are the group 'white people's–men's sexual inferiors'.

Unlike *white* men, Black men have, *qua* Black, been denied the status of 'people'. But, like white *men*, they have, *qua* men, been entitled to this status. It is not arbitrary that the abolitionist image of the slave was an image of a Black *man* asking: 'Am I not a man and a brother?'[54] As a condemnation of slavery, the abolitionist image was an image of a *slave* in a particular sense: the normative sense of *human being rightfully free and wrongfully enslaved*, rather than the merely descriptive sense of *human being enslaved*. The human being rightfully free, the human being in the moral sense, is the man. So the human being wrongfully enslaved was the Black *man*. Abolition was the movement designed to end slavery for all, Black men and women alike, but it was premised upon a conception of humanity as man, of freedom as the freedom owed to a man ('and a brother'), and of enslavement as the deprivation of such freedom. In line with this, abolitionists conceived of freedom as partly consisting in the right to a wife. Uriah Boston objected to the description of free Black people as wage *slaves* on the grounds that they, unlike slaves, had a right to a wife and children.[55] Abolitionists conceived of freedom as a Black man's freedom, and of a Black man's freedom as (in part) husbandly and fatherly mastery.

This offers another explanation of why, as Hazel Carby writes, '[t]he institutionalized rape of black women has never been as powerful a symbol of black oppression as the spectacle of lynching'.[56] If the human being in the moral sense is the man, then the paradigmatic abuse of the Black human being is the paradigmatic abuse of the Black man. The paradigmatic abuse of the man is physical abuse, while the paradigmatic abuse of the woman is sexual abuse. The symbol of the oppression of Black *people* is thus lynching,[57] while the symbol of the oppression of Black *women* is rape.

The Combahee River Collective assert the need to 'struggle together with black men against racism'.[58] But, so long as 'people' means men, the struggle against racism – against the mistreatment of a *people* as inferior by virtue of their race – will be a struggle against the mistreatment of *men* and for their recognition as *men*, and consequently as the *masters of women*.

I am not suggesting that the struggle against racism does not improve the lives of black women, or that it is merely insufficient, since it addresses the racial injustice but not the sexual injustice that Black women suffer, for this assumes that racial justice is sex-neutral – justice for all members of the race *qua* members of the race. Rather I am suggesting that racial justice is justice for members of the race *qua* men and, since 'man' means master of woman, that justice for members of the race *qua* men is injustice for members of the race *qua* women. In other words, it is not that racial justice is not sexual justice; it is that racial justice is necessarily sexual injustice.

The Collective writes of the sexism of racial justice movements (civil rights, Black nationalism, Black Panthers), a sexism not only of individual members but of the very visions of those movements, quoting for example from a Black nationalist pamphlet:

> We understand that it is and has been traditional that the man is the head of the house. He is the leader of the house/nation because his knowledge of the world is broader, his awareness is greater, his understanding is fuller and his application of this information is wiser ... Women can not do the same things as men – they are made by nature to function differently. Equality of men and women is something that can not happen even in the abstract world. Men are not equal to other men, i.e. ability, experience or even understanding. The value of men and women can be seen as in the value of gold and silver – they are not equal but both have great value. We must realize that men and women are a complement to each other because there is no house/family without a man and his wife. Both are essential to the development of any life.[59]

For the Mumininas of Committee for Unified Newark, the family is a microcosm of the nation.[60] The family consists of husband–father, wife–mother, and children. The husband–father's role is of ruler (over wife and children) and the wife–mother's role is of nurturer (of husband and children). Interestingly, when we transpose the family onto the nation, women disappear: 'husband–father' becomes 'ruler' and 'children' becomes 'citizenry', but what does 'wife–mother' become? Like 'children', 'wife–mother' becomes 'ruler's subject'; but, unlike 'children', it does not become 'citizen'. As wife–mother is integral to the family, women are integral to the nation, but integral as what? Pateman offers an answer to this question: the subjects of citizens.[61] Citizens consent to be governed by the ruler on condition that, in exchange for their loss of freedom, they receive sexual access to and sexual sovereignty over a woman. Mumininas allow Black women to depart from their role as nurturers only in the transition to freedom. Or, more accurately, they *demand* that women depart from their role and learn whatever skills are needed to achieve national liberation. Amusingly, they identify the following skills for this purpose: stenographer, notetaker; typing; telephone, switchboard, deskboard; accounting, bookkeeping; filing.[62] (In their defence, they do also identify weaponry.)[63] Mumininas demand Black women's commitment to struggle for a liberation that entails their subjection to Black men.

The Combahee River Collective is aware that sexism is intrinsic to racial justice movements, so that a new movement – Black feminism – for racial justice for Black women is needed.[64] Yet, in contradiction to this perception, it then expresses solidarity with Black men in their struggle for racial justice. Why? What grounds could exist for such a solidarity? I do see that sometimes, for instance under slavery, racial injustice may be the most immediate threat to the lives of Black women, and hence the problem most urgently in need of addressing. Black women must then join Black men in the struggle against racial injustice. But, as this struggle will secure only Black men's freedom, Black women's reason for struggling will not be the same as Black men's; it will be survival, not freedom. Once they have suppressed the immediate threat to their lives, what reason do Black women have to continue to struggle alongside Black men rather than to begin their own struggle? The Collective might argue that the two are not mutually exclusive and that Black women must do both. I am suggesting that the two are mutually exclusive: if Black men struggle for a freedom that entails Black women's subjection, and if Black women struggle for their own freedom, then Black women's struggle conflicts with Black men's,[65] as I think the Mumininas understood when they accused Black women who did not 'support their men in whatever they do in Nationalism' of 'holding back the progress of all Black people'[66] – Black people, of course, being Black men. They were right: the Black women who refuse to do stenography for a movement that envisions their wifely subjection, the

Black women who became the Combahee River Collective, do frustrate this movement's pursuit of the restoration of Black men to the position of rulers in the Black family and nation. I also see how Black women might believe that, besieged as they are, they cannot afford to forgo the alliance of Black men. But when Black women struggle with Black men, it is they who ally with Black men in the struggle for Black men's freedom. An alliance that requires that they sacrifice the pursuit of their own freedom to the pursuit of Black men's is not an alliance. In short, it seems to me that at a certain point Black women's solidarity with Black men becomes an impediment to Black women's liberation.

Women are members of other oppressed groups. But, so long as the reference point for oppression is the freedom owed to a *person* and 'person' here means man, the struggle against oppression and for freedom is one against the oppression and for the freedom of *men*. (If this were not so, would we regard abolition as the end of slavery and the beginning of freedom for all Black people, despite the production of pornography in which a white man holds a whip over naked and chained Black women?[67]) And, as 'man' means master of woman, the struggle against the oppression and for the freedom of men is a struggle against the oppression and for the freedom of *masters of women*.

Alice Walker beautifully illustrates this in a short story titled 'Coming Apart'. In one vignette, a Black middle-aged man arrives home from work, is greeted at the door by his wife, who has just finished preparing dinner, and proceeds to the bathroom, where he looks at pornographic magazines containing images of Black and white women.[68] In another vignette, the man, on a business trip to New York, is taking his wife down Forty-Second Street. At the sight of 'blonde, spaced-out hookers, with their Black pimps', he cries, 'Look! . . . how *free* everything is! A far cry from Bolton!'[69] Later, reading about feminists ('white women – those overprivileged hags')[70] who protest pornography in Times Square, he remembers 'only the *freedom* he felt there'.[71] In a third vignette, the wife is watching television in the hotel room. On the TV programme, two Black women are singing their latest hits. The first woman, who wears a chain around her ankle, sings 'Free me from my freedom, chain me to a tree!', the second 'Ready, aim, fire, my name is desire' and 'Shoot me with your love!' (a lyric that the husband thinks 'explains everything'), while guns fire around her.[72] In a fourth vignette, the wife, having resolved to fight, hands her husband his pornographic magazines and reads from Audre Lord's essay 'The Uses of the Erotic'. He 'realizes he can never have her again sexually, the way he has had her since their second year of marriage, as though her body belonged to someone else ... He feels *oppressed* by her incipient struggle, and feels somehow as if her struggle to change the pleasure he has enjoyed is a violation of his rights.'[73] In the first vignette, the husband consumes images of women coiled, for his pleasure, at the feet of men. In the second, the husband's freedom is Black women's sexual servitude – the hookers' servitude to their pimps and customers, and perhaps his wife's servitude to him and the men of his choosing (she is mistaken for a prostitute).[74] In the third, Black women gain freedom by relinquishing it. In the fourth, when the wife lays claim to her body, she violates her husband's sex right, oppressing him.[75] The abolition of slavery, Walker suggests, was the liberation of Black men, and the liberation of Black men was the subjection of women – *Black and white* – to them. Indeed, the measure of the freedom of men is the race of the women subjected to them. As Walker writes in the preface to the first edition of 'Coming Apart', '[m]any Black men see pornography as progressive because the white woman, formerly taboo, is, via pornography, made available to them. Not simply available, but in a position of vulnerability to all men.'[76]

If the reference point for oppression is the freedom owed to a *person* and 'person' here means man, then the demand that women choose women over the other oppressed groups of which they are members is a demand that they choose women over the *men* in the other oppressed groups of which they are members. Why does this demand strike even many feminists as obviously improper? Why, if not because even many feminists believe that women owe allegiance first and foremost, in the words of the Mumininas, to '*their* men'?[77]

These feminists might object that, just as the demand that women choose women over other downtrodden groups to which they belong is in truth a demand that women choose women over the *men* in those downtrodden groups, the demand that women choose women is in truth a demand that they choose *privileged* – white, middle-class – women.[78] It is because the reference point for oppression is the freedom owed to a *man* that, for women, to choose other downtrodden groups to which they belong is to choose *men*. In other words, it is for a conceptual reason that such a choice has this meaning. What conceptual reason could explain why, for women, to choose women is to choose *privileged* women? When Sojourner Truth said, '[t]hat man over there says that women need to be helped into carriages, and lifted over ditches, and to have the best place everywhere. Nobody ever helps me into carriages, or over mud-puddles, or gives me any best place! And ain't I a woman?',[79] she pointed to the implicit whiteness and middle-classness of the paradigmatic woman of 'that man over there'. But his paradigmatic woman (a thoroughly feminine female person) is precisely this: *his*, or rather man's. As feminism's woman is a member of the female sex class, feminism's paradigmatic woman is the woman whose condition exemplifies the condition of a member of the female sex class, which is a condition of subjection to members of the male sex class.

Feminists have treated the prostituted woman[80] and the wife[81] as the paradigmatic woman, the former because her function is to serve men's sexual desires, the latter because one of her duties is to serve her husband's sexual desires (once encoded in law, this duty remains encoded in our concepts, so that 'marital rape' is legally possible but practically inconceivable). If the prostituted woman and the wife alike have the function of serving men's sexual desires, and if men's sexual desire is for dominance, then the prostituted woman and the wife alike have the function of subjection, the prostituted woman to the class of men, the wife to one particular man.

If feminism's paradigmatic woman is the woman whose condition exemplifies the condition of subjection to men, then the demand that women choose women is a demand that they identify with women least spared their fate and that they struggle for these women and for these women in all women.

These women will be women whose circumstances least buttress them against their fate. On the one hand, they will be women with little money, with little recourse to the law, living on the margins, and, more often than not, migrant women and women from downtrodden racial groups. On the other hand, as no circumstances can make a woman not be a woman, no circumstances can guarantee her protection against her fate. Class privilege cannot ensure that a girl is not sexually abused or driven into prostitution, that a woman is not battered by her male partner or raped. Contemporary feminists assume that relative privilege in domains other than sex (such as class and race) becomes relative privilege in the domain of sex ('privileged *women*'), shielding women somewhat from the abuse that accompanies membership of the class 'woman'. In doing so, they treat women's oppression more or less as Marxists do, as a function of another kind of oppression, class-based or race-based – that is, a real kind.

Consider Larissa Behrendt's wariness of the claim that white Australian and Indigenous Australian women have in common, *qua* women, oppression exerted by men *qua* men on the grounds that '[w]hite women stand in a much better position in society than Aboriginal women. They have access to more resources, they are better educated, they earn more money and enjoy a better standard of living.'[82] The resources to which one has access, the level of one's education, the amount of money one earns, and the standard of living one enjoys are all functions of one's economic class. Behrendt's claim, then, is that white Australian women are, *qua* women, freer than Indigenous Australian women are, *qua* women, because they are relatively privileged economically. In Marxist fashion, Behrendt equates economic privilege with privilege *simpliciter*: because one has more resources, is better educated, earns more money, and enjoys a better standard of living, one stands in a better position in society. Behrendt can then see the privilege of women *qua* women only as a function of the privilege of women *qua* members of an economic class. Why is it not that one stands in a better position because one has sexual sovereignty over oneself – because one is inviolable, because one's violation is a wrong, because the law redresses that wrong, because one has reproductive autonomy, because one is accustomed to using others sexually – as all men *qua* men are, be they white or Indigenous Australian, but no woman *qua* woman is, be she white or Indigenous Australian? Why is the power that men *qua* men have and women *qua* women do not have unreal *qua* power? Why are 'those forms of harm that are not common to all women – those from which some women, by virtue of their wealth, race, citizenship status or caste, are insulated – . . . the most grievous to the women who suffer them'?[83] Why are the harms done to women *qua* women – the harms from which no woman is insulated, the endless forms of sexual violation – the least grievous ones? In addition, Behrendt's claim, quoted earlier, that 'white women stand in a much better position in society than Aboriginal women' conflates 'economically privileged white woman' with 'white woman'. This conflation is reminiscent of the left's dismissal of women *qua* women as bourgeois.[84] It seems that, for Behrendt, *real* white women are bourgeois, just as, for the left, *real* women are bourgeois. Is this because, for Behrendt, real white women are *ladies*, just as, for the left, real women are *ladies*?

Behrendt argues that white women have at best neglected Indigenous Australian women. As an example, when white Australian women were campaigning for accessible and safe contraception and abortion, Indigenous Australian women were being dispossessed of their children and sterilised.[85] Behrendt's suggestion is that in a particular historical period (the twentieth century) white Australian women and Indigenous Australian women faced, *qua* women, different primary problems – the former, forced motherhood, the latter, theft of motherhood – and that, because white Australian women mistook their own situation as women – that is, a situation in which the right to motherhood was assured – for the universal situation of women, they did not struggle for Indigenous Australian women's right to motherhood. Behrendt is right to consider this a failure. By neglecting Indigenous Australian women *qua* women, feminism neglected its constituents. It failed.

As another example, white women have not supported Indigenous Australian women by protecting female sacred sites. Behrendt explains that, because anthropologists did not consult Indigenous women, they recorded only male sacred sites. Unrecorded and therefore unprotected, female sacred sites have been destroyed more than male sacred sites.[86] In truth, I was not sure at first that this was an example of feminism failing Indigenous women, for I was not convinced that feminism had an obligation to support them on this issue. The destruction of female sacred sites is an erosion of culture and, as such, is clearly part of the dispossession of Indigenous people *qua* Indigenous people. In the beginning it looked to me less clearly like being part of the oppression of women *qua* women. On reflection, however, the destruction of Indigenous female sacred sites is of a piece with the disregard for what is women's – a disregard that runs across cultures but takes culturally specific forms: in Indigenous cultures, it takes the form of destruction of female sacred sites; in western cultures, it takes the form of replacement of women-only spaces with gender-inclusive spaces. Consequently it is part of the oppression of women *qua* women. Behrendt is therefore once again right to criticise white women. Notice, however, that conceiving of this as a feminist issue requires framing it in a particular way, namely as an instance of the erosion of *women's culture*. This is not to say that it is not an erosion of *Indigenous people's* culture; it is to say that, for feminism, it is of concern as an erosion of *Indigenous women's* culture. Behrendt may be dissatisfied with this. But just as, for feminism, this issue is of concern as an erosion of Indigenous women's culture, for an Indigenous rights movement it is of concern as an erosion of Indigenous people's culture. So it is not the case that, because *feminism* does not address this issue in a particular way, the issue will continue not to be addressed in that way. If it is not addressed in that way, this is the failure of the Indigenous rights movement. Interestingly, Behrendt makes no mention of Indigenous men's actual or proper role in this matter – she does not comment either on why Indigenous men seemingly did not inform anthropologists of female sacred sites or on whether they have supported women by resisting the destruction of these sites.

If feminists have an obligation of principle to support Indigenous Australian women in protecting female sacred sites, then it seems to me that they also have an obligation of principle to support, for example, Catholic women in their pursuit of appointing women to decision-making roles within the Catholic Church. For, just as the destruction of Indigenous female sacred sites is a specific instance of the general disregard for what belongs to women *qua* women, so the formal exclusion of Catholic women from decision-making roles is a specific instance of the general exclusion of women *qua* women from (or at least underrepresentation in) decision-making roles. Yet

Catholic women do not demand the support of feminists in general, and feminists in general do not feel shame for not providing this support. Why would this be? Feminists might argue that Catholicism is inherently patriarchal, so that to support the empowerment of women within the Catholic Church is, oxymoronically, to support the empowerment of women within an institution that disempowers women. But, insofar as all worldviews except the feminist – the Catholic, the liberal,[87] the Marxist, the white Australian, the Indigenous Australian – are inherently patriarchal,[88] to support the empowerment of women within the Catholic Church is not to support the empowerment of women within an institution that disempowers women any more than it is to support the empowerment of women within a liberal democratic state. Showing feminist willingness to support the empowerment of women within a liberal democratic state (say, through female suffrage) but refusal to support the empowerment of women within the Catholic Church is unjustified on feminist grounds. It is simply leftist bias.

Behrendt's description of the women's movement as having failed Indigenous Australian women is right.[89] It is also revealing. The idea that feminism has failed Indigenous women implies that feminism has a duty to these women, and the idea that feminism has a duty to these women implies that these women are rightfully, *qua* women, members of feminism's constituency. Behrendt's suggestion that white Australian and Indigenous Australian women do not, *qua* women, 'have a shared experience'[90] – meaning that they do not belong to the one female sex class – appears to be false, if not disingenuous. Why does Behrendt see a feminism that has not struggled for Indigenous Australian women as a feminism that has failed – if not because she herself believes that feminism ought to serve all members of the female sex class and that Indigenous Australian women are, *qua* women, no less members of this class than are white Australian women *qua* women?

Contemporary feminists reject the demand that women choose women, which they hear as white middle-class women's demand that Black women choose them.[91] These feminists are disdainful of white middle-class women, more so of them, it sometimes seems, than of the men responsible for the wrongs that these women failed to prevent. Behrendt writes that '[w]hite women were the wives, mothers and sisters of those who violently raped Aboriginal women and children and brutally murdered Aboriginal people'[92] – placing primary emphasis not on the men who raped Indigenous women and girls but on the women who were their wives, mothers, and sisters. Behrendt represents these women as standing in a relation of accomplice to these men and omits that they stood also in a relation of victim to them. My initial reaction to this contempt for white middle-class women is that it seems disproportionate, and my initial account of this disproportionateness is that it reflects a hatred of women *qua* women: white middle-class women are women whose race and class do not render them pitiable, thereby modulating their contemptibleness as women; they are women who consequently bear the full force of misogyny. On further thought, however, another interpretation occurs to me: this disproportionateness reflects the particular expectation that women have of women. Perhaps women feel particularly aggrieved by women who stand by as men rape them, because they regard women as their kin and expect solidarity from them. This accounts for the bitterness characteristic of women's anger with women. On this interpretation, Behrendt's anger with Anglo-Celtic Australian women who turned a blind eye as their husbands and sons raped Indigenous Australian women is proportionate and justified, as is the shame of Anglo-Celtic Australian women.

Feminists, contemporary and second-wave, understand white women's failure of Black women as the result of racism – whether the conscious and overt racism of white women who believed that Black women were, *qua* Black, lesser human beings or the race blindness of white women who mistook their set of issues for the set of all women's issues.[93] On this understanding, white women's disloyalty to Black women has meant loyalty to their race – to white people or to white women. But the white women who stood by as white men raped Aboriginal women (the wives, mothers, and sisters of whom Behrendt writes) were loyal to white men specifically. They chose the men of their race over the women of another race. To notice this is to perceive a similarity where previously we have perceived a difference – namely between the white women who stood by as white men raped Aboriginal women and the leftist white women who, in the name of anti-racism, stand by as Aboriginal men batter Aboriginal women.[94] Just as the former chose the men of their race over the women of another race, the latter choose the men of another race over the women of another race. The difference between the two positions is in the men to whom women are loyal. White women's failure of Black women is, I am suggesting, the product of both racial and sexual loyalties.

Precisely because Behrendt's anger is justified, precisely because women are right to expect solidarity from women and to feel aggrieved when they do not receive it, the contemporary feminist conclusion that women are not members of the one female sex class, that they are not a 'we' in the sense of a class in itself – and therefore cannot become a 'we' in the sense of a class for itself[95] – is wrong. Such a conclusion is the false inference that if we have not yet done something – chosen women, thereby becoming a 'we' in the sense of a class for itself and revealing ourselves as a 'we' in the sense of a class in itself – that something cannot be done. It is the redescription of choosing women as an impossibility, and of striving and failing to choose women as striving and failing to achieve what we mistakenly believed to be achievable. It is the redescription of our failure as theoretically and historically inevitable and as a *non-failure*.

When made by members of a group of women (say, white

Australian) that has repeatedly failed the members of another group of women (say, Indigenous Australian) and addressed to the members of that group, the demand that women choose women is the demand that the latter (the Indigenous) do for the former (the white Australian) what the former have not done for the latter. That this demand galls the latter and embarrasses the former is reasonable. But to succumb to our indignation and shame and reject this demand is to meet failure with failure. For if women do not choose women, we shall never be free. So, along with doing better ourselves, we who have failed other women must ask of them that they do better than we have done.

III

Reading this, one could be forgiven for forming the belief that the history of women's relations is a history of disloyalties. But such a belief would be false. If women have lied to one another, they have also, Rich reminds us, told the truth to one another.[96] Equally, if women have betrayed one another, they have also been faithful to one another.

Consider the marriage resistance movement in rural Guangdong.[97] From the early 1800s to the early 1900s, women in this region – at least, it is speculated, one in ten[98] – were members of a sisterhood that resisted marriage: they refused to marry (took vows never to marry) or, having ceremonially married, they refused to consummate their marriages and live with their husbands.[99] These women did not simply reject men, as the description 'marriage resisters' suggests; they committed to women. Indeed, many were 'sworn sisters', 'mutually tied by oath'.[100]

Think of the image of Amy and Sethe, 'two throw-away people, two lawless outlaws – a slave and a barefoot white-woman with unpinned hair – wrapping a ten-minute-old baby in the rags they wore',[101] in Toni Morrison's *Beloved*. Running from the plantation where she had been a slave, Sethe encounters 'whitegirl' Amy, who is kind to her, rubbing her feet, making shoes for her, and helping her to deliver her baby.[102]

Or think of the suffragettes. In order that women might have the right to vote in the United Kingdom, the suffragettes lobbied, paraded, picketed, smashed windows, orchestrated a bombing and arson campaign, and staged hunger strikes.[103]

Or think of what Mrs Peters and Mrs Hale do for Mrs Wright in Susan Glaspell's play *Trifles*.[104] Two men – Mr Hale and the sheriff, Mr Peters – are attending the scene of Mr Wright's death accompanied by their wives. While the men inspect the house, the two women realise that it was Mrs Wright who strangled her abusive husband. Together they then conceal the evidence from their husbands, deceiving them to protect Mrs Wright.

Or think of the Women's War of 1929. In 1925 the British introduced direct taxation – of adult men – in Nigeria in order to create the Native Treasury. The collection of taxes occurred without widespread trouble. But when in 1929 an assistant district officer set about recounting households and property, including women and their property, the women became suspicious that they were to be taxed. Suspicious and already aggrieved by the native administration, which had diminished their power, they organised. They informed other women in neighbouring provinces and, together, they descended on the District Office, where they succeeded in securing an assurance that they would not be taxed, along with the arrest and conviction of Okugo, the warrant chief (the Igbo man from each village chosen by the British to be a member of the Native Court), for spreading news likely to cause alarm and for physically assaulting women. Their victory inspired other women to attempt to get rid of their warrant chiefs and native administration. In total, thousands of women participated in the 'war'.[105]

Or think of the Ford sewing machinists strike of 1968. On 7 June 1968, angered by the reclassification of their work as 'semi-skilled', the female sewing machinists at Ford's River plant in Dagenham – 187 in total – went on strike. They did so despite the initial unwillingness of their union and their male colleagues to support them.[106]

Or think of the consciousness-raising groups in which women spoke truthfully of what the patriarchal code of honour for women requires them to lie about: their feelings of inadequacy, their discontentment, their unsatisfying sexual relations, the lies that they tell men, their abuse.[107]

Or think of the Black women (and of the white women, too) who supported Anita Hill when she accused Clarence Thomas, then a US Supreme Court nominee, of having sexually harassed her while he was her supervisor.[108]

Or think of the Gulabi Gang. When Sampat Pal Devi saw a man mercilessly beating his wife, she pleaded with him to stop. He abused her as well. So, the next day she and five other women returned and gave him a thrashing. When other women heard, they joined her. Thus was the Gulabi Gang born – a female vigilante group dedicated to protecting women of all castes from male violence.[109]

Or think of the women who attended Let Women Speak. In 2023, Kellie-Jay Keen hosted Let Women Speak events in the United States, Australia, and New Zealand. Held in public spaces, these events were an opportunity for gender-critical women to defy the systematic efforts to silence them, and to speak as women and for women. These women braved seething and threatening protests, the certainty of public censure, the possibility of assault, the not unreal prospect of job loss.[110]

Or think of the countless other instances of female solidarity that have not been recorded, or have been misrecorded because female solidarity is unintelligible.[111]

The marriage resisters are assumed to have been motivated by fear of 'the evils of the Chinese system of marriage'.[112] On this view, it is not that women chose women but that they fled an excessively brutal relation to a man.

The suffragettes were considered hysterical, fanatical, mad, suicidal, masochistic, seekers of cheap martyrdom.[113] Men who are willing to die for their people are regarded as heroes, women who are willing to die for *their* people are regarded as lunatics. When men revolt on behalf of men, their actions are understood as political, performed with the goal of obtaining justice for a particular group. When women revolt on behalf of women, their actions are understood as thoughtless ('reckless'), performed to no end at all, or as thoughtful, performed with the goal of obtaining individual glory.[114]

As Mrs Peters and Mrs Hale piece together what has happened and hide the evidence, Mr Peters and Mr Hale see them as 'worrying over trifles'.[115] They hear Mrs Hale's question, 'I wonder if she was goin' to quilt it or just knot it?',[116] as a question about Mrs Wright's quilt, not about Mr Wright's murder.

Judith Van Allen observes that the British refer to the Women's War of 1929 as 'the Aba Riots'. 'Riot' connotes spontaneity, disorder, irrationality, an eruption of emotion, not an orchestrated political action; 'Aba' (the name of a city in Nigeria) suggests that the riots were contained within one city, when in fact the political action was carried out across southeastern Nigeria; and the label 'Aba Riots' obscures the fact that it was women who, in pursuit of their shared interest, orchestrated and carried out the political action.[117] The British viewed the riots as an expression of Igbo dissatisfaction with the native administration in general rather than as an expression of Igbo women's dissatisfaction with the way in which the native administration disempowered them. They accounted for its being women who rioted by arguing that women were reacting to a rumour that they were to be taxed in a context of declining profits from the palm products trade, and that they were banking on the British showing less willingness to fire on women than on men. In other words, Igbo women were acting as an economic class, not as a sex class; they were acting on behalf of Igbo people, not of Igbo women; and they were acting at the behest of Igbo men, who assumed that the women would be safer. The British[118] could not conceive of the possibility of Igbo women organising and acting as women for women.

Gender-critical feminists are seen as 'peddling the far-right agenda'.[119] When women defend without qualification the interests of women, when they engage without qualification in feminism, they are seen as the pawns of other political actors, not as being such actors themselves.

IV

To ask women to choose women is to ask too much of them. Very well: we must ask too much of them. But we must also be honest with ourselves and with them about this. As Frye writes, '[p]erhaps, in our requirements and expectations on each other, we err only when we ask too little ... Perhaps what we have to ask is that all women assume responsibility for choosing things and constructing selves that are *not* possible.'[120] If we must ask too much of women, then we must see the failure to choose women as precisely that: a failure. Forgivable, I am sure, tolerable, I think, but nonetheless a failure. Forgivable but intolerable is the (contemporary feminist) lie that failure is success, that the desertion of women is an appropriately poststructural struggle for them, that the sacrifice of their interest is an appropriately intersectional pursuit of all oppressed people's interests – intolerable because it is a lie that the possibility of women's liberation will not survive. So long as we admit our failure, we preserve the standard by which it is failure – the standard of loyalty to women; and, so long as we preserve this standard, we look forward to the possibility of success. Once we begin to redescribe our failure as success – as acknowledgement of women's differences, recognition of their agency, respect for their choices, acceptance of their truth, inclusion – we can no longer strive to succeed, and so we can no longer succeed.

All feminists have lied about the benefits and costs of their project. I do not think that feminism will 'sav[e] the fragile blue and green biosphere named Earth',[121] that it will secure 'human liberation',[122] or that it will create 'a society without domination'.[123] I do think that feminism will cost men their sex right – their sexual access to women. From the feminist perspective, men never rightfully had sexual access to women, and so the loss of it is not a genuine cost. But from a patriarchal perspective, men do rightfully have sexual access to women, and so the loss of it is a genuine cost. To assert that it is not is simply to assert the feminist perspective. I do think that feminism will cost women much of what they have found their value in – the roles of wife and mother. I do think that it will cost trans women inclusion and authenticity. I do think that the pursuit of women's liberation will entail cruelty to men, who will find themselves made examples of in the establishment of new – feminist – norms. I do think that it will cost feminists work, success, recognition, relationships, pleasure.

In lying about the benefits and costs of our project, we fail women. We fail to demand of them unconditional commitment to the struggle for women's freedom, commitment not because this struggle will end all evils but in spite of the fact that it will not, not because it is costless but in spite of the fact that it is not, not because its outcome is certain but in spite of the fact that it is not. We fail to insist that women's freedom is a goal worthy of great sacrifice.

Conclusion

'Man' and 'woman' are the categories in relation to which *other* categories – 'state' and 'citizen', 'master' and 'slave', 'capitalist' and 'worker' – are political, and legitimate or illegitimate. It is through similitude to the rightfully hierarchical relationship between father and children and, implicitly, husband and wife that Filmer presents the hierarchical relationship between king and subject as legitimate,[1] just as it is through difference from the naturally hierarchical relationship between husband and wife that Locke presents the consensually hierarchical relationship between magistrate and subject as political and legitimate.[2] It is in a relation of dependence upon the family that Hegel presents the state:[3] as the husband 'has his actual substantive life in the state, in learning, and so forth, as well as in labour and struggle with the external world and with himself', whereas the wife 'has her substantive destiny in the family, and to be imbued with family piety is her ethical frame of mind', and as the relationship between husband and wife is rightfully hierarchical, the dependence of the state upon the family is the dependence of the citizenship of men *qua* men upon the denial of citizenship to women *qua* women, the dependence of the freedom of men *qua* men upon the denial of freedom to women *qua* women.[4] It is in a relation of dependence upon the subjection of the wife that Rousseau presents the citizenship of men *qua* men: a man becomes a citizen of his country when he is the head of a family, the master of a wife.[5] Finally, it is through difference from the implicitly rightfully hierarchical relationship between husband and wife that Engels presents the hierarchical relationship between capitalist and worker as illegitimate. Consider his claim that the worker 'is his employer's slave in still other respects. If his wife or daughter finds favour in the eyes of the master, a command, a hint suffices, and she must place herself at his disposal.'[6] The wrongful subjection of the worker to the employer consists partly in the subjection of the worker's wife or daughter to the employer. Unpacked, this means that, because a man *qua* man is the master of himself insofar as he is the master of his wife and daughter, an employer's mastery of a worker's wife and daughter is the employer's wrongful denial of the worker's mastery of his wife and daughter, in other words the employer's wrongful denial of the worker's self-mastery. It is in relation to the rightful subjection of a wife to her husband that the subjection of a worker to an employer is wrongful. If the condition of the worker's wife or daughter is wrongful, it is not because it is one of subjection to a man but because it is one of subjection to a man *who is not her husband or her father*. For the worker, freedom means, in part, respect for his mastery of his wife and daughter. For the wife or daughter, freedom means, in part, respect for her subjection to her husband or father.

When second-wave feminists claimed that 'man' and 'woman' are political and illegitimate categories, they did not add one more – man and woman – to a series of pairings – master and slave, white and Black, capitalist and worker. They added the rightfully hierarchical relationship between man and woman to a series of wrongfully hierarchical relationships between one class of men and another: master and slave, white and Black, capitalist and worker are all implicitly or paradigmatically male, and these relationships are *wrongfully* hierarchical precisely because they are between man and man ('Am I not a man and a brother?'), not man and woman. They treated 'woman' as a subclass of 'man' and 'natural subject' as a subclass of 'natural master'. They exploded the categories in relation to which other categories are political and legitimate or illegitimate; if a husband is not the rightful master of his wife, then an employer who has mastery over a worker's wife does not thereby deny the worker's rightful mastery of his wife.

This is why intersectional feminists are wrong to assert the need to struggle against 'capitalism, racism, and sexism'. Insofar as the accounts of capitalism and racism are accounts of oppression (oppression suffered by men) that conceptually depend upon the rightfulness of the subjection of women to men, the struggle against sexism entails the retheorisation of capitalism and racism as systems of oppression.

Like all revolutionaries, second-wave feminists spoke a language not yet invented,[7] a language in which 'woman' is a class of 'man', in which 'prostitution' is the sexual enslavement of women,[8] in which the sexual enslavement of women is the enslavement of human beings, a paradigm of slavery. Our mothers and grandmothers, these women 'dreamed dreams that no one knew – not themselves, in any coherent fashion – and saw visions no one could stand'.[9] As time passed, as the revolution did not arrive, these women, whom we had taken for prophets, began to appear as lunatics. We grew 'embarrassed'[10] with them, and because we were embarrassed we dismissed them (although not without first appropriating them). Men were not the enemy, women were not the friend, misogyny was not hatred of women,[11] rape was not sexual,[12] prostitution was not slavery. *If* we women were oppressed, we were so *qua* poor, or *qua* Black, or *qua* occupants of the feminine role, not *qua* women. Indeed, *qua* women, we did not exist. From within a disenchanted present, this appears to be progression. From the vantage point of the second wave, it is the exchange of dreams – the dream of freedom – for false respect from men.

Notes

Notes to Introduction

1. Ti-Grace Atkinson, *Amazon Odyssey* (New York: Links Books, 1974), 41.
2. Denise Riley, *'Am I That Name?' Feminism and the Category of 'Women' in History* (Minneapolis: University of Minnesota Press, 1988), 1.
3. Sheldon S. Wolin, *Politics and Vision: Continuity and Innovation in Western Political Thought* (Princeton, NJ: Princeton University Press, 2016), 257–263.
4. 'In the first place we must distinguish the state from society. To identify the social with the political is to be guilty of the grossest of all confusions, which completely bars any understanding of either society or the state'. R. M. MacIver, *The Modern State* (London: Oxford University Press, 1926), 4–5.
5. Martin Buber, 'Society and the State', in his *Pointing the Way: Collected Essays*, trans. Maurice Friedman (New York: Harper & Brothers, 1957), 161.
6. Bertrand Russell, *Power: A New Social Analysis* (London: Routledge, 2004 [1938]) 4 (emphasis added).
7. Buber, 'Society and the State', 161.
8. Buber (ibid.) writes: 'The primary element must not be superseded by the secondary element – association by subordination, fellowship by domination or, schematically speaking, the horizontal structure by the vertical.'

9 Walter Benjamin, 'Theses on the Philosophy of History', in his *Illuminations: Essays and Reflections*, trans. Harry Zohn, ed. Hannah Arendt (Boston, MA: Mariner Books, 2019 [1968]), 255.
10 Ibid.
11 Holly Lawford-Smith, *Gender-Critical Feminism* (Oxford: Oxford University Press, 2022), 22 (emphasis added).
12 Ibid., 21.

Notes to Chapter 1

1 Simone de Beauvoir, *The Second Sex*, trans. Constance Borde and Sheila Malovany-Chevallier (London: Vintage Books, 2010 [1949]), 293.
2 Catharine A. MacKinnon, *Toward a Feminist Theory of the State* (Cambridge, MA: Harvard University Press, 1989), 109.
3 Mary Wollstonecraft, *A Vindication of the Rights of Woman*, rev. edn (London: Penguin, 2004 [1792]), 11.
4 'As always in history, a formula that had outlived itself served to cover a political content which was the direct opposite of that which the formula had served in its day.' Leon Trotsky, 'Introduction', in Harold R. Isaacs, *The Tragedy of the Chinese Revolution* (Chicago, IL: Haymarket Books, 2009 [1938]), xix.
5 Christine Delphy identifies the 'first and common postulate underlying the whole of the new feminism' as the claim that 'women's oppression is not an individual phenomenon and not a natural phenomenon. It is political.' For Delphy, the antithesis of 'natural' is not 'social'; it is 'political'. See Christine Delphy, 'Patriarchy, Feminism, and Their Intellectuals', in her *Close to Home: A Materialist Analysis of Women's Oppression* (Amherst: University of Massachusetts Press, 1984), 140.
6 Kate Millett, *Sexual Politics* (Urbana: University of Illinois Press, 2000), 24.
7 New York Radical Feminists, 'Politics of the Ego: A Manifesto for NY Radical Feminists', in Anne Koedt, Ellen Levine, and Anita Rapone, eds, *Radical Feminism* (New York: Quadrangle Books, 1973), 379.
8 Shulamith Firestone, *The Dialectic of Sex: The Case for Feminist Revolution* (New York: William Morrow, 1970), 1.
9 Adrienne Rich, 'Translations', in her *Diving into the Wreck: Poems, 1971–1972* (New York: W. W. Norton, 1973), 41.
10 Atkinson, *Amazon Odyssey*, 25.
11 Monique Wittig, 'One Is Not Born a Woman', in Henry Abelove, Michèle Aina Barale, and David M. Halperin, eds, *The Lesbian and Gay Studies Reader* (New York: Routledge, 1993), 105.

12 Andrea Dworkin, 'Woman-Hating Right and Left', in Dorchen Leidholdt and Janice G. Raymond, eds, *The Sexual Liberals and the Attack on Feminism* (New York: Teachers College Press, 1990), 30.
13 MacKinnon, *Toward a Feminist Theory of the State*, 161.
14 Millett, *Sexual Politics*, 23.
15 Marx expresses the paradigmatically non-political nature of sexual relations: 'The direct, natural, and necessary relation of person to person is the relation of man to woman.' Karl Marx, *Economic and Philosophic Manuscripts of 1844* (Moscow: Progress Publishers, 1977), 95.
16 Millett, *Sexual Politics*, 25 (emphasis added).
17 Ibid., 22.
18 Ibid., 25.
19 Henry Miller, *Sexus: The Rosy Crucifixion* (New York: Grove Press, 1965), 482–483.
20 Norman Mailer, *The Naked and the Dead* (New York: Henry Holt, 1981), 415–416.
21 Henry Miller, *Black Spring* (New York: Grove Press, 1963), 228.
22 MacKinnon, *Toward a Feminist Theory of the State*, 111.
23 Beauvoir, *The Second Sex*, 397.
24 Ibid., 397–398.
25 Atkinson, *Amazon Odyssey*, 85–86.
26 Ibid.
27 Adrienne Rich, 'Compulsory Heterosexuality and Lesbian Existence', *Signs: Journal of Women in Culture and Society* 5.4 (1980), 645.
28 Andrea Dworkin, *Intercourse* (New York: Basic Books, 2007 [1987]), 79–80.
29 See e.g. Juliet Mitchell, *Woman's Estate* (Harmondsworth: Penguin, 1971); Heidi I. Hartmann, 'The Unhappy Marriage of Marxism and Feminism: Towards a More Progressive Union', *Capital and Class* 3.2 (1979): 1–33; Christine Delphy, 'The Main Enemy', *Feminist Issues* 1.1 (1980): 25 (originally published in a special double issue of the journal *Partisans*, entitled *Libération des Femmes: Année Zéro*, 1970); and Iris Young, 'Beyond the Unhappy Marriage: A Critique of the Dual Systems Theory', in Lydia Sargent, ed., *Women and Revolution: A Discussion of the Unhappy Marriage of Marxism and Feminism* (London: Pluto Press, 1981), 43–69.
30 'We must develop a class analysis of women', writes Delphy ('The Main Enemy', 25).
31 In Engels's words, 'capitalists cannot exist without wage-workers'.

Friedrich Engels, *Socialism: Utopian and Scientific*, trans. Edward Aveling (Chicago, IL: Charles H. Kerr, 1914), 50.
32 Karl Marx and Friedrich Engels, *The Communist Manifesto* (Harmondsworth: Penguin Books, 1967), 79.
33 Carole Pateman, *The Sexual Contract* (Stanford, CA: Stanford University Press, 1988), 6. Similarly, Delphy writes: 'the situation of being dominated was for me the major characteristic of women as a social group, just as the situation of being dominant was the major characteristic of men as a social group'. Christine Delphy, 'Preface: Critique of Naturalizing Reason', *South Atlantic Quarterly* 114.4 (2015), 852.
34 Engels, *Socialism: Utopian and Scientific*, 91–92.
35 Firestone, *The Dialectic of Sex*, 5.
36 Ibid., 8–11.
37 Engels, *Socialism: Utopian and Scientific*, 76–83.
38 Firestone, *The Dialectic of Sex*, 8.
39 Ibid.
40 Ibid.
41 Ibid., 205 (emphasis added).
42 MacKinnon, *Toward a Feminist Theory of the State*, 3–4.
43 Nancy Fraser and Linda Nicholson, 'Social Criticism without Philosophy: An Encounter between Feminism and Postmodernism', *Social Text* 21 (1989), 92.
44 MacKinnon, *Toward a Feminist Theory of the State*, 3.
45 Susan Brownmiller, *Against Our Will: Men, Women, and Rape* (New York: Bantam Books, 1976), 5.
46 Ibid., 4.
47 Ibid.
48 Ibid.
49 Randy Thornhill and Craig T. Palmer, *A Natural History of Rape: Biological Bases of Sexual Coercion* (Cambridge, MA: MIT Press, 2000).
50 Brownmiller, *Against Our Will*, 5.
51 Max Weber, 'The Nature of Social Action', in *Max Weber: Selections in Translation*, ed. W. G. Runciman (Cambridge: Cambridge University Press, 1978), 7.
52 Or perhaps the first rape, which is motivated by a 'psychologic urge', is purely reactive, not an action at all.
53 Carl Schmitt, *The Concept of the Political*, trans. George Schwab (Chicago, IL: University of Chicago Press, 2007), 32–37. For the Brownmiller quotations, see Against Our Will, 5.

54 Dworkin, *Intercourse*.
55 MacKinnon, *Toward a Feminist Theory of the State*, 117.
56 Sheila Rowbotham, *Woman's Consciousness, Man's World* (Harmondsworth: Penguin Books, 1973), 34.
57 Wittig, 'One Is Not Born a Woman', 107.
58 Kathleen Stock, *Material Girls: Why Reality Matters for Feminism* (London: Fleet, 2021), 46.
59 Ibid., 47.
60 Ibid., 50–53.
61 Ibid., 71.
62 Pateman, *The Sexual Contract*, 41.
63 Stock, *Material Girls*, 102–103.
64 MacKinnon, *Toward a Feminist Theory of the State*, 136.
65 'Women and men are ... made into the *sexes as we know them.*' MacKinnon, *Toward a Feminist Theory of the State*, 113 (emphasis added).
66 She identifies Wittig and MacKinnon as theorists of 'the dominance model'. Stock, *Material Girls*, 69.
67 Ibid.
68 Atkinson, *Amazon Odyssey*, 135.
69 Millett, *Sexual Politics*, 29.
70 Catharine A. MacKinnon, *Feminism Unmodified: Discourses on Life and Law* (Cambridge, MA: Harvard University Press, 1987), 51. Notice that MacKinnon suggests that in the feminist future 'sex' will not have the meaning that it has under male dominance – not that it will have no meaning.
71 Christine Delphy, 'Rethinking Sex and Gender', *Women's Studies International Forum* 16.1 (1993): 1–9, here 6–7.
72 Wittig, 'One Is Not Born a Woman', 103.
73 Ibid., 104.
74 Monique Wittig, 'The Category of Sex', *Feminist Issues* 2 (1982), 64.
75 Wolin, *Politics and Vision*, 18.
76 Ibid., 20.
77 Wittig, 'One Is Not Born a Woman', 104.
78 Ibid.
79 Wittig, quoting Dworkin, writes: 'Thus, as long as we will be "unable to abandon by will or impulse a lifelong and centuries-old commitment to childbearing as *the* female creative act", gaining control of the production of children will mean much more than the mere control of the material means of this production: women will have to abstract

themselves from the definition "woman" which is imposed upon them.' Andrea Dworkin, 'Biological Superiority: The World's Most Dangerous and Deadly Idea', in *Letters from a War Zone: Writings 1976–1989* (New York: E. P. Dutton, 1989), 115. The emphasis on 'the' occurs in both Dworkin and Wittig.

80 Andrea Dworkin, *Woman Hating* (New York: Plume, 1974), 183. See generally pp. 175–184.
81 Wittig, 'The Category of Sex', 64.
82 '[F]anciful statements are not of the same status as propositions that seek to prove or disprove. Fancy neither proves nor disproves; it seeks, instead, to illuminate, to help us become wiser about political things.' Wolin, *Politics and Vision*, 18.
83 Stock, *Material Girls*, 11–43.
84 'The theoretical and social transformation required if women and men are to be full members of a free, properly democratic (or properly "civilized") society is as far-reaching as can be imagined . . . To create a properly democratic society, which includes women as full citizens, it is necessary to deconstruct and reassemble our understanding of the body politic. This task extends from the dismantling of the patriarchal separation of private and public, to a transformation of our individuality and sexual identities as feminine and masculine beings.' Carole Pateman, *The Disorder of Women: Democracy, Feminism, and Political Theory* (Cambridge: Polity, 1989), 52–53.

Notes to Chapter 2

1 '"Sex" is a word that refers to the biological differences between male and female: the visible difference in genitalia, the related difference in procreative function. "Gender" however is a matter of culture: it refers to the social classification into "masculine" and "feminine".' Ann Oakley, *Sex, Gender, and Society* (London: Maurice Temple Smith, 1972), 16.
2 Judith Butler, *Gender Trouble: Feminism and the Subversion of Identity* (New York: Routledge, 2006 [1990]), 152.
3 'Every female human being is not necessarily a woman; to be considered so she must share in that mysterious and threatened reality known as femininity.' Beauvoir, *The Second Sex*, 3.
4 See Moira Gatens, *Imaginary Bodies: Ethics, Power, and Corporeality* (London: Routledge, 1996), 9–10, 14.
5 Marilyn Frye, *The Politics of Reality: Essays in Feminist Theory* (Berkeley, CA: Crossing Press, 1983), 131.
6 Ibid.

7 Michel Foucault, *The History of Sexuality*, trans. Robert Hurley, vol. 1 (New York: Pantheon Books, 1978), 135.
8 Ibid., 136.
9 Ibid.
10 Michel Foucault, *Power/Knowledge: Selected Interviews and Other Writings 1972–1977*, ed. Colin Gordon (New York: Pantheon Books, 1980), 89.
11 Ibid., 88.
12 Michel Foucault, 'The Subject and Power', *Critical Inquiry* 8.4 (1982): 777–795, here 781.
13 Peter Dews argues that Foucault's equation of production as subject–subjectification with subjection undercuts his theory of power *qua* theory of power in the political sense (i.e. as having 'critical political import'). Power in the political sense must crush, subdue, or repress that from which it is desirable for all to be liberated. A power that *produces* the subject cannot crush, subdue, or repress. Foucault's is thus a depoliticised theory of power, an account 'of the constitutive operation of *social* systems' rather than one of power. It is a theory of the horizontal, not of the vertical. See Peter Dews, 'Power and Subjectivity in Foucault', *New Left Review* 144 (1984), 88 (emphasis added).
14 Hekman writes of the 'subjugating categories of sex, gender, and sexuality' and of the 'subjection constituted by sexual categories': see Susan J. Hekman, 'Editor's Introduction', in Susan J. Hekman, ed., *Feminist Interpretations of Michel Foucault* (University Park: Pennsylvania State University Press, 1996), 6.
15 Susan Bordo, *Unbearable Weight: Feminism, Western Culture, and the Body* (Berkeley: University of California Press, 2003 [1993]), 28.
16 Atkinson, *Amazon Odyssey*, 47.
17 Ibid.
18 Delphy, 'The Main Enemy', 23–40.
19 Ibid., 39.
20 Ibid.
21 Bordo, *Unbearable Weight*, 28.
22 A multicontributor collection of essays titled *Feminism and Foucault* is introduced by its editors with the following questions: 'Why this volume? Is this yet another attempt to authorize feminism by marrying it into respectability? Are we trying to arrange a final divorce from Marxism – or Freudianism or Lacanian analysis – for a happier union with Foucauldian genealogy?' Irene Diamond and Lee Quinby, 'Introduction', in Irene Diamond and Lee Quinby, eds, *Feminism*

and Foucault: Reflections on Resistance (Boston, MA: Northeastern University Press, 1988), ix.
23 'Thinking that our man is the exception, and, therefore, we are the exception among women.' Irene Peslikis, 'Resistances to Consciousness', in Robin Morgan, ed., *Sisterhood Is Powerful: An Anthology of Writings from the Women's Liberation Movement* (New York: Vintage Books, 1970), 337.
24 'Respectful Relationships', State Government of Victoria, 8 February 2024, https://www.vic.gov.au/respectful-relationships.
25 Harold Dwight Lasswell, *Politics: Who Gets What, When, How* (New York: Peter Smith, 1950).
26 'Marxists do not refer to capitalists as "the capitalist role".' Carol Anne Douglas, *Love and Politics: Radical Feminist and Lesbian Theories* (San Francisco, CA: ism press, 1990), 56.
27 Gatens, *Imaginary Bodies*, 4.
28 'This neutralizing process is not novel; it can be traced to nineteenth-century liberal environmentalism where "re-education" is the catchcry of radical social transformation. Much of contemporary radical politics is, perhaps unwittingly, enmeshed in this liberal tradition.' Ibid.
29 Thus Komter writes of 'the *old* idea of "oppression"': Aafke Komter, 'Gender, Power, and Feminist Theory', in Kathy Davis, Monique Leijenaar, and Jantine Oldersma, eds, *The Gender of Power* (London: Sage, 1991), 46 (emphasis added).
30 Nancy Fraser, 'Beyond the Master/Subject Model: Reflections on Carole Pateman's *Sexual Contract*', *Social Text* 37 (1993), 180.
31 Susan Bordo, 'Feminism, Foucault, and the Politics of the Body', in Janet Price and Margrit Shildrick, eds, *Feminist Theory and the Body: A Reader* (Edinburgh: Edinburgh University Press, 1999), 190.
32 Butler, *Gender Trouble*, xxx.
33 Ibid., xxvii.
34 Nicola Gavey, *Just Sex: The Cultural Scaffolding of Rape*, 2nd edn (London: Routledge, 2019), 130.
35 Ibid., 135.
36 Ibid., 130.
37 Ibid., 132.
38 Ibid., 133.
39 Ibid., 134.
40 Ibid., 135.
41 As Morgan puts it, 'the pressure is there, and it need not be a knife blade against the throat; it's in his body language, his threat of sulking,

his clenched or trembling hands, his self-deprecating humor or angry put-down or silent self-pity at being rejected'. Robin Morgan, 'Theory and Practice: Pornography and Rape', in Laura Lederer, ed., *Take Back the Night: Women on Pornography* (New York: William Morrow, 1980), 136.

42 Foucault, *Power/Knowledge*, 98.
43 Foucault, *The History of Sexuality*, 99. I am therefore not convinced that Bordo is right when she claims: 'For Foucault, modern (as opposed to sovereign) power is non-authoritarian, non-conspiratorial, and indeed non-orchestrated; *yet it nonetheless produces and normalizes bodies to serve prevailing relations of dominance and subordination.*' She continues: 'Dominance here, however, is sustained not by decree or design "from above" (as sovereign power is exercised) but through multiple "processes, of different origin and scattered location", regulating the most intimate and minute elements of the construction of space, time, desire, embodiment.' Bordo, *Unbearable Weight*, 26–27 (emphasis added). I am not sure that Foucault could accept Bordo's claim that modern power aims to 'serve prevailing relations of dominance and subordination'. The term 'serve' suggests that relations of dominance are the origin of power, which they issue for their continuation. On one reading, Foucault rejects this. He says, for example: 'the question we must address, then, is not ... Neither is [it] the question: *What over-all domination was served* by the concern, evidenced since the eighteenth century, to produce true discourses on sex?' On his view, power serves only power and produces individuals only in order to circulate through them. Another reading, however, complicates this one. Having said that the question is not 'what overall domination was served' by this particular concern, he continues: 'In a specific type of discourse on sex, in a specific form of extortion of truth, appearing historically and in specific places (around the child's body, apropos of women's sex, in connection with practices restricting births, and so on), *what were the most immediate, the most local power relations at work? How did they make possible these kinds of discourses, and conversely, how were these discourses used to support power relations?*' Foucault, *The History of Sexuality*, 97 (emphasis added). What is more, he writes elsewhere that '[t]he systems of domination and the circuits of exploitation certainly interact, intersect and support each other, but they do not coincide', and that '[i]t is certain that the mechanisms of subjection cannot be studied outside their relation to the mechanisms of exploitation and domination'. Foucault, *Power/Knowledge*, 72; Foucault, 'The Subject and Power', 782.

44 'The individual, that is, is not the vis-à-vis of power; it is, I believe, one of its prime effects. The individual is an effect of power, and at the same time, or precisely to the extent to which it is that effect, it is the element of its articulation. The individual which power has constituted is at the same time its vehicle.' Foucault, *Power/Knowledge*, 98.
45 Pateman, *The Sexual Contract*, 207.
46 See Sigmund Freud, 'Female Sexuality', in *The Standard Edition of the Complete Psychological Works of Sigmund Freud*, vol. 21, trans. James Strachey, 225–243 (London: Hogarth Press, 1961); Sigmund Freud, 'Three Essays on Sexuality', in *The Standard Edition of the Complete Psychological Works of Sigmund Freud*, vol. 7, trans. James Strachey, 123–243 (London: Hogarth Press, 1953), esp. pp. 220–221; and Helene Deutsche, *The Psychology of Women: A Psychoanalytic Interpretation*, vol. 1 (New York: Grune & Stratton, 1944), 229–230.
47 Monique Plaza, 'Our Damages and Their Compensation: Rape: The Will Not to Know of Michel Foucault', *Feminist Issues* 1.3 (1981): 30 (originally published in *Questions féministes* 3 of 1978).
48 See Butler, *Gender Trouble*, viii, xxiv. Butler (ibid., xxiii) also writes of a 'gendered life . . . foreclosed by certain habitual and violent presumptions' and of a 'naturalised knowledge of gender' that 'operates as a preemptive and violent circumscription of reality'.
49 John Locke, 'The Second Treatise: An Essay Concerning the True Original, Extent, and End of Civil Government', in *Two Treatises of Government and A Letter Concerning Human Understanding*, ed. Ian Shapiro (New Haven, CT: Yale University Press, 2003), 101.
50 '[N]either Foucault nor any other poststructuralist thinker discovered or invented the idea . . . that the "definition and shaping" of the body is "the focal point for struggles over the shape of power". *That* was discovered by feminism, and long before it entered into its marriage with poststructural thought.' Bordo, *Unbearable Weight*, 17.
51 Wollstonecraft, *A Vindication of the Rights of Woman*, 55–59. Cited in Bordo, *Unbearable Weight*, 18.
52 Fraser, 'Beyond the Master/Subject Model', 180.
53 Ibid., 178 (emphasis added).
54 Ibid., 174.
55 Ibid., 179.
56 Pateman, *The Disorder of Women*, 72.
57 This statement, made by Sir Matthew Hale CJ in his *History of the Pleas of the Crown*, published in 1736 (vol. 1, p. 629), is still quoted in court cases.

Notes to pp. 43–46   193

58 Pateman, *The Sexual Contract*, 2; Pateman takes this term from Rich, 'Compulsory Heterosexuality and Lesbian Existence', 645. For a discussion of the relationship between the marriage contract and male sex right, see Pateman, *The Sexual Contract*, 154–188.
59 MacKinnon, *Feminism Unmodified*.
60 'All feminism is also radically feminist in that woman's identity as a sexual class underlies this claim.' Zillah H. Eisenstein, *The Radical Future of Liberal Feminism* (New York: Longman, 1981), 4.
61 MacKinnon, *Toward a Feminist Theory of the State*, 85.
62 Ibid., 86.
63 Margaret Benston, 'The Political Economy of Women's Liberation', *Monthly Review* 21.4 (1969): 13–27; Mariarosa Dalla Costa and Selma James, *The Power of Women and the Subversion of the Community* (Bristol: Falling Wall, 1975); Martha E. Gimenez, 'Marxism and Feminism', *Frontiers: A Journal of Women Studies* 1.1 (1975): 61–80; Robin Morgan, 'Goodbye to All That', in her *Going Too Far: The Personal Chronicle of a Feminist* (New York: Vintage Books, 1978), 121–130; Zillah R. Eisenstein, 'Developing a Theory of Capitalist Patriarchy and Socialist Feminism', in Zillah R. Eisenstein, ed., *Capitalist Patriarchy and the Case for Socialist Feminism* (New York: Monthly Review Press, 1979), 5–40; Hartmann, 'The Unhappy Marriage of Marxism and Feminism'; Delphy, 'The Main Enemy'; Young, 'Beyond the Unhappy Marriage'; and MacKinnon, *Toward a Feminist Theory of the State*.
64 Some, perhaps many, feminist theorists understood that poststructuralism threatened feminism itself. Here is an example: 'Foucault's ontology includes only bodies and pleasures, and he is notorious for not including gender as a category of analysis. If gender is simply a social construct, the need and even the possibility of a feminist politics becomes immediately problematic.' Linda Alcoff, 'Cultural Feminism versus Post-Structuralism: The Identity Crisis in Feminist Theory', *Signs: Journal of Women in Culture and Society* 13.3 (1988), 420.
65 Georg Wilhelm Friedrich Hegel, 'Preface to *The Philosophy of Right*', in his *The Philosophy of Right: The Philosophy of History* (Chicago, IL: William Benton, 1952), 7.

Notes to Chapter 3
1 Lesley Stern, 'Introduction to Plaza', *m/f* 4 (1980), 23. See also Biddy Martin, 'Feminism, Criticism, and Foucault', *New German Critique* 27 (1982), 16–17.
2 Astonishingly, Butler writes: 'Within feminism, it seems as if there is

some political necessity to speak as and for *women*, and I would not contest that necessity. Surely, that is the way in which representational politics operates, and in this country, lobbying efforts are virtually impossible without recourse to identity politics. So we agree that demonstrations and legislative efforts and radical movements need to make claims in the name of women.' Here Butler admits that feminists must in their *politics* do precisely what she denounces. Her project, it seems, is to convince feminists to proceed differently in theory while they continue the same way in practice. Judith Butler, 'Contingent Foundations: Feminism and the Question of "Postmodernism"', in Seyla Benhabib, Judith Butler, Drucilla Cornell, and Nancy Fraser, *Feminist Contentions: A Philosophical Exchange* (New York: Routledge, 1995), 49.

3 Karl Marx, 'Theses on Feuerbach', in Karl Marx and Friedrich Engels, *The German Ideology*, ed. C. J. Arthur (New York: International Publishers, 1972), 121–123.

4 Martin suggests as much: 'it is imperative that we not dismiss the importance of the concepts patriarchy and oppression as they have been developed by radical feminist thinkers. The radical feminist articulation of the universality and totality of the oppression of women constitutes the condition of possibility for feminist deconstructive work.' Martin, 'Feminism, Criticism, and Foucault', 16.

5 Stern, 'Introduction to Plaza', 23.

6 Fraser and Nicholson, 'Social Criticism without Philosophy', 101.

7 Foucault speaks of biopower as 'micro-powers'. See Michel Foucault, *Discipline and Punish: The Birth of the Prison*, trans. Alan Sheridan (New York: Pantheon Books, 1977), 27.

8 'The urgency of feminism to establish a universal status for patriarchy in order to strengthen the appearance of feminism's own claims to be representative has occasionally motivated the shortcut to a categorial or fictive universality of the structure of domination.' Butler, *Gender Trouble*, 5.

9 For a critique of the postmodern concern with the 'local', see Teresa L. Ebert, 'The "Difference" of Postmodern Feminism', *College English* 53.8 (1991): 886–904.

10 As Denise Riley writes, 'Feminism of late has emphasised that indeed "women" are far from being racially or culturally homogeneous, and it may be thought that this corrective provides the proper answer to the hesitations I've advanced here about "women". But this is not the same preoccupation. 'Indeed there is a world of helpful difference between making claims in the name of an annoyingly generalised "women" and

doing so in the name of, say, "elderly Cantonese women living in Soho" ... However the specifications of difference are elaborated, they still come to rest on "women" and it is the isolation of this last which is in question.' (But, it is not obvious how 'there is a world of helpful difference between making claims in the name of an annoyingly generalised "women", and doing so in the name of, say, "elderly Cantonese women living in Soho".') Riley, *'Am I That Name?'*, 16–17.

11 Bordo similarly suggests that poststructural feminist scholarship stands on the shoulders of the earlier feminist scholarship that it repudiates: 'Could we now speak of the differences that inflect *gender* if gender had not first been shown to make a difference?' Susan Bordo, 'Feminism, Postmodernism, and Gender-Skepticism', in Linda J. Nicholson, ed., *Feminism/Postmodernism* (New York: Routledge, 1990), 141.

12 Butler, *Gender Trouble*, 5.

13 Ibid.

14 Alice Walker, 'Coming Apart', in her *The Complete Stories* (London: Women's Press, 1994), 171.

15 'The category of sex ... does not concern being but relationships (for women and men are the result of relationships).' Wittig, 'The Category of Sex', 66.

16 Sheldon S. Wolin, 'Political Theory as a Vocation', *American Political Science Review* 63.4 (1969), 1078.

17 Fraser and Nicholson, 'Social Criticism without Philosophy', 92 (emphasis added).

18 'Feminist critique ought to explore the totalizing claims of a masculinist signifying economy, but also remain self-critical with respect to the totalising gestures of feminism.' Butler, *Gender Trouble*, 18.

19 Fraser and Nicholson, 'Social Criticism without Philosophy', 92 (emphasis added).

20 Ibid.

21 Ibid.

22 Ibid.

23 Ibid., 101–102.

24 'What would distinguish this type of fallibilistic pragmatics of feminist theory from the usual self-understanding of empirical and value-free social science? Can feminist theory be postmodernist and still retain an interest in emancipation?' – asks Seyla Benhabib, 'Feminism and Postmodernism: An Uneasy Alliance' in *Feminist Contentions*, 24.

25 See Wolin, *Politics and Vision*, 257–263.

26 Ibid., 17–20.

27 Ibid., 18.
28 MacKinnon, *Toward a Feminist Theory of the State*, xi.
29 Ibid., 110.
30 Fraser and Nicholson, 'Social Criticism without Philosophy', 93 (emphasis added). Fraser and Nicholson are quoting Gayle Rubin, 'The Traffic in Women: Notes on the "Political Economy" of Sex', in Rayna R. Reiter, ed., *Toward an Anthropology of Women* (New York: Monthly Review Press, 1975), 160.
31 MacKinnon, *Toward a Feminist Theory of the State*, 101.
32 Sheldon S. Wolin, 'On Reading Marx Politically', in his *Fugitive Democracy and Other Essays* (Princeton, NJ: Princeton University Press, 2016), 180.
33 Ibid.
34 Ibid., 177.
35 Bordo, 'Feminism, Postmodernism, and Gender-Scepticism', 136.
36 Ibid., 153.
37 Marx, 'Theses on Feuerbach', 121 (emphasis added).
38 Bernick is therefore right to reject Bordo's distinction between theory and practice. See Susan E. Bernick, 'Philosophy and Feminism: The Case of Susan Bordo', *Hypatia* 7.3 (1992), 194.
39 Judith Butler, *Bodies That Matter: On the Discursive Limits of 'Sex'* (London: Routledge Classics, 2011), xi.
40 Butler, *Gender Trouble*, 151. Similarly, Foucault writes: 'It is through sex – in fact, an imaginary point determined by the deployment of sexuality – that each individual has to pass in order to have access to his own intelligibility (seeing that it is both the hidden aspect and the generative principle of meaning), to the whole of his body (since it is a real and threatened part of it, while symbolically constituting the whole), to his identity (since it joins the force of a drive to the singularity of a history).' *The History of Sexuality*, 155–156.
41 'The category of "sex" is, from the start, normative; it is what Foucault has called a "regulatory ideal". In this sense, then, "sex" not only functions as a norm, but is part of a regulatory practice that produces the bodies it governs, that is, whose regulatory force is made clear as a kind of productive power, the power to produce – demarcate, circulate, differentiate – the bodies it controls. Thus, "sex" is a regulatory ideal whose materialization is compelled, and this materialization takes place (or fails to take place) through certain highly regulated practices.' Butler, *Bodies That Matter*, xi–xii.
42 Bernard M. Dickens, 'Management of Intersex Newborns: Legal and

Ethical Developments', *International Journal of Gynaecology and Obstetrics* 143.2 (2018): 255–259; Alice Domurat Dreger, '"Ambiguous Sex" or Ambivalent Medicine? Ethical Issues in the Treatment of Intersexuality', *Hastings Centre Report* 28.3 (1998): 24–35.
43 Butler, *Bodies That Matter*, x.
44 Ibid.
45 Butler, *Gender Trouble*, 23.
46 Foucault, *The History of Sexuality*, 155 (emphasis added).
47 Butler, *Gender Trouble*, 23.
48 The distinction between class in itself and class for itself comes from Marx: 'Economic conditions had first transformed the mass of the people of the country into workers. The combination of capital has created for this mass a common situation, common interests. This mass is thus already a class as against capital, but not yet for itself. In the struggle, of which we have noted only a few phases, this mass becomes united, and constitutes itself as a class for itself. The interests it defends become class interests. But the struggle of class against class is a political struggle.' A class in itself is a group of people who share a relationship to the means of production, while a class for itself is a group of people with class consciousness and solidarity, a group of people united in pursuit of their common interest. Karl Marx, *The Poverty of Philosophy* (New York: International Publishers, 1963), 173.
49 Butler, *Gender Trouble*, xxi. *Gender Trouble* is a 'dogged effort to "denaturalize" gender' and *Bodies That Matter* an attempt to show that '"sex" is an ideal construct which is forcibly materialized through time'. Butler, *Gender Trouble*, xx and *Bodies That Matter*, xii.
50 Butler, *Gender Trouble*, viii.
51 Ibid., 203 (emphasis added).
52 Atkinson, *Amazon Odyssey*, 41.
53 Butler, *Gender Trouble*, viii.
54 Marx and Engels, *The Communist Manifesto*, 79.
55 Richard Rorty, 'Feminism, Ideology, and Deconstruction: A Pragmatist View', *Hypatia* 8.2 (1993), 96.

Notes to Chapter 4
1 Butler, *Gender Trouble*, xxv.
2 Ibid., viii.
3 Frye, *The Politics of Reality*, 165 (emphasis added).
4 Wendy Brown, 'Wounded Attachments', *Political Theory* 21.3 (1993), 399, quoting from an early draft of a public document from Santa Cruz,

California titled 'An Ordinance of the City of Santa Cruz: Adding Chapter 9.83 to the Santa Cruz Municipal Code Pertaining to the Prohibition of Discrimination' (Mun. Code §§ 9.83.01 and 9.83.08(6)).
5 Ibid., 395.
6 Ibid., 398.
7 Ibid., 395.
8 Ibid., 399.
9 Ibid., 395.
10 Jordi Lippe-McGraw, 'Meet Your Cover Model: Leyna Bloom', *Sports Illustrated Swimsuit*, 19 July 2021, https://swimsuit.si.com/swimnews/meet-your-cover-model-2021-leyna-bloom.
11 'Gender-Neutral Sex Toys Are Here Just in Time for Trans Day of Visibility', *Queer Forty*, 18 March 2021, https://queerforty.com/gender-neutral-sex-toys-are-here-just-in-time-for-trans-day-of-visibility.
12 Pateman, *The Sexual Contract*.
13 Robin Morgan, 'Light Bulbs, Radishes, and the Politics of the 21st Century', in Diane Bell and Renate Klein, eds, *Radically Speaking: Feminism Reclaimed* (North Melbourne: Spinifex Press, 1996), 5.
14 Gayle Greene, 'Feminist Fiction and the Uses of Memory', *Signs: Journal of Women in Culture and Society* 16.2 (1991): 290–321. According to Marx, 'An oppressed class is the vital condition for every society founded on the antagonism of classes. The emancipation of the oppressed class thus implies necessarily the creation of a new society.' 'The Metaphysics of Political Economy', 173.
15 'This "something new" is more than individual freedom or fulfillment; it is the creation of a better world, an alternative to a death-bound society, a "four-gated city".' Greene, 'Feminist Fiction and the Uses of Memory', 303.
16 Marx and Engels, *The Communist Manifesto*, 79.
17 '*Gender Trouble* seeks to expand the realm of gender possibilities'; 'dissonant adjectives work retroactively to redefine the substantive identities they are said to modify and, hence, to expand the substantive categories of gender to include possibilities that they previously excluded'; 'The productions swerve from their original purposes and inadvertently mobilize possibilities of "subjects" that do not merely exceed the bounds of cultural intelligibility, but effectively expand the boundaries of what is, in fact, culturally intelligible.' Butler, *Gender Trouble*, xxi, 33–34, 40.
18 Butler (ibid., viii, xxv) also writes of 'opening up possibilities' and 'exten[ding] . . . legitimacy'.
19 'This exclusionary matrix by which subjects are formed thus requires the

simultaneous production of a domain of abject beings, those who are not yet "subjects", but who form the constitutive outside to the domain of the subject.' Butler, *Bodies That Matter*, xiii.
20 Wendy Tuohy, 'Inclusive Language Risks "Dehumanising Women", Top Researchers Argue', *The Sydney Morning Herald*, 29 January 2022, https://www.smh.com.au/national/inclusive-language-risks-dehumanising-women-top-researchers-argue-20220126-p59red.html.
21 Butler, *Bodies That Matter*, 25.
22 Ibid.
23 For example, Stock acknowledges that '[m]issexing in single-sex spaces happens, and it is a highly regrettable cost of the current system'. Stock, *Material Girls*, 108.
24 If, as Sarah Hoagland argues, the patriarchal conceptual scheme cannot admit the existence of a lesbian, a woman-identified-woman, then the inclusion of lesbians is necessarily the reduction of 'lesbian' from a political identity to a sexual orientation (or a male fetish), the elimination of the threat that 'lesbian' poses to patriarchy. See Hoagland as quoted in Frye, *The Politics of Reality*, 152. (Frye quotes from 'Lesbian Epistemology', a paper delivered by Hoagland in 1978 at the Midwestern Division of the Society for Women in Philosophy.) 1978,)
25 See Martha C. Nussbaum, 'The Professor of Parody: The Hip Defeatism of Judith Butler', *New Republic*, 22 February 1999, https://newrepublic.com/article/150687/professor-parody.
26 Delphy argues that Anglo-American scholars invented 'French feminism', and that they did so to 'pass off as feminist a "theory" in which feminism and feminists need not figure any longer'. Christine Delphy, 'The Invention of French Feminism: An Essential Move', *Yale French Studies* 97 (2000): 190–221. The quotation is from p. 195.
27 'I sought to counter those views that made presumptions about the limits and propriety of gender ... Some of these kinds of presumptions were found in what was called "French Feminism" at the time, and they enjoyed great popularity among literary scholars and some social theorists.' Butler does not cite a single work of French feminism or a single literary scholar or social theorist with whom such work enjoyed popularity. Butler, *Gender Trouble*, viii.
28 On this forgetting, see Dale Spender, *For the Record: The Making and Meaning of Feminist Knowledge* (London: Women's Press, 1985), 1–6, and Dale Spender, *Women of Ideas and What Men Have Done to Them: From Aphra Behn to Adrienne Rich* (London: Routledge & Kegan Paul, 1982), 3–13.

29 Kathleen Barry, *Female Sexual Slavery* (New York: NYU Press, 1984).
30 Andrea Dworkin, *Pornography: Men Possessing Women* (London: Women's Press, 1981).
31 Dworkin, *Woman Hating*; Mary Daly, *Gyn/Ecology: The Metaethics of Radical Feminism* (London: Women's Press, 1991 [1978]).
32 Dworkin, *Woman Hating*; Daly, *Gyn/Ecology*.
33 Daly, *Gyn/Ecology*.
34 Ibid.
35 Diana E. H. Russell, *Rape in Marriage* (New York: Macmillan, 1982).
36 Catharine A. MacKinnon, *Sexual Harassment of Working Women: A Case of Sex Discrimination* (New Haven, CT: Yale University Press, 1979).
37 Naomi Wolf, *The Beauty Myth: How Images of Beauty Are Used against Women* (London: Chatto & Windus, 1990); Sheila Jeffreys, *Beauty and Misogyny: Harmful Cultural Practices in the West* (London: Routledge, 2014).
38 Benston, 'The Political Economy of Women's Liberation'; Pat Mainardi, 'The Politics of Housework', Redstockings, 1970 (see https://www.cwluherstory.org/classic-feminist-writings-articles/the-politics-of-housework and https://womenwhatistobedone.wordpress.com/wp-content/uploads/2021/08/1969-06-27-pat-mainardi-politicsofhousework-redstockings.pdf); Peggy Morton, 'A Woman's Work Is Never Done', in Edith Hoshino Altbach, ed., *From Feminism to Liberation* (Cambridge: Schenkman Books, 1971), 211–227; Dalla Costa and James, *The Power of Women and the Subversion of the Community*; Silvia Federici, *Wages against Housework* (Bristol: Power of Women Collective and Falling Wall Press, 1975); Ann Oakley, *Woman's Work: The Housewife, Past and Present* (New York: Pantheon Books, 1975).
39 In MacKinnon's terminology, these are 'difference feminists' and 'dominance feminists'. See Catharine MacKinnon, 'Difference and Dominance: On Sex Discrimination', in her *Feminism Unmodified*, 32–45.
40 Scott, for instance, argues that 'equality is not the elimination of difference, and difference does not preclude equality'. Joan W. Scott, 'Deconstructing Equality-versus-Difference: Or, the Uses of Poststructuralist Theory for Feminism', *Feminist Studies* 14.1 (1988), 38.
41 In Marxian language, the 'additive' framework is the 'metaphysical' framework and the 'holistic' framework the 'dialectical' framework. As Engels writes, 'capitalists cannot exist without wage-workers' (see p. 186, n. 31.
42 'For women to affirm difference, when difference means dominance, as

it does with gender, means to affirm the qualities and characteristics of powerlessness.' MacKinnon, 'Difference and Dominance', 39.
43 Delphy, 'The Invention of French Feminism', 186.
44 Katharine Jenkins, 'Amelioration and Inclusion: Gender Identity and the Concept of Woman', *Ethics* 126.2 (2016): 394–421.
45 For another critique of Jenkins and another argument for the incoherence of trans-inclusionary feminism, see Tomas Bogardus, 'Some Internal Problems with Revisionary Gender Concepts', *Philosophia* 48.1 (2020): 55–75.
46 Catharine A. MacKinnon, 'Exploring Transgender Law and Politics', *Signs: Journal of Women in Culture and Society* (2023), https://signsjournal.org/exploring-transgender-law-and-politics.
47 Jenkins, 'Amelioration and Inclusion', 411. Jenkins assumes that to take norms to apply to oneself is to be subject to norms. As Lawford-Smith points out, norms by definition are expectations imposed from without. Lawford-Smith, *Gender-Critical Feminism*, 53.
48 Sally Haslanger, 'Gender and Race: (What) Are They? (What) Do We Want Them to Be?' *Noûs* 34, no. 1 (2000): 39.
49 Jenkins, 'Amelioration and Inclusion', 394.
50 Ibid., 395.
51 Ibid., 394.
52 Delphy, 'The Invention of French Feminism', 185.

Notes to Chapter 5
1 Butler, *Gender Trouble*, vii.
2 Ibid., vii–viii.
3 Dalla Costa and James, *The Power of Women and the Subversion of the Community*.
4 Butler, *Gender Trouble*, viii. I am not quite sure what Butler means by '*produce new* forms of hierarchy and exclusion': does she mean that feminism ought not to *perpetuate other forms* of exclusion, whether old or new, or does she mean that feminism ought not to *bring new forms into being*? Her reference to 'homophobic consequences' suggests the former but, if this is read literally, she means the latter. To my mind, the only new form of exclusion that can be said to be the product of feminism is the exclusion of trans women from the female sex class.
5 Butler, *Gender Trouble*, 26.
6 In a bitter irony, Wittig saw it as 'our historical task ... to make it evident that women are a class', but Butler exploited Wittig's words to efface precisely this. 'One Is Not Born a Woman', 106.

7 Interestingly, she continues to identify 'women' as the subject of feminism. Butler, *Gender Trouble*, 2–8.
8 Schmitt, *The Concept of the Political*, 24.
9 'The efforts to denaturalize sexuality and gender have taken as their main enemy those normative frameworks of compulsory heterosexuality that operate through the naturalization and reification of heterosexist norms.' Butler, *Bodies That Matter*, 58.
10 '[A] postmodern-feminist form of critical inquiry ... would be the theoretical counterpart of a broader, richer, more complex, and multilayered feminist solidarity, the sort of solidarity that is essential for overcoming the oppression of women in its "endless variety and monotonous similarity".' Fraser and Nicholson, 'Social Criticism without Philosophy', 102.
11 A report published in 2019 found that '[s]exual violence and coercion were much more common among participants who had been assigned female at birth – trans men and nonbinary people – compared with those assigned male (61.8% vs 39.3%, p<0.001)'. D. Callander, J. Wiggins, S. Rosenberg, V. J. Cornelisse, E. Duck-Chong, M. Holt, M. Pony, E. Vlahakis, J. MacGibbon, T. Cook, *The 2018 Australian Trans and Gender Diverse Sexual Health Survey: Report of Findings* (Sydney: The Kirby Institute, University of New South Wales, 2019), 10.
12 Butler, 'Contingent Foundations', 49.
13 'The opening discussion in this chapter argued that this globalizing gesture has spawned a number of criticisms from women who claim that the category of "women" is normative and exclusionary and is invoked with the unmarked dimensions of class and racial privilege intact.' Butler, *Gender Trouble*, 19.
14 Ibid., viii.
15 Mary Daly, *Beyond God the Father: Toward a Philosophy of Women's Liberation* (Boston, MA: Beacon Press, 1985), 56.
16 Andrea Dworkin, *Scapegoat: The Jews, Israel, and Women's Liberation* (New York: Free Press, 2000), 246.
17 For New York Radical Women, the first principle is loyalty to women: 'We take the woman's side in everything.' New York Radical Women, 'Principles', in *Sisterhood Is Powerful*, 520.
18 Ellen Willis, 'Radical Feminism and Feminist Radicalism', *Social Text* 9/10 (1984), 105.
19 MacKinnon, *Toward a Feminist Theory of the State*, 9.
20 Alcoff, as quoted in Teresa de Lauretis, 'The Essence of the Triangle

or, Taking the Risk of Essentialism Seriously: Feminist Theory in Italy, the U.S., and Britain', *differences: A Journal of Feminist Cultural Studies* 1, no. 2 (1989): 13. These words constitute one answer to de Lauretis's question: 'But why do it at all? What is the purpose, or the gain, of supplying a missing premise (innate female essence) in order to construct a coherent image of feminism which thus becomes available to charges (essentialism) based on the very premise that had to be supplied? What motivates such a project, the suspicion, and the inferences?'

21 Elizabeth V. Spelman, *Inessential Woman: Problems of Exclusion in Feminist Thought* (Boston, MA: Beacon Press, 1988), ix.

22 '[T]here are many junctures at which, for example, women of color and white women discover profound commonalities in their experience (as well as profound differences). One can, of course, adjust one's methodological tools so that these commonalities become indiscernible under the finely meshed grid of various "inflections" (or the numerous counterexamples that can always be produced). When it comes to issues of race, however, intellectuals have no problem allowing that color (that is, the experience of being a person of color in a racist culture) creates some similarities of position across class and gender, and that these can be retrieved and discussed. What is not clear is why we have such a problem when it comes to issues of gender.' Susan Bordo, 'Feminist Skepticism and the "Maleness" of Philosophy', *Journal of Philosophy* 85.11 (1988), 625–626.

23 Butler, *Gender Trouble*, 4.

24 '[T]he concepts which emerged in the feminist discourse were mostly struggle concepts, not based on theoretical definitions worked out by an ideological mastermind of the movement ... They are derived from our struggle experiences and the reflection on these experiences, and have thus a certain explanatory value.' Maria Mies, *Patriarchy and Accumulation on a World Scale: Women in the International Division of Labour* (London: Zed Books, 1998), 35–36.

25 hooks observes a similar shift in language with respect to race: 'Words like *Other* and *difference* are taking the place of commonly known words deemed uncool or too simplistic, words like *oppression, exploitation,* and *domination.*' bell hooks, *Yearning: Race, Gender, and Cultural Politics* (Boston, MA: South End Press, 1990), 51–52.

26 Marilyn French, *The Women's Room* (New York: Ballantine Books, 1988), 462.

27 Joan Wallach Scott writes:

> In its simplest recent usage, 'gender' is a synonym for 'women'. Any number of books and articles whose subject is women's history have, in the past few years, substituted 'gender' for 'women' in their titles. In some cases, this usage, though vaguely referring to certain analytic concepts, is actually about the political acceptability of the field. In these instances, the use of 'gender' is meant to denote the scholarly seriousness of a work, for 'gender' has a more neutral and objective sound than does 'women'. 'Gender' seems to fit within the scientific terminology of social science and thus dissociates itself from the (supposedly strident) politics of feminism. In this usage, 'gender' does not carry with it a necessary statement about inequality or power nor does it name the aggrieved (and hitherto invisible) party. Whereas the term 'women's history' proclaims its politics by asserting (contrary to customary practice) that women are valid historical subjects, 'gender' includes, but does not name women, and so seems to pose no critical threat. This use of 'gender' is one facet of what might be called the quest of feminist scholarship for academic legitimacy in the 1980s. (Joan Wallach Scott, *Gender and the Politics of History*, New York: Columbia University Press, 1988, 31–32)

Similarly, Mies writes:

> It is not surprising that this terminology [gender] has immediately been adopted by all kinds of people who may not otherwise feel much sympathy for, or even be hostile to, feminism. If, instead of 'sexual violence', we talk of 'gender violence', the shock is somewhat mitigated by an abstract term, which removes the whole issue from the realm of emotionality and political commitment to that of scientific and apparently 'objective' discourse. If the woman's question is again removed to that level, many men and women, who do not want to change the status quo, will again feel quite comfortable with the women's movement. (Mies, *Patriarchy and Accumulation on a World Scale*, 23)

See also Pateman, *The Sexual Contract*, 225. For all their critique of the ideal of neutrality, by using the neutral (masculine) language of 'gender' rather than 'women', poststructural feminists may be attempting to acquire the appearance of neutrality, of disinterestedness. The position of neutrality is, by definition, the position of the noncombatant. This is how poststructural feminism's form mirrors its depoliticised substance.

As Susan Bernick writes with respect to gender scepticism, '[s]kepticism is ironic; it is detached. Skepticism is, in short, male in at least the way Bordo claims philosophy is male. Skepticism requires a place outside, a place from which to survey the passing scene and from which to criticize it. The only people who have this place are by definition noncombatants. In the context of women and men, feminism and male dominance, it is not clear feminists could fill this role.' 'Philosophy and Feminism', 193.

28 Donna Haraway, 'A Manifesto for Cyborgs: Science, Technology, and Socialist Feminism in the 1980s', *Australian Feminist Studies* 2.4 (1987), 9.

29 Butler, *Gender Trouble*, xxii (emphasis added).

30 Butler, 'Contingent Foundations', 50. She also says (p. 41): 'Inasmuch as poststructuralism offers a mode of critique that effects this contestation of the foundationalist move, it can be used as a part of such a radical agenda. Note that I have said, "It can be used": I think there are no necessary political consequences for such a theory, but only a possible political deployment.' According to her, '[t]he problem emerges, though, that what one means by "the universal" will vary, and the cultural articulation of that term in its various modalities will work against precisely the trans-cultural status of the claim. This is not to say that there ought to be no reference to the universal or that it has become, for us, an impossibility.' Judith Butler, 'For a Careful Reading', in *Feminist Contentions*, 129.

31 'If deconstruction is the theory, postmodernism is the practice ... Is there any reason why Progressive political people should take either the theory or the practice seriously unless it is necessary to do so in order to get tenure? I am going to argue that we do ... My contention is that socialist feminists need to make a break with this practice and go beyond the successes it has made possible if we are to address the concerns of young women who find the feminism of an earlier generation unnecessary at best, *embarrassing at worst*.' Kate Ellis, 'Stories without Endings: Deconstructive Theory and Political Practice', *Socialist Review* 89.2 (1989), 38 (emphasis added).

32 Fraser and Nicholson, 'Social Criticism without Philosophy', 98 (the second emphasis is my own).

33 Josephine Bartosch, 'Ordinary Women Are Rejecting an Elite Feminism That Cannot Even Define Them', *The Telegraph*, 2 December 2022, https://archive.md/TB3Yt; and Victoria Smith, 'Dirty Feminism: You Can't Have Feminism without Femaleness', *The Critic*, 13 December

2022, https://thecritic.co.uk/dirty-feminism/?fbclid=IwAR1-rU4SgLyZ BfS5V5noFVZLNi4Ulc9CEAaAMnyl09pYJTQxmvtAk8U1_Vg.

34 Bordo writes:

> It is no accident, I believe, that feminists are questioning the integrity of the notion of 'female reality' just as we begin to get a foothold in those professions which could be most radically transformed by our (historically developed) Otherness and which have been historically most shielded from it. Foucault constantly reminded us that the routes of individual interest and desire do not always lead where imagined and may often sustain unintended and unwanted configurations of power. Could feminist gender-scepticism, in all its multifaceted 'deployment' (to continue the Foucauldian motif), now be operating in the service of the reproduction of white, male knowledge/power?
>
> If so, it will not be the result of conspiracy, but a 'strategy', as Foucault would say, 'without strategists', operating through numerous, noncentralized processes: through the pleasure of joining an intellectual community and the social and material rewards of membership; through the excitement of engagement in culturally powerful and dominant theoretical enterprises; through our own exhaustion with maintaining an agonistic stance at the institutions where we work; through intellectual boredom with stale, old talk about male dominance and female subordination; through our postmodern inclination to embrace the new and the novel; through the genuine insights that new theoretical perspectives offer; through our feminist commitments to the representation of difference; even (most ironically) through our 'female' desire to heal wounds of exclusion and alienation. (Bordo, 'Feminism, Postmodernism, and Gender-Scepticism', 151)

35 Nancy K. Miller, 'The Text's Heroine: A Feminist Critic and Her Fictions', *Diacritics* 12.2 (1982): 48–53; see esp. p. 49.
36 Tania Modleski, *Feminism without Women: Culture and Criticism in a 'Postfeminist' Age* (New York: Routledge, 1991), 6.
37 Ibid., 14–15.
38 '[W]hat distinguishes this moment from other moments of backlash is the extent to which it has been carried out not against feminism but in its very name.' Ibid., x.
39 Ibid., 5. Modleski is here quoting Elaine Showalter: 'While men's studies, gaystudies, and feminist criticism have different politics and priorities, together they are moving beyond "male feminism" to raise challeng-

ing questions about masculinity in literary texts, questions that enable gender criticism to develop.' Cf. Elaine Showalter, 'Introduction: The Rise of Gender', in Elaine Showalter, ed., *Speaking of Gender* (New York: Routledge, 1989), 8.
40 Modleski, *Feminism without Women*, 5.
41 Ibid.
42 Lauretis, 'The Essence of the Triangle', 5.
43 Ibid., 32. See also Bordo, 'Feminism, Postmodernism, and Gender-Skepticism', 147.
44 Ibid.
45 Modleski, *Feminism without Women*, 18.
46 Benhabib, 'Feminism and Postmodernism', 30.
47 Ibid.
48 Ibid., 20.
49 Bordo, 'Feminism, Postmodernism, and Gender-Skepticism', 142.
50 Somer Brodribb, *Nothing Mat(t)ers: A Feminist Critique of Postmodernism* (North Melbourne: Spinifex, 1992).
51 Toril Moi, 'Power, Sex and Subjectivity: Feminist Reflections on Foucault', *Paragraph* 5 (1985), 95.
52 Ibid.
53 Nancy Hartsock, 'Foucault on Power: A Theory for Women?', in *Feminism/Postmodernism*, 169, 165.
54 Sabina Lovibond, 'Feminism and Postmodernism', *New Left Review* 178 (1989), 12.
55 Bernick, 'Philosophy and Feminism', 194.
56 'I want to ... suggest that not only "woman" but also "women" is troublesome – and that this extension of our suspicions is *in the interest of feminism.*' Riley, *'Am I That Name?'*, 1 (emphasis added). What, I wonder, is feminism if the doubt that women exist is in its interest? Similarly, Butler writes: 'Is the construction of the category of women as a coherent and stable subject an unwitting regulation and reification of gender relations? And is not such a reification *precisely contrary to feminist aims?*' *Gender Trouble*, 7 (emphasis added).

Notes to Chapter 6
1 Schmitt, *The Concept of the Political*, 20.
2 Ibid., 25–26.
3 Ibid.
4 Ibid., 37.

5 While this feminism repudiates the notion of enemy, it embraces that of ally. It seeks allies in its struggle against no one. What would Schmitt make of this, I wonder – a friend–enemy grouping in which the enemy has disappeared.
6 Schmitt, *The Concept of the Political*, 38.
7 '[W]omen – even feminists – are intimidated into Self-deception, becoming the only Self-described oppressed who are unable to name their oppressor, referring instead to vague "forces", "roles", "stereotypes", "constraints", "attitudes", "influences". This list could go on. The point is that no agent is named – only abstractions.' Daly, *Gyn/Ecology*, 29.
8 See Atkinson, *Amazon Odyssey*, xxii. Another answer, according to hooks, is 'sexist thought and behavior'. bell hooks, *Feminism Is for Everybody: Passionate Politics* (Cambridge, MA: South End Press, 2000), 12. Even Atkinson wrote: 'I always understood that it was male *behaviour* that was the enemy.' *Amazon Odyssey*, xxii.
9 Bordo, *Unbearable Weight*, 28.
10 hooks, *Feminism Is for Everybody*, x.
11 'Identity categories are never merely descriptive, but always normative, and as such, exclusionary.' Butler, 'Contingent Foundations', 50.
12 In contrast to Butler, Wittig sees in exclusion 'a shadow of victory': 'Lesbians should always remember and acknowledge how "unnatural", compelling, totally oppressive, and destructive being "woman" was for us in the old days before the women's liberation movement. It was a political constraint, and those who resisted it were accused of not being "real" women. But then we were proud of it, since in the accusation there was already something like a shadow of victory: the avowal by the oppressor that "woman" is not something that goes without saying, since to be one, one has to be a "real" one.' 'One Is Not Born a Woman', 104.
13 Daly, *Gyn/Ecology*, 72.
14 Alcoff, 'Cultural Feminism versus Post-Structuralism', 408.
15 Daly, *Gyn/Ecology*, 57.
16 'Loyalty and identity are so closely connected as to be almost just two aspects of one phenomenon.' Marilyn Frye, 'History and Responsibility', *Women's Studies International Forum* 18.3 (1985), 216.
17 MacKinnon, 'Exploring Transgender Law and Politics'.
18 It is loyalty to 'all the women you don't want to be around, including all the women who used to be your best friends whom you don't want anything to do with anymore'. Dworkin, 'Woman-Hating Right and Left', 30–31.

19 Moira Gatens, *Feminism and Philosophy: Perspectives on Difference and Equality* (Bloomington: Indiana University Press, 1991), 79.
20 For a thoughtful critique of the feminist rejection of the concept of false consciousness, see Lovibond, 'Feminism and Postmodernism'. Lovibond (ibid., 27) suggests that 'the occasional moralism or "moral elitism" of radical movements will have to be understood as a vice of excess rather than as a symptom of fundamental wrong-headedness: the danger lies, in other words, not in wishing to bring our (felt, empirical) desires into line with our rational understanding, but in tackling the job in a ham-fisted way that is doomed to provoke disgust and reaction.'
21 Butler, 'Contingent Foundations', 54.
22 Ibid., 49.
23 Butler, *Gender Trouble*, 7.
24 Rowbotham, *Woman's Consciousness, Man's World*, xi; Daly, *Beyond God the Father*, 9; Frye, *The Politics of Reality*, 165.
25 Frye, *The Politics of Reality*, 48.
26 Ibid., 45–51.
27 The paradigm of such treatment is sexual penetration. See Jonathan Walters, 'Invading the Roman Body: Manliness and Impenetrability in Roman Thought', in Judith P. Hallett and Marilyn B. Skinner, eds, *Roman Sexualities* (Princeton, NJ: Princeton University Press, 1997), 29–43. A study examining the sexual self-concept of men and women survivors of child sexual abuse concluded that 'women are found in greater number within the Confident and non-preoccupied profile while men are found in greater number in the Demeaning and depressive profile, which highlights that men tend to have a more detrimental sexual self-concept than women'. Perhaps male victims are experientially demeaned by sexual abuse in a way female victims are not, because women are the proper object of sexual penetration and violation. Roxanne Guyon, Mylène Fernet, Cloé Canivet, Monique Tardif, Natacha Godbout, 'Sexual Self-Concept among Men and Women Child Sexual Abuse Survivors: Emergence of Differentiated Profiles', *Child Abuse and Neglect* 104 (2020), 9.
28 Seiya Morita, 'From Feminism to Transgenderism: Catharine MacKinnon and Her Political Transition', On the Woman Question: A Critical Approach to Marx and Feminism, 1 August 2023, https://onthewomanquestion.com/2023/08/01/from-feminism-to-transgenderism-catharine-mackinnon-and-her-political-transition.

29 Catharine A. MacKinnon, *Are Women Human? And Other International Dialogues* (Cambridge, MA: Harvard University Press, 2007).
30 MacKinnon, 'Exploring Transgender Law and Politics'.
31 Morita, 'From Feminism to Transgenderism'.
32 Butler, 'Contingent Foundations', 50.
33 Ibid., 49.
34 Ibid.
35 Schmitt, *The Concept of the Political*.
36 Lawford-Smith, *Gender-Critical Feminism*, 143–164.
37 Natalie Stoljar, 'Essence, Identity, and the Concept of Woman', *Philosophical Topics* 23.2 (1995): 261–293.
38 Lawford-Smith, *Gender-Critical Feminism*, 30–31.
39 Monique Wittig, *The Straight Mind and Other Essays* (Boston, MA: Beacon Press, 1992), 29.
40 'To the metaphysician, things and their mental reflexes, ideas, are isolated, are to be considered one after the other and apart from each other, are objects of investigation fixed, rigid, given once for all.' Engels, *Socialism: Utopian and Scientific*, 79.
41 'It is the fate of women to perform three-quarters of the work of society (in the public as well as in the private domain) plus the bodily work of reproduction according to a preestablished rate. Being murdered, mutilated, physically and mentally tortured and abused, being raped, being battered, and being forced to marry is the fate of women.' Wittig, 'The Category of Sex', 65.
42 Butler, *Gender Trouble*, 9.
43 Ibid., 10.
44 'To use the language of gender reinforces the language of the civil, the public and the individual, language that depends on the repression of the sexual contract.' Pateman, *The Sexual Contract*, 225.
45 Adapting Pateman (ibid., 229), one could say: 'Their argument remains caught within the dichotomies that are under attack, bouncing back and forth within the boundaries established by the story of the original contract.'
46 Judith Butler, 'Against Proper Objects', *differences: A Journal of Feminist Cultural Studies* 6.2–3 (1994), 7.
47 Srinivasan represents the critique of prostitution as one in which 'the prostitute calls out to be *saved*'. Second-wave feminists saw prostitution as the sexual *enslavement* of women, and so were committed to the *abolition* of prostitution. They saw women in prostitution as *slaves* in need of *liberation*, not as *sinners* in need of *redemption* (of being

'saved'). See Amia Srinivasan, *The Right to Sex* (London: Bloomsbury, 2021), 151.
48 This is how MacKinnon finds herself having to argue that pornography is a political, not a moral issue. See MacKinnon, 'Not a Moral Issue', in her *Feminism Unmodified*, 146–162.
49 Dworkin, *Intercourse*, 154.
50 Gatens, *Imaginary Bodies*, 78.
51 Ibid., 79.
52 Dworkin, *Intercourse*, 131, 132.
53 Gatens, *Imaginary Bodies*, 79.
54 Ibid., 79.
55 Ibid., 89.
56 Dworkin, *Scapegoat*, 246.
57 Daly, *Gyn/Ecology*, 39.
58 Jean Grimshaw, *Feminist Philosophers: Women's Perspectives on Philosophical Traditions* (Brighton: Wheatsheaf Books, 1986), 120–121.
59 In his overview of Schmitt's 'On the Concept of the Political', Lars Vinx writes:

> Any distinction that can serve as a marker of collective identity and difference will acquire political quality if it has the power, in a concrete situation, to sort people into two opposing groups that are willing, if necessary, to fight against each other. Whether a particular distinction will come to play this role is not determined by its own intrinsic significance but by whether a group of people relies on it to define its own collective identity and comes to think of that identity, as based on that distinction, as something that might have to be defended against other groups by going to war. (Lars Vinx, 'Carl Schmitt', in Edward N. Zalta, ed., *The Stanford Encyclopedia of Philosophy* (2019), https://plato.stanford.edu/archives/fall2019/entries/schmitt)

In the writings of second-wave feminists such as Dworkin and Daly, the sex distinction acquires a political quality, ceasing to be a biological distinction and becoming a political one: a distinction on the basis of which men persecute women, and hence a distinction on the basis of which women must defend themselves against men or attack them.
60 Gatens, *Feminism and Philosophy*, 81.
61 'It [war] does not have to be common, normal, something ideal, or desirable. But it must nevertheless remain a real possibility for as long

as the concept of the enemy remains valid.' Schmitt, *The Concept of the Political*, 33.
62 Andrea Dworkin, *Right-Wing Women* (New York: Perigee Books, 1983), 20.
63 'There are feminist works which provide abundant examples of misogynistic statements from authorities in all "fields", in all major societies, throughout the millennia of patriarchy. Feminists have also written at length about the actual rapist behavior of professionals, from soldiers to gynecologists. The "custom" of widow-burning (suttee) in India, the Chinese ritual of footbinding, the genital mutilation of young girls in Africa ... the massacre of women as witches in "Renaissance" Europe, gynocide under the guise of American gynaecology and psychotherapy – all are documented facts accessible in the tomes and tombs (libraries) of patriarchal scholarship. The contemporary facts of brutal gang rape, of wife-beating, of overt and subliminal psychic lobotomizing – all are available. What then can the label anti-male possibly mean when applied to works that expose these facts and invite women to free our Selves?' Daly, *Gyn/Ecology*, 28.
64 Consider the titles of Dworkin's books: *Life and Death: Unapologetic Writings on the Continuing War against Women* and *Letters from a War Zone*.
65 Gatens, *Feminism and Philosophy*, 81.
66 Ibid.
67 Schmitt, *The Concept of the Political*, 27.
68 Ibid.
69 In Australia, the strategy for preventing male violence against women is education – consent education and respectful relationships education.
70 I am reminded of an amusing passage in Mary Ellmann, *Thinking about Women* (New York: Harcourt Brace Jovanovich, 1968), xii:

> Me: Or think of the official successes. I am afraid of the ideal unions toward which counsellors propel us. You take an intolerable man and an intolerable woman and put them in an apartment together, and then if they are both *mature*, and each tries to *understand* the other's monstrous nature, a *good marriage* results.
> I: It cannot be wrong to urge understanding.
> Me: No, it must be right in social work. But in novels, say, misunderstanding reasserts itself. Its resilience is apparent, and one feels a grudging admiration for resilience, the admiration one might feel for a viral strain which all the aspirin in the world won't eradicate.

71 Jean Améry, 'On the Necessity and Impossibility of Being a Jew', *New German Critique* 20 (1980), 15–16.
72 Ibid., 18.
73 Ibid., 21.
74 Ibid.
75 Ibid., 17.
76 Butler, *Gender Trouble*, xxxi.
77 Riley, *'Am I That Name?'*.
78 Améry, 'On the Necessity and Impossibility of Being a Jew', 22.
79 Fraser, 'Beyond the Master/Subject Model', 173–181.
80 Améry, 'On the Necessity and Impossibility of Being a Jew', 23.
81 Ibid., 21–22.
82 Butler, *Gender Trouble*.
83 Améry, 'On the Necessity and Impossibility of Being a Jew', 29. See also p. 20: 'The first step must be the unqualified recognition that the verdict of the social group is a given reality.'
84 Butler, *Gender Trouble*, xxiii.
85 This evasion at the level of substance is mirrored at the level of form. See Brodribb, *Nothing Mat(t)ers*.
86 Schmitt, *The Concept of the Political*, 27.
87 Ibid.
88 'To be rapable, a position that is social not biological, defines what a woman is.' MacKinnon, *Toward a Feminist Theory of the State*, 178.
89 MacKinnon, 'Exploring Transgender Law and Politics'.
90 'Suddenly a desire to violate tears through his body like an electric shock, six thousand volts of violence, sacrilege, the lust to desecrate, destroy. His thumbs unite between the crack of her ass, nails inwards, knuckle hard on knuckle, and plunge up to the palms into her. A submarine scream rises from the deep green of her dreaming, and she snaps towards waking, half-waking, half-dreaming with no sense of self, just a raw consciousness of moving images against a dark background, and a hard pain stabbing at her entrails. The scream surfaces now, breaking the water-skin into the other world, and she struggles, writhing to get away from the probing fingers, jerking her hips forward in a wild pelvic thrust. But she can't escape, Macrae has too much of her . . . He can feel the thin membrane tighten and relax as her muscles flex to dislodge the invaders from her, invaders she doesn't know or recognize, as slowly the fragmentary world begins to resolve around her, and she knows for the first time that she is Isabelle Lantier, a

stranger in a stranger's bed in New York. She jerks and twists again, but Macrae is too deeply in, his thumbs almost a part of her now, he can feel the blood knocking on the walls, as though at any moment it will damburst through, come flooding out. Isabelle opens her eyes, still not knowing where or what or why, her face jammed hard against the cracking plaster, her breathing wrenched out in hot thick pants, as Macrae digs deeper dragging another scream from her viscera, and her jerking head cracks hard on the wall. Her own hands are busy now, twisting behind her back, around her buttocks, and her palms touch Macrae's hands, still clamped tight around her ass, kneading, working on it, with a violence born of desperation and desire, desire to have her so completely that their separate flesh might coalesce and occupy the same space, that it seems as if he would tear the flesh from her to absorb it, crush it, melt it into his own hands, become his hands . . . Isabelle knows at last the identity of her violator, and is calmed by the knowing . . . And Isabelle, feeling tautened flesh relaxing, hears a voice calling out "don't stop; don't stop", a voice called from somewhere deep within her from ages past, ancestral voices from a time the world was young, "don't stop, don't stop". It's nearer now, this atavistic voice, and she realises with surprise that it is coming from her mouth, it is her lips that are moving, it is her voice.' Laurence St Clair, *Isabelle and Véronique: Four Months, Four Cities* (New York: Blue Moon Books, 1989), 2–5.

91 'A human being has a body that is inviolate; and when it is violated, it is abused. A woman has a body that is penetrated in intercourse: permeable, its corporeal solidness a lie. The discourse of male truth – literature, science, philosophy, pornography – calls that penetration violation. This it does with some consistency and some confidence. Violation is a synonym for intercourse. At the same time, the penetration is taken to be a use, not an abuse; a normal use; it is appropriate to enter her, to push into ("violate") the boundaries of her body.' Dworkin, *Intercourse*, 154.

92 'Sometimes men are used sexually by other men as if they were women. Typically these are young boys or men in prison, that is, men who, by virtue of their youth or incarceration lack power. Yet, as MacKinnon states, even men in such a position do not "experience or share the meaning of being a woman". They remain men. They experience their violation as embodied men, with all that the embodiment entails for their political position as a sex.' Carole Pateman, 'Sex and Power', *Ethics* 100.2 (1990), 402.

93 Quoted in Stock, *Material Girls*, 245–246.
94 E.g. Rebecca Solnit, 'Trans Women Pose No Threat to Cis Women, but We Pose a Threat to Them if We Make Them Outcasts', *The Guardian*, 10 August 2020, https://www.theguardian.com/commentisfree/2020/aug/10/trans-rights-feminist-letter-rebecca-solnit; Jennifer Wright, 'Transgender Women Are Women: Transgender Men Are Men', *Harper's Bazaar*, 23 October 2018, https://www.harpersbazaar.com/culture/politics/a24109933/transgender-women-are-women-transgender-men-are-men; Jill Stark, 'For Some Transgender Students, the School Bathroom Is a Battleground', ABC News, 1 April 2017, updated 9 May 2017, https://www.abc.net.au/news/2017-04-01/transgender-students-bathroom-battleground/8395782; Paris Lees, 'Fears around Gender-Neutral Toilets Are All in the Mind', *The Guardian*, 3 December 2016, https://www.theguardian.com/commentisfree/2016/dec/02/fears-gender-neutral-toilets-women-trans-people-violence; Rachael Thorn, 'Why Toilets Are a Battleground for Transgender Rights', BBC News Online, 8 June 2016, https://www.bbc.com/news/uk-england-36395646; Gabrielle Bellot, 'A Trans Woman Enters the Restroom', Slate, 20 January 2016, https://slate.com/human-interest/2016/01/how-the-trans-bathroom-myth-makes-life-difficult-for-trans-women.html.
95 MacKinnon, 'Exploring Transgender Law and Politics'.
96 Améry, 'On the Necessity and Impossibility of Being a Jew', 23.
97 The second-wave feminists share this lexicon with the suffragettes. Emmeline Pankhurst, for example, said: 'I am here as a soldier who has temporarily left the field of battle in order to explain . . . what civil war is like when civil war is waged by women.' 'Freedom or Death', speech delivered on 13 November 1913 in Hartford, Connecticut.
98 The epigraph to Andrea Dworkin, *Life and Death: Unapologetic Writings on the Continuing War against Women* (London: Virago, 1997) is: 'Let there be no mention of the war. If it were not for those few who could not repress their experiences, the victims themselves would have denied the horror.' Aharon Appelfeld, *Beyond Despair: Three Lectures and a Conversation with Philip Roth* (New York: Fromm International, 1994), 35.
99 Recall Rich:

> You show me the poems of some woman
> my age, or younger
> translated from your language

> Certain words occur: *enemy, oven, sorrow*
> enough to let me know
> she's a woman of my time. (Rich, 'Translations', 40)

100 'The political meaning of intercourse for women is the fundamental question of feminism and freedom: can an occupied people – physically occupied inside, internally invaded – be free; can those with a metaphysically compromised privacy have self-determination; can those without a biologically based physical integrity have self-respect?' Dworkin, *Intercourse*, 156.
101 Dworkin, *Pornography*.
102 'Physically, the woman in intercourse is a space inhabited, a literal territory occupied literally.' Dworkin, *Intercourse*, 168.
103 'Because of our participation in the middle-class lifestyle we were the oppressors of other people, our poor white sisters, our Black sisters, our Chicana sisters – and the men who in turn oppressed them.' Dworkin, *Woman Hating*, 21.
104 'This book is an action, a political action where revolution is the goal. It has no other purpose. It is not cerebral wisdom, or academic horseshit, or ideas carved in granite or destined for immortality.' Ibid., 17.
105 'Could women's liberation ever be a revolutionary movement, not rhetorically but on the ground?' Dworkin, *Scapegoat*, 248.
106 'The emptiness of Butler's conception of resistance-as-subversion is pointed up by her overall strategy of argument, namely her choice to not debate competing accounts of political resistance, but rather cast her argument in terms of epistemological/ontological issues divorced from political debate.' Kathy Miriam, 'Re-Thinking Radical Feminism: Opposition, Utopianism and "Moral Imagination"' (PhD diss., University of California, 1998), 135.
107 Catharine A. MacKinnon, 'Points against Postmodernism', *Chicago-Kent Law Review* 57.3 (2000), 693.
108 'At the heart of current debates lie divergent understandings of the *ontology* of the categories of "sex" and "gender" and conflicting understandings of their relationship.' Sally Hines, 'Sex Wars and (Trans) Gender Panics: Identity and Body Politics in Contemporary UK Feminism', *Sociological Review Monographs* 68.4 (2020): 699–717, here 700 (emphasis added).
109 MacKinnon, *Feminism Unmodified*, 82.
110 Admittedly, this is not quite how MacKinnon (ibid.) puts it. She writes: 'You might think that's too broad. I'm not talking about sending all of

you men to jail for that. I'm talking about attempting to change the nature of the relations between women and men by having women ask ourselves: "Did I feel violated?" To me, part of the culture of sexual inequality that makes women not report rape is that the definition of rape is not based on our sense of our violation.'
111 Améry, 'On the Necessity and Impossibility of Being a Jew', 21.
112 Ellis, 'Stories without Endings', 45.

Notes to Chapter 7
1. As MacKinnon writes, 'by comparison with our agenda, it was playing with, or within, blocks'. MacKinnon, 'Points against Postmodernism', 691.
2. Butler explicitly rejects the possibility of something new: 'the postmodern ought not be confused with the new; after all, the pursuit of the "new" is the preoccupation of high modernism; if anything, the postmodern casts doubt upon the possibility of a "new" that is not in some way already implicated in the "old".' 'Contingent Foundations', 39. Foucault does more than cast doubt when he claims that 'to imagine another system is to extend our participation in the present system'. Michel Foucault, *Language, Counter-Memory, Practice: Selected Essays and Interviews* (Ithaca: Cornell University Press, 1977), 230.
3. See Catharine A. MacKinnon, 'Does Sexuality Have a History?', *Michigan Quarterly Review* 30.1 (1991), 2.
4. Ibid., 5.
5. Richard Rorty, 'Feminism and Pragmatism', *Michigan Quarterly Review* 30.2 (1991), 234.
6. For a man to have sex with a woman is for him to *have* her. See Beauvoir, *The Second Sex*, 397; Dworkin, *Intercourse*, 79–80; Millett, *Sexual Politics*, 6.
7. Sara Garcia, 'Most Australian Women Still Take Husband's Name after Marriage, Professor Says', ABC Radio Adelaide, 26 April 2016, https://www.abc.net.au/news/2016-03-31/most-australian-women-still-take-husbands-name-after-marriage/7287022.
8. 'We find ourselves having to *teach* – through programs such as Respectful Relationships – men that they are obligated to respect women's refusal and women that they are entitled to refuse.' Victorian Government, 'Respectful Relationships', 20 December 2022, https://www.vic.gov.au/respectful-relationships#for-educators.
9. In the television series *Les Papillons Noirs* (*Black Butterflies*), a woman's boyfriend murders men who attempt to rape her.

10. See Tamara L. Tompkins, 'Prosecuting Rape as a War Crime: Speaking the Unspeakable', *Notre Dame Law Review* 70.4 (1994): 845–890.
11. MacKinnon, 'Does Sexuality Have a History?', 6.
12. Butler, *Gender Trouble*, 43.
13. Ibid.
14. Ibid.
15. Ibid., xxxi.
16. Sheila Jeffreys, *Gender Hurts: A Feminist Analysis of the Politics of Transgenderism* (London: Routledge, 2014), 42–43.
17. Butler, *Gender Trouble*, 169. 'Performativity describes this relation of being implicated in that which one opposes, this turning of power against itself to produce alternative modalities of power, to establish a kind of political contestation that is not a "pure" opposition, a "transcendence" of contemporary relations of power, but a difficult labour of forging a future from resources inevitably impure.' Butler, *Bodies That Matter*, 184.
18. Delphy, 'Rethinking Sex and Gender', 6.
19. 'I am not interested in delivering judgments on what distinguishes the subversive from the unsubversive.' Butler, *Gender Trouble*, xxii.
20. Nancy Fraser, 'False Antitheses', in *Feminist Contentions*, 71.
21. 'I prefer to reserve the term Lesbian to describe women who are woman-identified, having rejected false loyalties to men on all levels. The terms gay or female homosexual more accurately describe women who, although they relate genitally to women, give their allegiance to men and male myths, ideologies, styles, practices, institutions, and professions.' Daly, *Gyn/Ecology*, 26.
22. Wittig, 'One Is Not Born a Woman', 108.
23. Butler, *Gender Trouble*, 42.
24. Ibid.
25. 'Radical feminism is not reconciliation with the father. Rather it is affirming our original birth, our original source, movement, surge of living. This finding of our original integrity is re-membering our Selves. Daly, *Gyn/Ecology*, 39. Similarly, Radicalesbians wrote: 'Together we must find, reinforce, and validate our authentic selves ... We feel a real-ness, feel at last we are coinciding with ourselves. With that real self, with that consciousness, we begin a revolution to end the imposition of all coercive identifications, and to achieve maximum autonomy in human expression.' Radicalesbians, 'The Woman-Identified Woman', Duke University, 1970, https://repository.duke.edu/dc/wlmpc/wlmms0 1011.

26 Butler, *Gender Trouble*, 42.
27 Daly, *Gyn/Ecology*, 1.
28 Ibid., 340.
29 Ibid., 353.
30 Ibid., 340.
31 Ibid., 337.
32 Gatens, *Feminism and Philosophy*, 83.
33 Rorty speaks of 'creative misuses of language – familiar words used in ways which initially sound crazy'. 'Feminism and Pragmatism', 233.
34 Butler, *Gender Trouble*, 42.
35 Ailbhe Smyth, 'Haystacks in My Mind or How to Stay SAFE (Sane, Angry and Feminist) in the 1990s', in Gabriele Griffin, ed., *Feminist Activism in the 1990s* (London: Routledge, 1995), 194.
36 'As a society, we are more progressive: two-thirds of young women identify as feminists; to say so when I was a teen would have been unthinkable.' Sirin Kale, '"I Was Worried Lindsay, Paris, or Britney Would Die": Why the 00s Were So Toxic for Women', *The Guardian*, 6 March 2021, https://www.theguardian.com/culture/2021/mar/06/why-the-00s-were-so-toxic-for-women. Kale cites the results of a survey carried out for Young Women's Trust: 'Young Women's Feminism and Activism 2019', https://www.youngwomenstrust.org/wp-content/uploads/2020/11/Young-womens-feminism-and-activism-2019-report.pdf.

Notes to Chapter 8

1 Kathleen Stock, 'Is Womanhood a Social Fact?', in Alice Sullivan and Selina Todd, eds, *Sex and Gender: A Contemporary Reader* (Abingdon: Routledge, 2024), 51–68. Stock concludes (66): 'In some quarters, including many feminist ones, it has become popular to say that womanhood is a social fact. Prolonged examination of this claim has established no good reason to agree. Womanhood is a natural fact, if any is.'
2 Iris Marion Young, 'Throwing Like a Girl: A Phenomenology of Feminine Body Comportment, Motility, and Spatiality', in her *On Female Body Experience: Throwing Like a Girl and Other Essays* (New York: Oxford University Press, 1990), 27–45.
3 Caroline Criado-Perez, *Invisible Women: Exposing Data Bias in a World Designed for Men* (London: Chatto & Windus, 2019).
4 Alyson J. McGregor, *Sex Matters: How Male-Centric Medicine Endangers Women's Health and What We Can Do about It* (New York: Hachette, 2020); Gabrielle Jackson, *Pain and Prejudice: A Call to Arms for Women and Their Bodies* (Sydney: Allen & Unwin, 2019).

5 MacKinnon, 'Exploring Transgender Law and Politics'.
6 Quoted in Stock, *Material Girls*, 245–246.
7 Stock, *Material Girls*, 102–103.
8 Ibid., 103.
9 Janice Raymond distinguishes sex separation from sex segregation, defining the former as separation by women's choice and the latter as separation imposed on women. See Janice Raymond, *A Passion for Friends: Toward a Philosophy of Female Affection* (North Melbourne: Spinifex Press, 2001), 143.
10 Daly captures the difference between minority group and class and argues that women are the latter: 'I am suggesting that the women's movement is more than a group governed by central authority in conflict with other such hierarchical groups. If it were only this it would be only one more subgroup within the all-embracing patriarchal "family". What we are about is the human becoming of that half of the human race that has been excluded from humanity by sexual definition.' Daly, *Beyond God the Father*, 35.
11 Ellen Pence and Melanie Shepard, 'Integrating Feminist Theory and Practice: The Challenge of the Battered Women's Movement', in Kersti Yllö and Michele Bograd, eds, *Feminist Perspectives on Wife Abuse* (Newbury Park, CA: Sage Publications, 1988), 285, quoting Ellen Pence, *Criminal Justice Response to Domestic Assault Cases: A Guide for Policy Development* (Duluth, MN: Domestic Abuse Intervention Project, 1985), 2. According to Baldwin, '[t]he feminist shelter movement was the "first line" mobilization of these insights, founded on the understanding that new feminist institutions and strategies for women's empowerment were necessary to provide women with options other than to "stay", or to move on to other domestic arrangements where she would be vulnerable to the same treatment. Shelters were envisioned as the necessary first step; the overall vision the crafting of intervention politics intended structurally "to alter the power system which creates the foundation of battering behavior".' Margaret A. Baldwin, 'Split at the Root: Prostitution and Feminist Discourses of Law Reform', *Yale Journal of Law and Feminism* 5 (1992): 74–75.
12 '[T]he public representations of claims by subordinate groups, even in situations of conflict, nearly aways have a strategic or dialogic dimension that influences the form they take.' James C. Scott, *Domination and the Arts of Resistance: Hidden Transcripts* (New Haven, CT: Yale University Press, 1990), 92.

Notes to pp. 127–137   221

13 Susan Schechter, *Women and Male Violence: The Visions and Struggles of the Battered Women's Movement* (Boston, MA: South End Press, 1982), 42–43.
14 Ibid., 241–255.
15 Stock, *Material Girls*, 15–16.
16 'When the constructed status of gender is theorized as radically independent of sex, gender itself becomes a free-floating artifice, with the consequence that man and masculine might just as easily signify a female body as a male one, and woman and feminine a male body as easily as a female one.' Butler, *Gender Trouble*, 10.
17 Lili Elbe is the name adopted by Einar Wegener. As recounted in his 'memoir', Wegener was told by a doctor that he probably had both male and female organs; see Niels Hoyer, ed., *Man into Woman: The First Sex Change: A Portrait of Lili Elbe* (London: Blue Boat Books, 2004), 12–13, 27–28. The reliability of the memoir is questionable, as it was, we are told, compiled by Niels Hoyer 'partly from his own knowledge, partly from material dictated by Lili herself, partly from Lili's diaries, and partly from letters written by Lili and other persons concerned'. The doctor is said to have verified the account provided in the memoir (14).
18 Brownmiller, *Against Our Will*, 13–14.
19 MacKinnon, *Toward a Feminist Theory of the State*, 110.
20 Brownmiller, *Against Our Will*, 12.
21 MacKinnon, *Toward a Feminist Theory of the State*, 4.
22 Ibid., 140.
23 Delphy suggests that the difference between the two is a difference in certainty: the latter is 'prepared to abandon our certainties and to accept the (temporary) pain of an increased uncertainty about the world'. Delphy, 'Rethinking Sex and Gender', 1.
24 Mary Harrington, *Feminism against Progress* (Hampshire: Forum, 2023), 164. Harrington is quoting Nicolás Gómez Dávila: 'The true reactionary is not a seeker after abolished pasts, but a hunter of sacred shades on the eternal hills.'
25 Ibid., 199.
26 Ibid., 200.
27 'Acknowledging the biological differences between women and men is important if we are to understand their distinct needs and vulnerabilities (for example, women are on average physically weaker than men).' Alice Sullivan and Selina Todd, 'Introduction', in Alice Sullivan and Selina Todd, eds, *Sex and Gender: A Contemporary Reader* (Abingdon: Routledge, 2024), 2.

28 'There was a time when you were not a slave, remember that. You walked alone, full of laughter, you bathed bare-bellied. You say you have lost all recollection of it, remember ... You say there are no words to describe this time, you say it does not exist. But remember. Make an effort to remember. Or, failing that, invent.' Monique Wittig, *Les Guérillères* (London: Peter Owen, 1971), 89. The novel *Les Guérillères* is itself an act of such invention.

29 'Women's oppression is firstly based on their reproductive capacities, *because it is these capacities that mean they can be turned into a reproductive resource*. Women's oppression is not, however, biologically determined by these capacities, because the socio-cultural system which treats women as an appropriable resource is a historical development and is, therefore, contingent rather than necessary.' Jane Clare Jones, 'The History of Sex: Sex Denial and Gender Identity Ideology', in Alice Sullivan and Selina Todd, eds, *Sex and Gender: A Contemporary Reader* (Abingdon: Routledge, 2024), 75–76 (emphasis added).

30 MacKinnon, *Toward a Feminist Theory of the State*, 110.

31 Louise Perry, *The Case against the Sexual Revolution: A New Guide to Sex in the 21st Century* (Cambridge: Polity, 2022), 166–167; Harrington, *Feminism against Progress*, 211.

32 Harrington, *Feminism against Progress*, 212.

33 The following story, written by a student, emerged in the #MeToo movement:

> He slid inside me and I didn't say a word. At the time, I didn't know why. Maybe I didn't want to feel like I'd led him on. Maybe I didn't want to disappoint him. Maybe I just didn't want to deal with the 'let's do it, but no, we shouldn't' verbal tug-of-war that so often happens before sleeping with someone. It was easier to just do it. Besides, we were already in bed, and this is what people in bed do. I felt an *obligation*, a *duty* to go through with it. I felt guilty for not wanting to. I wasn't a virgin. I'd done this before. It shouldn't have been a big deal – it's just sex – so I didn't want to make it one. (https://medium.com/@totalsratmove?p=2194a96bdbb6, cited in Perry, *The Case against the Sexual Revolution*, 12; emphasis added)

The student was right to feel a sense of obligation, of duty. As the sexual subject of a man, she has a sexual duty to him.

34 Celia Kitzinger and Helen Frith, 'Just Say No? The Use of Conversation Analysis in Developing a Feminist Perspective on Sexual Refusal', *Discourse and Society* 10.3 (1999): 303–304.

35 Friedrich Nietzsche, 'On the Uses and Disadvantages of History for Life', in his *Untimely Meditations*, trans. R. J. Hollingdale (Cambridge: Cambridge University Press, 1983), 59.
36 Ibid., 62–63, esp. 63: 'This, precisely, is the proposition the reader is invited to meditate upon: the unhistorical and the historical are necessary in equal measure for the health of an individual, of a people, and of a culture'.
37 Harrington, *Feminism against Progress*, 195.
38 'We have no time or place to look back to.' Rowbotham, *Woman's Consciousness, Man's World*, 36.
39 'But nothing less than the most radical imagination will carry us beyond this place, beyond the mere struggle for survival, to that lucid recognition of our possibilities which will keep us impatient, and unresigned to mere survival.' Adrienne Rich, 'Motherhood: The Contemporary Emergency and the Quantum Leap', in her *On Lies, Secrets, and Silence: Selected Prose, 1966–1978* (New York: Norton, 1979), 273.
40 MacKinnon, *Toward a Feminist Theory of the State*, 104–105.
41 Andrea Dworkin, *Our Blood: Prophecies and Discourses on Sexual Politics* (New York: Perigee Books, 1981), 70.
42 Ibid.
43 Ibid.
44 Ibid., 71.
45 This would be consistent with Frye's claim that women are considered human in the sense of belonging to the species *Homo sapiens*, not in the sense of being a full person. A member of the species *Homo sapiens* is to be treated humanely; a full person is to be treated with respect. Frye, *The Politics of Reality*, 48.

Notes to Chapter 9
1 Dworkin, *Our Blood*, 61.
2 Daly, *Beyond God the Father*, 54.
3 Ibid.
4 Lawford-Smith, *Gender-Critical Feminism*, 143–164.
5 MacKinnon, *Toward a Feminist Theory of the State*, 116–117.
6 Ibid., 124.
7 Ibid.
8 'Men say women desire to be degraded; feminism sees female masochism as the ultimate success of male supremacy.' Ibid., 125.
9 Ibid., xvi.
10 Ibid.

11 Robin Morgan, 'Monster', in her *Monster* (New York: Vintage Books, 1972), 82.
12 Wollstonecraft, *A Vindication of the Rights of Woman*, 186.
13 Alexis Carrel, *Man, the Unknown* (New York: Harper & Brothers, 1939), 302.
14 Wittig, 'One Is Not Born a Woman', 105.
15 Adrienne Rich, 'Women and Honour: Some Notes on Lying' in her *On Lies, Secrets, and Silence: Selected Prose, 1966–1978* (New York: Norton, 1979), 188.
16 Jillian Spencer, child and adolescent psychiatrist, said: 'I think after the years of pressure and not being able to express these concerns, I just felt that I couldn't miss an opportunity to say them out loud. It's a really hard thing as a doctor to be in a position where you feel that you need to do an intervention that you don't agree with. And being able to speak aloud about it was a relief.' *Four Corners*, 'Blocked: The Battle over Youth Gender Care', ABC, 11 July 2023, https://www.abc.net.au/news/2023-07-11/blocked:-the-battle-over-youth-gender-care/102587506.
17 Rich, 'Women and Honour', 191.
18 Dworkin, *Intercourse*, 169.
19 'The first requirement for raising class consciousness is honesty, in private and in public, with ourselves and other women.' Redstockings, *Redstockings Manifesto* (New York: Redstockings, 7 July 1970). See also Kathie Sarachild, 'Consciousness-Raising: A Radical Weapon', in Redstockings, ed., *Feminist Revolution: An Abridged Edition with Additional Writings* (New York: Random House, 1978), 144–150; Kathie Sarachild, 'A Program for Feminist "Consciousness Raising"', in Shulamith Firestone and Anne Koedt, eds, *Notes from the Second Year: Women's Liberation: Major Writings of the Radical Feminists* (New York: Radical Feminism, 1970), 78–80; Lynn O'Connor, 'Defining Reality', *Tooth and Nail* 1.2 (1969): 8–11; Pamela Allen, *Free Space: A Perspective on the Small Group in Women's Liberation* (New York: Times Change Press, 1970); and Catharine A. MacKinnon, 'Consciousness Raising', in her *Toward a Feminist Theory of the State*, 83–105.
20 I am referring in general to Kellie-Jay Keen's Let Women Speak tour, and in particular to Let Women Speak in Melbourne, which took place on the steps of Parliament House and which I attended. A general description of the purpose of this tour can be found later in this chapter (p. 175).

21 Combahee River Collective, 'The Combahee River Collective: A Black Feminist Statement', in Zillah R. Eisenstein, ed., *Capitalist Patriarchy and the Case for Socialist Feminism* (New York: Monthly Review Press, 1979), 365–366.
22 Rowbotham, 'A Woman's Work Is Never Done', in her *Woman's Consciousness, Man's World*, 67–80; Pateman, *The Sexual Contract*, 136–41; Benston, 'The Political Economy of Women's Liberation', 13–27; Oakley, *Woman's Work*; Joan Acker, 'Gendered Organisations and Intersectionality: Problems and Possibilities', *Equality, Diversity and Inclusion: An International Journal* 31.3 (2012): 214–224.
23 MacKinnon, *Toward a Feminist Theory of the State*, 109.
24 Pateman, T*he Disorder of Women*, 9; Pateman, *The Sexual Contract*, 137–138. See Locke, 'The Second Treatise', 111.
25 Pateman, *The Sexual Contract*, 14.
26 Angela Y. Davis, *Women, Race, and Class* (London: Women's Press, 2001 [1981]), 5.
27 Ibid., 6: 'Expediency governed the slaveholders' posture toward female slaves: when it was profitable to exploit them *as if they were men*, they were regarded, in effect, *as genderless*, but when they could be exploited, punished and repressed in ways suited only for women, they were locked into their exclusively female roles' (emphasis added). Notice that Davis slides from 'as if they were men' to 'as genderless'. To be treated as *men* is to be treated as *genderless*, while to be treated as *women* is to be treated as *gendered*. This slide accurately reflects the duality of 'man': man as humanity and as male. As humanity, man is the genderless gender. As a departure from humanity, woman is the gendered gender.
28 Ibid., 7.
29 Ibid.
30 Angela Y. Davis, 'Rape, Racism, and the Capitalist Setting', *The Black Scholar* 12.6 (1981), 42 (emphasis added).
31 Ibid., 40.
32 Ibid., 39.
33 For discussion of this phenomenon, see Emily West, 'Reflections on the *History and Historians* of the Black Woman's Role in the Community of Slaves: Enslaved Women and Intimate Partner Sexual Violence', *American Nineteenth Century History* 19.1 (2018): 1–21; David Stefan Doddington, '"He Am Big and 'Cause He So He Think Everybody Do What Him Say"', in his *Contesting Slave Masculinity in the American South* (Cambridge: Cambridge University Press, 2018), 127–170;

and Herbert G. Gutman, *The Black Family in Slavery and Freedom, 1750–1925* (New York: Pantheon Books, 1976), 84–85.

34 'Working-class men, whatever their color, can be motivated to rape by the belief that their maleness has accorded them the privilege of dominating women.' Davis, 'Rape, Racism and the Capitalist Setting', 44.

35 Ibid.

36 Fraser, 'Beyond the Master/Subject Model', 179.

37 Miriam, 'Re-Thinking Radical Feminism', 11.

38 Antonio Gramsci, 'Discorso agli anarchici', *L'Ordine Nuovo* 4, 3–10 April 1920: 339–340, http://www.centrogramsci.it/riviste/nuovo/ordine%20nuovo%20p4.pdf. (An English translation under the title 'An Address to Anarchists' can be found at https://redsails.org/discorso-agli-anarchici.) Gramsci explicitly attributes this phrase to Romain Rolland.

39 Davis, *Women, Race, and Class*, 23.

40 Ibid., 175.

41 Davis, 'Rape, Racism and the Capitalist Setting', 42 (emphasis added).

42 Davis, *Women, Race and Class*, 24.

43 Ibid., 23.

44 It puts me in mind of the epigraph in Federici's *Wages against Housework* (1): 'They say it is love. We say it is unwaged work. They call it frigidity. We call it absenteeism.'

45 Dalla Costa and James, *The Power of Women and the Subversion of the Community*; Gimenez, 'Marxism and Feminism', 67; Nancy Chodorow, 'Mothering, Male Dominance, and Capitalism', in Zillah R. Eisenstein, ed., *Capitalist Patriarchy and the Case for Socialist Feminism* (New York: Monthly Review Press, 1979), 97.

46 Federici, *Wages against Housework*, 2.

47 Ibid., 1–2.

48 Ibid., 1.

49 Linda Babcock, Maria P. Recalde, and Lise Vesterlund, 'Why Women Volunteer for Tasks That Don't Lead to Promotions', *Harvard Business Review*, 16 July 2018, https://hbr.org/2018/07/why-women-volunteer-for-tasks-that-dont-lead-to-promotions; Linda Babcock, Maria P. Recalde, Lise Vesterlund, and Laurie Weingart, 'Gender Differences in Accepting and Receiving Requests for Tasks with Low Promotability', *American Economic Review* 107.3 (2017): 714–747.

50 Butler, 'Contingent Foundations', 49.

51 Federici, *Wages against Housework*, 8.

52 Combahee River Collective, 'The Combahee River Collective', 365.

53 'Hence one of the reasons for the surge of Afro-American women's writing during the 1970s and its emphasis on sexism in the black community is precisely that when the ideologues of the 1960s said *black*, they meant *black male*.' Barbara Christian, 'The Race for Theory', *Cultural Critique* 6 (1987), 60.
54 Mary Guyatt, 'The Wedgwood Slave Medallion: Values in Eighteenth-Century Design', *Journal of Design History* 13.2 (2000): 93–105. This may account for the neglect of rape in the 'traditional' literature on slavery. Davis, *Women, Race, and Class*, 25.
55 Amy Dru Stanley, 'Home Life and the Morality of the Market', in Melvyn Stokes and Stephen Conway, eds, *The Market Revolution in America: Social, Political, and Religious Expressions, 1800–1880* (Charlottesville: University Press of Virginia, 1996), 89.
56 Hazel V. Carby, *Reconstructing Womanhood: The Emergence of the Afro-American Woman Novelist* (New York: Oxford University Press, 1987), 39.
57 In Walker's short story 'Coming Apart' (177), a Black wife reads the following passage to her Black husband: 'After the Civil War, "popular justice" (which meant there usually was no trial and no proof needed) began its reign in the form of the castration, burning at the stake, beheading, and lynching of Black men. As many as 5,000 white people turned out to witness these events, as though going to a celebration ... Over 2,000 Black men were lynched in the ten-year period from 1889–1899 [sic]. There were also a number of Black women who were lynched. (*She reads this sentence quickly and forgets it.*)' Her husband, the narrator tells us, 'cannot imagine a woman being lynched. He has never even considered the possibility. Perhaps this is why the image of a Black woman chained and bruised excites rather than horrifies him?'. Lynching is the symbol of the oppression of Black *people*, and yet the lynching of Black *women* cannot be countenanced, either by the 'womanist' wife or by her husband (ibid., 175).
58 Combahee River Collective, 'The Combahee River Collective', 366.
59 Mumininas of Committee for Unified Newark, *Mwanamke Mwananchi (The Nationalist Woman)* (Newark, NJ: Mumininas of CFUN, 1971), 4, 5.
60 'The house/family is the smallest example of how the nation works.' Ibid., 3.
61 Pateman, *The Sexual Contract*.
62 Mumininas of Committee for Unified Newark, *Mwanamke Mwananchi*, 12–14.

63 Ibid., 8.
64 Combahee River Collective, 'The Combahee River Collective', 368–369.
65 Frances Beal is wrong when she writes that 'black women are not resentful of the rise to power of black men. We welcome it. We see in it the eventual liberation of all black people from this oppressive system of capitalism. Nevertheless, this does not mean that you have to negate one for the other. This kind of thinking is a product of miseducation; that it's either X or it's Y. It is fallacious reasoning that in order for the black man to be strong, the black woman has to be weak.' Frances Beal, 'Double Jeopardy: To Be Black and Female', *Meridians: Feminism, Race, Transnationalism* 8.2 (2008), 169. Black men's freedom *is* Black women's subjection to Black men.
66 Mumininas of Committee for Unified Newark, *Mwanamke Mwananchi*, 6.
67 Luisah Teish, 'A Quiet Subversion', in Laura Lederer, ed., *Take Back the Night: Women on Pornography* (Toronto: Bantam Books, 1982), 107.
68 Walker, 'Coming Apart', 169–170.
69 Ibid., 171.
70 Ibid., 175.
71 Ibid.
72 Ibid., 172.
73 Ibid., 173.
74 Ibid., 171.
75 'What we see in the panic surrounding Mumsnet and grassroots organisations such as Fair Play for Women and For Women Scotland is an effort to depict the refusal of female people to be "unconditionally accessible" as an act of dominance rather than the challenge to "unconditional access" that it actually is.' Victoria Smith, *Hags: The Demonisation of Middle-aged Women* (London: Fleet, 2023), 223: just as the husband in 'Coming Apart' feels *oppressed* by his wife's denial of access, so trans women, Smith suggests in *Hags*, feel *dominated* by women's denial of access. I would make the point, though, that under patriarchy a woman who denies a man access to her *is* a woman who denies him his freedom. Neither the husband nor trans women are wrong to feel oppressed or dominated. This does not vindicate their demands of women as much as it exposes the operative conception of freedom: freedom is the freedom of men to access women and the freedom of women to grant men access. Women who deny men access exercise a freedom above and beyond that to which they are entitled;

men who are denied access by women are deprived of a freedom to which they are entitled. As Smith (222) writes, '[a]nger at modern-day covens is anger at the failure of members to behave as non-people should.'

76 Alice Walker, 'Coming Apart', in Laura Lederer, ed., *Take Back the Night: Women on Pornography* (Toronto: Bantam Books, 1982), 84. All the other quotations are from the 1994 volume listed earlier, in chapter 3.

77 Mumininas of Committee for Unified Newark, *Mwanamke Mwananchi*, 6.

78 'White western feminisms are predicated on sex and gender differences; they are part of the ontological basis of feminism that informs theory making. An effect of theorising about sex and gender differences is the creation of the universal woman: white, middle-class and heterosexual, whose life is oppressed under patriarchy.' Aileen Moreton-Robinson, *Talkin' up to the White Woman: Indigenous Women and Feminism* (Minneapolis: University of Minnesota Press, 2021), 32.

79 Sojourner Truth, 'Ain't I a Woman?' Speech delivered at the Women's Convention in Akron, Ohio, 1851.

80 'Prostitution isn't like anything else. Rather, everything else is like prostitution because it is the model for women's condition.' Evelina Giobbe, 'Confronting the Liberal Lies about Prostitution', in Dorchen Leidholdt and Janice G. Raymond, eds, *The Sexual Liberals and the Attack on Feminism* (New York: Teachers College Press, 1990), 76.

81 See for example Pateman, *The Sexual Contract*. The Marxist feminist literature that focuses on the housewife also implicitly treats the wife as the paradigmatic woman.

82 Larissa Behrendt, 'Aboriginal Women and the White Lies of the Feminist Movement: Implications for Aboriginal Women in Rights Discourse', *Australian Feminist Law Journal* 1 (1993), 37.

83 Srinivasan writes:

> On its face, the notion of 'common oppression' contains a promise of universal women's solidarity. The rich woman and the poor woman, the citizen and the refugee, the white woman and the black and brown woman, the high-caste woman and the Dalit woman: all women are oppressed on the basis of their sex, and this will be the foundation of their empathetic and strategic alliance. But it is precisely those forms of harm that are not common to all women – those from which some women, by virtue of their wealth, race, citizenship status or caste, are

insulated – that are the most grievous to the woman who suffer them
... Carceral approaches to gender justice tend to presuppose a subject
who is a 'pure' case of women's 'common oppression', uncomplicated by
such factors as class and race. The ... belief that incarceration is the way
to deal with domestic violence does not take into account the women
whose fates are bound up with the men who perpetrate it: the women
who are financially dependent on the men who beat them, and who
have a large stake in how the men in their community are treated by the
police, courts or prisons. (Srinivasan, *The Right to Sex*, 162)

It does not occur to Srinivasan that feminists might take into account the women whose fates are bound up with the men who perpetrate domestic violence, that they might conclude that an unimprisoned violent partner is a graver threat to a woman than the loss of income (assuming that he shares his income with her) – presumably because it does not occur to her that an unimprisoned violent partner can be a graver threat to a woman than the loss of income. In addition, to say that the imprisonment of a violent partner means loss of income for the victim assumes that it is not he who is responsible for her financial dependence. Often he is. He forbids her from working, sabotages her efforts to get work (e.g. by refusing to provide childcare while she attends a job interview), sabotages her efforts to go to work (e.g. by stealing her car keys), and, if she does succeed, demands that she give him her pay. His imprisonment, then, is the removal of a major impediment to her financial independence. See Adrienne E. Adams, Cris M. Sullivan, Deborah Bybee, and Megan R. Greeson, 'Development of the Scale of Economic Abuse', *Violence Against Women* 14.5 (2008): 563–588, esp. 565–566, 571. Similarly, Beal writes: 'Any white group that does not have an anti-imperialist and anti-racist ideology has *absolutely nothing in common* with the black women's struggle'; 'If the white groups do not realise that they are[,] in fact, fighting capitalism and racism, we do not have common bonds.' 'Double Jeopardy', 174. Why are anti-imperialism, anti-racism, and anti-capitalism common causes, but anti-patriarchy is not?

84 'Most of the women's groups are *bourgeois*, unconscious or unconcerned with class struggle and the exploitation of working women ... their direction leads to a middle-class single-issue movement ... Instead of integrating (not submerging) the struggles of women into the broader revolutionary movement, these women are flailing at their own middle class images. To focus only on sexual exploitation ... does

not develop a mass understanding of the causes of oppression, and it does not accurately point at the enemy.' Bernardine Dohrn, 'Toward a Revolutionary Women's Movement', *New Left Notes* 4.9 (8 March 1969) (emphasis added).
85 Behrendt, 'Aboriginal Women and the White Lies of the Feminist Movement', 29–30.
86 Ibid., 28.
87 Pateman, *The Sexual Contract*.
88 MacKinnon, 'Points against Postmodernism', 699; Susan Moller Okin, Joshua Cohen, Matthew Howard, and Martha C. Nussbaum, *Is Multiculturalism Bad for Women?* (Princeton, NJ: Princeton Unuiversity Press, 1999); Katha Pollitt, 'Whose Culture?', *Boston Review*, 1 October 1997, https://www.bostonreview.net/forum_res ponse/katha-pollitt-whose-culture.
89 Behrendt, 'Aboriginal Women and the White Lies of the Feminist Movement', 34, 37, 44.
90 Ibid., 43.
91 'The emphasis on Sisterhood was often seen as the emotional appeal masking the opportunism of manipulative bourgeois white women.' bell hooks, 'Sisterhood: Political Solidarity between Women', *Feminist Review* 23 (1986), 127.
92 Behrendt, 'Aboriginal Women and the White Lies of the Feminist Movement', 31.
93 Rich writes of the race blindness of white women: 'Marginalized though we have been as women, as white and Western makers of theory, we also marginalize others because our lived experience is thoughtlessly white.' Adrienne Rich, 'Notes toward a Politics of Location', in her *Blood, Bread, and Poetry* (New York: Norton, 1994), 219.
94 Judith Kelly, 'Talk Given at the 2022 Women Lawyers' Drinks on the Supreme Court Balcony', talk delivered to the Supreme Court of the Northern Territory, 26 August 2022, https://supremecourt.nt.gov.au/__data/assets/pdf_file/0013/1132015/2022-Women-Lawyers-drinks.pdf.
95 'The difficulty of saying "I" – a phrase from the East German novelist Christa Wolf. But once having said it, as we realize the necessity to go further, isn't here a difficulty of saying "we"? You cannot speak for me. I cannot speak for us. Two thoughts: *there is no liberation that only knows how to say "I"*; there is no collective movement that speaks for each of us all the way through.' Rich, 'Notes toward a Politics of Location', 224 (emphasis added).

96 "'Women have always lied to each other." "Women have always whispered the truth to each other." Both of these axioms are true.' Rich, 'Women and Honor', 189.
97 See Raymond, *A Passion for Friends*, 117–147.
98 Maria H. A. Jaschok, 'On the Lives of Women Unwed by Choice in Pre-Communist China: Research in Progress', *Republican China* 10.1A (1984), 43.
99 Marjorie Topley, 'Marriage Resistance in Rural Kwangtung', in Jean DeBernardi, ed., *Cantonese Society in Hong Kong and Singapore: Gender, Religion, Medicine, and Money* (Aberdeen, Hong Kong: Hong Kong University Press, 2011 [1978]), 423–446, esp. 423.
100 Raymond, *A Passion for Friends*, 126; Topley, 'Marriage Resistance in Rural Kwangtung', 432. Yet Jaschok writes of marriage resisters as 'women who resisted marriage, who formed sisterhoods, who lived in separate women's houses, who lived in lesbian relationships, *who purchased mooijai (slave-girls) to perform the role of wife and mother on their behalf*'. 'On the Lives of Women Unwed by Choice in Pre-Communist China', 43 (emphasis added). This complicates the claim that marriage resisters were loyal to women.
101 Toni Morrison, *Beloved* (London: Vintage, 2005), 38–42, 92–100.
102 We are made to understand (ibid., 90) that it was in Amy's economic interest to turn Sethe over: 'She took Ma'am to that lean-to and rubbed her feet for her, so that was one thing. And Ma'am believed she wasn't going to turn her over. You could get money if you turned a runaway over, and she wasn't sure this girl Amy didn't need money more than anything, especially since all she talked about was getting hold of some velvet.'
103 E. Sylvia Pankhurst, *The Suffragette: The History of the Women's Militant Suffrage Movement, 1905–1910* (Boston, MA: The Woman's Journal, 1911), 24–39; Andrew Rosen, *Rise Up, Women! The Militant Campaign of the Women's Social and Political Union, 1903–1914* (London: Routledge & Kegan Paul, 1974); Laura E. Nym Mayhall, *The Militant Suffrage Movement: Citizenship and Resistance in Britain, 1860–1930* (Oxford: Oxford University Press, 2003).
104 Susan Glaspell, *Trifles* (New York: Frank Shay, 1916).
105 Judith Van Allen, 'Aba Riots or the Igbo Women's War? Ideology, Stratification and the Invisibility of Women', *Ufahamu: A Journal of African Studies* 6.1 (1975), 11–39.
106 Jonathan Moss, 'The Ford Sewing Machinists' Strike, 1968, Dagenham', in his *Women, Workplace Protest and Political Identity*

in England, 1968–85 (Manchester: Manchester University Press, 2019), 56–81.
107 O'Connor, 'Defining Reality', 8–11; Allen, *Free Space*; MacKinnon, 'Consciousness Raising', 83–105; Susan Brownmiller, *In Our Time: Memoir of a Revolution* (New York: Dial Press, 1999).
108 'African American Women in Defence of Ourselves', *New York Times*, 17 November 1991.
109 Gulabi Gang website, 'History', 2016, https://gulabigang.in/history.php.
110 Brendan O'Neill, 'The Shameful Persecution of Posie Parker in New Zealand', *Spectator*, 25 March 2023, https://www.spectator.co.uk/article/the-shameful-persecution-of-posie-parker-in-new-zealand; Amy Landsey, '"Worst Place": Anti-Trans Rights Activist Posie Parker Hits Out at New Zealand after Fleeing the Country', Sky News, 26 March 2023, https://www.skynews.com.au/australia-news/politics/worst-place-antitrans-rights-activist-posie-parker-hits-out-at-new-zealand-after-fleeing-the-country/news-story/2054d3619e3423281c05c4540baba67d; Liam Beatty, 'Anti-Trans Activist Posie Parker's Parting Shots after Fleeing NZ Protests', *Australian*, 26 March 2023, https://www.theaustralian.com.au/news/latest-news/antitrans-activist-posie-parkers-parting-shots-after-fleeing-nz-protests/news-story/776167c8110a8660ba44c730c5c6cfcf; Lauren Ferri, 'Independent-Liberal MP Moira Deeming Opens Up on "Public Stoning"', *Australian*, 19 August 2023, https://www.theaustralian.com.au/breaking-news/independentliberal-mp-moira-deeming-opens-up-on-public-stoning/news-story/21d099a400d1afe024051ac09ca6530d; Reilly Sullivan, 'University of Melbourne Lecturer Targeted by Trans Activists after Attending Let Women Speak Rally', Sky News, 15 May 2023, https://www.skynews.com.au/australia-news/university-of-melbourne-lecturer-targeted-by-trans-activists-after-attending-let-women-speak-rally/news-story/6a3da4c444ee5fdea23fc8eb40f57a4f.
111 Smith identifies another instance in Mumsnet; see Victoria Smith, 'Plotting Hag', in her *Hags*, 196–229.
112 Arthur Smith, *Village Life in China: A Study in Sociology* (New York: Revell, 1899), 287, as quoted in Raymond, *A Passions for Friends*, 119.
113 Gay L. Gullickson, 'When Death Became Thinkable', *Journal of Social History* 51.2 (2017): 364–386.
114 Emmeline Pankhurst observed that Irish men who revolted against the British were deemed *political* criminals, while Irish women were deemed *ordinary* criminals. Interestingly, this was so even though

Irish women fought for the independence of Irish *people*, which is to say, Irish *men* ('when women, helping the men, got into the coils of the law, all those women in Ireland who were helping the men to get home rule, were invariably treated as ordinary criminals and got ordinary criminals' treatment'). Pankhurst, 'Freedom or Death'. Imagine, then, how women who fight for *women* might be seen.

115 Glaspell, *Trifles*, 10.
116 Ibid., 16.
117 Van Allen, 'Aba Riots or the Igbo Women's War?', 11–12: 11–39.
118 Interestingly, the Igbo call it 'the Women's War': ibid., 11.
119 Sophia Siddiqui, 'Feminism, Biological Fundamentalism and the Attack on Trans Rights', Race and Class Blog, Institute of Race Relations, 3 June 2021, https://irr.org.uk/article/feminism-biological-fundamentalism-attack-on-trans-rights.
120 Frye, 'History and Responsibility', 216–217.
121 Morgan, 'Light Bulbs, Radishes, and the Politics of the 21st Century', 8.
122 Roxanne Dunbar, 'Female Liberation as the Basis for Social Revolution', in Robin Morgan, ed., *Sisterhood Is Powerful: An Anthology of Writings from the Women's Liberation Movement* (New York: Vintage Books, 1970), 492.
123 Adrienne Rich, 'Notes toward a Politics of Location', 217.

Notes to Conclusion

1 Robert Filmer, *Patriarcha and Other Political Works* (Oxford: Basil Blackwell, 1949).
2 'This was part and parcel of Locke's liberal politics – the family was a private association which preceded civil society and into which the state should not intrude. Precisely because he did view it as distinct from the political association, perhaps, Locke was able to maintain that the husband should exercise rule as "the abler and the stronger", while he rejected any such argument with respect to political authority.' Mary Lyndon Shanley, 'Marriage Contract and Social Contract in Seventeenth Century English Political Thought', *Western Political Quarterly* 32.1 (1979), 91.
3 Hegel, *The Philosophy of Right*, 172.
4 Ibid., 59–60.
5 Jean-Jacques Rousseau, *Emile or On Education*, trans. Allan Bloom (New York: Basic Books, 1979).
6 Frederick Engels, *Condition of the Working Class in England in 1844* (New York: J. W. Lovell, 1887), 122.

7 Joyce Trebilcot, 'Conceiving Women: Notes on the Logic of Feminism', *Sinister Wisdom* 11 (1979): 43–50; Dale Spender, *Man Made Language* (London: Routledge & Kegan Paul, 1980); Adrienne Rich, 'Power and Danger: *The Work of a Common Woman* by Judy Grahn', in *The Work of a Common Woman: The Collected Poetry of Judy Grahn, 1964–1977* (Trumansburg, NY: Crossing Press, 1980), 7; Daly, *Beyond God the Father*; Frye, *The Politics of Reality*, 105–108, 81; and Mary Daly, *Websters' First New Intergalactic Wickedary of the English Language* (Boston, MA: Beacon Press, 1987).
8 Barry, *Female Sexual Slavery*.
9 Alice Walker, 'In Search of Our Mothers' Gardens', in Angelyn Mitchell, ed., *Within the Circle: An Anthology of African American Literary Criticism from the Harlem Renaissance to the Present* (Durham, NC: Duke University Press, 1994), 401–409, here 402.
10 Ellis, 'Stories without Endings', 38.
11 Kate Manne, *Down Girl: The Logic of Misogyny* (Oxford: Oxford University Press, 2018). Manne defines misogyny as 'the "law enforcement" branch of a patriarchal order, which has the overall function of policing and enforcing its governing ideology' (63). Compare this with Dworkin: 'repulsion for woman . . . is literal and linear: directed especially against her genitals, also her breasts, also her mouth newly perceived as a sex organ. It is a goose-stepping hatred of cunt.' *Intercourse*, 9.
12 Maria Eriksson Baaz and Maria Stern, 'Curious Erasures: The Sexual in Wartime Sexual Violence', *International Feminist Journal of Politics* 20.3 (2018): 295–314. Baaz and Stern observe the erasure of the sexual nature of rape in theorisations of wartime rape. This erasure is curious, given the feminist criticism (see MacKinnon, *Toward a Feminist Theory of the State*, 173–174) of the theorisation of rape as violence, not as sex (see Brownmiller, *Against Our Will*, 439).

Index

Aba riots 176–7
abolitionism 159–60, 163, 164
Alcoff, Linda 81
Améry, Jean 112
  political conception of Jews 106–7, 108, 110
Atkinson, Ti-Grace 1, 7, 10, 33–4, 76, 90
Australia
  white Australian and Indigenous Australian women 166–73

Barbour, Almanina 33–4, 90
bathrooms
  and gender inclusion 63, 109
Beauvoir, Simone de 5, 6, 9–10, 20, 30, 39, 76, 129
Behrendt, Larissa 166–8
Benenson, Joyce 140
Benhabib, Seyla 86
Benjamin, Walter 3
biology
  biological organisms and sex 23, 24
  and gender-critical feminism 3, 4, 124–5, 128–30, 132, 134–8
  and rape 17–20, 134
  and sex classes 13–14, 17
biopower 32, 43, 45, 48

bisexual bodies 57
Black feminism
  Combahee River Collective 151–2, 159–61, 162–3
Black Lives Matter 79
Black men 159–60, 161, 162–4
Black women
  enslaved 152–5, 160
  and women choosing women 161–4, 173, 175
  see also Indigenous women
Bordo, Susan 36–7, 55, 86, 90
  Unbearable Weight 33, 34, 35
Boston, Uriah 159–60
Britain
  and the Women's War (1929) in Nigeria 174, 176–7
Brodribb, Somar 86
Brown, Wendy 62–3
Brownmiller, Susan 17–20, 134, 153
Buber, Martin 2
Butler, Judith 73–82, 129, 158
  on culture and women's oppression 49
  and feminism 78–9, 82
  the displacement of 60–2
  and gender inclusion 64–6, 67, 74–5, 78
  Gender Trouble 37, 73–4, 75–6

Index

on the performance of a gender 117–19
on political lesbianism 119–20
and poststructural feminism 57, 58, 59
refusal to define 'woman' 90–9
on sex and gender 29–30, 100
on 'sex' as a regulatory ideal 56
on sexuality 101
see also poststructural feminism

capitalism
 and class 11–12, 13, 34
 and inclusion 62
 and Marxist theory 54
Carby, Hazel 160
Catholic women 169–70
childbirth 26
children
 biology and sex class 13–14
China
 marriage resistance movement 173, 175–6
chromosome account of sex 22
citizenship
 and difference feminism 68
 and male rights 31–2
 of men 180
class
 and capitalism 11–12, 13, 34
 and differences among women 86
 gender as 69–71
 and gender inclusion 64–5
 and gender-critical feminism 136
 and hierarchical relationships 180–1
 and the liberation of women 63–4
 and male dominance 154
 Marxism and the class struggle 10–11
 and second-wave feminism 112, 127
 and women choosing women 165, 167–8
 working-class women 71, 78
 see also sex class
class consciousness 110
cluster account of sex 22

Coleridge, Samuel Taylor 53
Combahee River Collective 151–2, 159–61, 162–3
consciousness-raising groups 91, 150, 175
contemporary feminism
 and second-wave feminism 79, 111–12
 and women choosing women 171–2
contraceptive pill 138, 139
cultural differences
 and poststructural feminism 49–50

Dahl, Robert 7
Dalla Costa, Mariarosa 74, 94
Daly, Mary 94, 106, 146
 Gyn/Ecology 91, 104–6, 120–1
Davis, Angela Y. 153–5
Delphy, Christine 25–6, 67–9, 76
 on difference feminists and equality feminists 67–9, 71–2
 'The Main Enemy' 34
Derrida, Jacques 112
difference feminists
 and equality feminists 67–9, 71–2
differences among women
 and poststructural feminism 82, 85–6
displacement of feminism 77, 84–7
displacement of politics 77
'dominance' model of the sexes 24
dual systems theory 44
Dworkin, Andrea 7, 26–7, 39, 58, 76, 79–80, 145, 150
 on the female person 101–4
 and gender-critical feminism 143–4

education
 and the social construction of women 5
Elbe, Lili 133
Elizabeth I, Queen 103
Ellis, Kate 112

enemies
  and extreme conflict 108
  men as the enemy 34–6, 76–7, 104
  see also friend–enemy distinction
Engels, Friedrich 13, 180
  Socialism: Utopian and Scientific 12
epicism, feminist 52
equality feminists
  and difference feminists 67–9, 71–2
erotic relations
  and the political 8–10
essentialism 85, 86–7, 99
  and gender-critical feminism 130–1

factionalisation
  and feminist attempts to define 'woman' 97–9
Federici, Sylvia
  Wages against Housework 156–7, 158
female body
  and sexual intercourse 101–2
  violability of 102–3
female sex
  and rape 17–20
  and sex class 9, 15–16, 17
femininity
  performance of 118
  and the sex–gender discourse 30–1, 33
Ferguson, Kathy 52
Filmer, Robert 179
Firestone, Shulamith 7, 12, 13–14, 35, 52, 76, 94, 130
  The Dialectic of Sex 74
Folbre, Nancy 52
Ford sewing machinists' strike 175
Foucault, Michel 34, 36, 43, 44, 114
  Butler on 75
  and the depoliticisation of feminism 86–7
  Foucauldian theory and feminism 47
  on power 38–41
  The History of Sexuality 32–3
Fraser, Nancy 36, 41–2, 43, 47–8, 53, 59, 154
  evaluation of second-wave feminism 50–2
  and Nicholson, Linda, 'Social Criticism without Philosophy' 82–4
freedom
  feminism as a political movement 1
  and gender-critical feminism 142
  and the history of sexuality 115
  and second-wave feminism 4, 182
  and women choosing women 178
  and women's liberation 63–4
  for workers 180
French feminism 67
Freud, Sigmund 114
friend–enemy distinction 76–80, 89–90, 108
  engagement with the political other 105–6
  and the female body 102
  and the feminist definition of 'woman' 97, 98
  and group identification 91–2
  and second-wave feminism 99–100
  and women as a political category 99
Frye, Marilyn 31, 61, 94, 95, 177

gamete account of sex 22
Gatens, Moira 102–3, 104–5, 120–1
  'A Critique of the Sex/Gender Distinction' 35–6
gender
  'butch' and 'femme' 64, 117–18
  diversification 60, 64, 65–6
  as identity and as class 69–71
  and poststructural feminism 58–9
  and sex 27, 29–32, 59
  sex–gender binary 63, 100–1, 128–9
gender affirmation 67
gender criticism 85
gender diversification 77–8, 80

Index

gender inclusion 60, 62–7, 74–5, 80, 108
gender injustice 71
gender-nonconforming people 76
gender studies 85
gender-critical feminism 3–4, 6, 123–44
  and biology 3, 4, 124–5
  conception of woman 1, 101
  definition of 'woman' 95–6, 99, 108
  and loyalty to women 92, 146
  and radical feminism 145–6
  and refuge for women 126–8
  and sex class 16, 69, 132, 135, 136, 139–41, 142–3, 145
  and sex as a construct 27–8
  and sex realism 135–6
  and trans women 66, 108–9, 110–11, 123–4, 128, 142–4
  and trans-inclusionary feminism 72, 123–5, 146
  and 'woman' as a gendered being 129–30
  and women choosing women 150–1, 177
  and women-only spaces 27–8, 124, 125–6
  and women's oppression 110
Glaspell, Susan
  Trifles 174, 176
Greer, Germaine 150
Grimshaw, Jean 104
Gulabi Gang 175

Harrington, Mary
  Feminism against Progress 135–6, 138, 140–1
Hartsock, Nancy 52, 87
health care
  and gender-critical feminism 124, 125
Hegel, G. W. F. 179–80
heterosexuality
  compulsory 76
  heterosexual relations 113–14, 147
Hill, Anita 175

history
  and gender-critical feminism 140–1
  and second-wave feminism 114–16
homosexual bodies 56–7
hooks, bell 90
housewives 155–9
human beings
  women as 61–2, 65, 94–6

Indigenous women
  Australian 166–73
  female sacred sites 168–9
inequality
  and sex class 21
intersectional feminists 98, 146–7, 181
intersex bodies 56, 57

James, Selma 74, 94
Jenkins, Katharine 69, 71
Jews, Améry's political conception of 106–7, 108, 110
Joan of Arc 102–3

Keen, Kellie-Jay 175

Lasswell, Harold 7
Lauretis, Teresa de 85, 86
Lawford-Smith, Holly 3, 29, 147, 150
lesbians 57
  political lesbianism 119–21
Let Women Speak 175
Locke, John 40, 179
love
  erotic love between man and woman 96–7
Lovibond, Sabina 87

MacIver, Robert 2
MacKinnon, Catharine 7, 15–17, 21, 23–4, 25–6, 39, 52, 53–4, 63, 92, 101, 103, 109–10
  on the dominant history of sexuality 114–15, 147–8
  on rape 134

MacKinnon, Catharine (*cont.*)
  Toward a Feminist Theory of the State 148
  on trans women 108
  on the violation of women 109–10, 111, 112
male bodies 108–9
  as human beings 61–2
male people
  and gender-critical feminism 123–4, 132–3, 140–1, 142
male sex class 8, 15–16
  and gender-critical feminism 142–3
man
  as a political category 7
marital rape 116, 166
marriage
  hierarchical relationship between husband and wife 179–80
  and second-wave feminism 116
Marx, Karl 35, 46, 145
  political reading of 54
Marxism 34, 44, 149
  class and second-wave feminism 10–12, 13, 15, 16–17
  and feminism 112
  and the poststructural turn 90
  and women choosing women 166, 167
Marxist feminism 44, 74, 145
  and housewives 155–7
masculinity
  and the sex–gender discourse 30–1, 33
mastery and subjection
  and sexual relations 41–3, 94, 115–16
maternity
  and attempts to define 'woman' 97, 98, 99
men
  Black men 159–61
  as the enemy 34–6, 105
  engaging with the political other 106
  and feminism as a political movement 1
  and gender-critical feminism 137–8, 140–1
  and hierarchical relationships 180–1
  and the sex–gender distinction 30
  and sexual relations as political 8–10
  and women choosing women 178
migrant women 166
Miller, Nancy 84
Millet, Kate 39, 58, 147
  on sexual relations as political 7, 8–9, 25
Miriam, Kathy 154
Modleski, Tania
  Feminism without Women 85–6
Moi, Toril 86–7
Morita, Seiya 96
morphological clusters 22, 23
Morrison, Tony
  Beloved 174
motherhood *see* maternity
Muminas of Committee for Unified Newark 161–2, 165

New York Radical Feminists 7
Nicholson, Linda 47–8, 50–2, 53, 59
  see also Fraser, Nancy
Nietzsche, Friedrich 121, 140
Nigeria
  Women's War (1929) 174, 176–7
nonbinary people 63
Norma, Caroline 150

the paradigmatic woman 165–6
Pateman, Carole 12, 39, 49, 63, 161
  The Sexual Contract 36
patriarchy 85
  and Catholic women 170
  definition of 'woman' 93–5, 96–7
  and feminist epicism 52
  Gatens on 35–6
  and gender-critical feminism 141, 142
  and Marxism 34
  and metaphors of war and invasion 103–4
  and poststructural feminism 49

and radical feminism 145
and sex classes 21–2, 24
and women's allegiance to men 149, 150
Perry, Louise 138
phallicism 117–18
Plaza, Monique 39
political category
  category of woman as 99–100
political kinds, women as 131–3, 134–6, 137
politics
  depolitisation of sex 32
  displacement of the political in feminism 1–3
  feminism as a political movement 1
  political lesbianism 119–21
  political nature of women as a class 1
  political theory and poststructural feminism 52–4
  rape as a political action 20
  and sex classes 7, 12, 17
  the sexual becomes political 5–28
pornography 113–14, 163, 164
postmodernism 86, 87
poststructural feminism 45, 46–59, 112
  and cultural differences 49–50
  and differences between women 82, 85–6
  and the enemy 89–90
  and gender 58–9
  and gender-critical feminism 128, 136
  and political lesbianism 120
  and political theory 52–4
  and power 154
  refusal to define 'woman' 98
  and second-wave feminism 48, 50, 55, 76, 83–4, 88, 113–17
  and sex class 16
  theory and practice 46–7, 55
  and trans women 108
  vision of the future 116–22
  and woman as a disunity 81
  and women choosing women 177

and women's subjection to men 111
  see also Butler, Judith
poststructuralism 1–2, 29–45
  friends and enemies 76–80, 89–90
  and power 32–3, 36–43, 87–8
  and second-wave feminism 44–5, 71
  shift from sex class to gender 29–32
power
  biopower 32, 43, 45
  feminists and male power 41–2
  Foucault's conception of 38–41
  and men as the enemy 35
  and phallicism 117–18
  and poststructural feminism 48, 57
  and the poststructural turn 32–3, 36–43, 86–7
  and rape 115
  and sex classes 12, 32
  and sexual relations 8, 37–9, 41–3, 115–16, 154
  and social science 2
pregnancy
  and gender-critical feminism 138, 139
prisons 63
prostitution 113–14, 147, 165–6, 181

queer community 56–7
queer theory and feminism 77–8

race
  and differences among women 86
  and gender 129
racial justice 160–1, 162
racism
  and women choosing women 171–2
radical feminism 3, 79
Ranke, Leopold von 3
rape
  Brownmiller on 17–20, 134

rape (*cont.*)
  criminalisation of marital rape 42–3
  of enslaved Black women 153–5, 160
  of Indigenous women 172
  MacKinnon on 109–10, 111, 112
  and the male and female body 108–10
  marital rape 116, 166
  and the poststructural turn 39
  and power 115
realism
  and gender-critical feminism 141
Rich, Adrienne 7, 10, 149
Rorty, Richard 59
Rosaldo, Michelle 52
Rowbotham, Sheila 21, 94
Russell, Bertrand
  Power 2

Schmitt, Carl
  The Concept of the Political 88–9, 98–9, 107–8, 110–11
second-wave feminism
  and compulsory heterosexuality 76
  and contemporary feminism 79, 111–12
  criticisms of 47
  critique of sexuality 101
  definition of 'woman' 90–1, 92–5
  description of women's condition 111–12
  epicism of 51–2
  and the future 113, 121–2
  and gender-critical feminism 4, 28, 128
  and hierarchical relationships 180–1
  and the inclusion or liberation of women 63–4, 71
  and the political 6
  and political lesbianism 119–21
  and poststructural feminism 48, 50, 55, 76, 83–4, 88, 113–17
  and the poststructural turn 44–5, 47

  scholarship 82–3
  and sex class 1, 3, 12–20, 24–8, 50–1, 58, 71
  and sexual relations 8–16, 58, 115–16
  and the social 6
  and women choosing women 171–2
  and women as oppressed 81–2, 147–9, 181–2
  and women as unified politically 80
separatism 151–2
sex
  and gender 27, 29–32, 35, 59
    and gender-critical feminism 128–9
  minimal descriptions of 22–3
sex binary
  and gender diversification 77–8
sex class 10–28
  and erotic relations 9
  and gender 29–32, 74
  and gender-critical feminism 16, 69, 132, 135, 136, 139–41, 142–3, 145
  and male victims of rape 109
  and the paradigmatic woman 165–6
  and the poststructuralist turn 44
  and rape 20, 134
  and second-wave feminism 1, 3, 12–20, 24–8, 50–1, 64, 71, 131
    definition of 'woman' 91, 92, 100
  and sex 21–8
  and sexuality 15–16
  and trans women 69–70, 108
  women as a sex class 1, 3, 6, 7, 10–16, 74, 79, 158
  women and victimisation 77
sex realism
  and gender-critical feminism 135–6
sex segregation 27–8, 63, 124, 125–6
sexism 79

sexless society 24–6
sexual harassment 158
sexual relations
  and the female person 101–2
  and gender-critical feminism 123, 138–9
  mastery and subjection in 41–3, 94, 115, 147
  and the paradigmatic woman 166
  power in 8, 37–9, 41–3, 115–16, 154
  and sex classes 7–10, 28
  and women's oppression 148
sexual reproduction
  and the 'female person' 101
  and gender-critical feminism 138–9
  and rape 18–20
  and sex classes 22
sexual violence 147
  and gender-critical feminism 124, 126
  see also rape
sexuality
  and inclusion 63
  second-wave critique of 101
  and sex classes 15–16, 16–17
slavery
  abolitionism 159–60, 163, 164
  Black men 159–60
  Black women 152–5
  and second-wave feminism 181
Smith, Victoria 150
Smyth, Ailbhe 122
the social
  and the displacement of the political 1–3
social construction, sex as 5–6, 27–8
social kinds
  and gender-critical feminism 130, 131
socialist feminism 44, 145
sport
  and gender-critical feminism 124, 125
  and the inclusion project 63

Stern, Lesley 46
Stock, Kathleen 22, 23, 24, 28, 126, 128–9, 150
structuralism
  and poststructuralism 43–4
suffragettes 174, 176

Thomas, Clarence 175
trans women 149, 178
  and the class 'woman' 69–70
  and gender-critical feminism 66, 108–9, 110–11, 123–4, 128, 142–4
  inclusion of 63, 65–7
  and the performance of femininity 118
  and the political definition of 'woman' 92, 95
  and poststructural feminism 108
  and trans-inclusionary feminism 108–9
trans-exclusionary feminists 67, 71, 72
  and the meaning of 'woman' 92, 108
  see also gender-critical feminists
trans-inclusionary feminism 3–4, 6, 65–6, 69
  concept of woman 1, 95
  and gender-critical feminism 72, 123–5, 143
  as intersectional 146–7
  and rape 108–10
  and trans women 108–9, 110–11
transexuality
  and inclusion 62
transgendered bodies 56, 57, 133
transphobia 66
transsexual bodies 56
Truth, Sojourner 165

wages for housework 156–8
Walker, Alice
  'Coming Apart' 50, 163–4
war metaphor 103–6
Weber, Max 19
Weinstein, Leo 148
Willis, Ellen 80

Wittig, Monique 7, 25–7, 51, 75–6, 99, 149
  'One Is Not Born a Woman' 25–7, 76
Wolin, Sheldon 2, 53, 55
  'On Reading Marx Politically' 54
Wollstonecraft, Mary 5, 41
woman
  as an essence 81
  defining 39–40
    Butler's refusal to define 'woman' 90–9
    feminist attempts to define 'woman' 97–9
    political definition of 91
  and feminism 85
  and gender-critical feminism 129–30
  as a political category 7
  as the social category of gender 101
women
  oppression of 71, 79, 147–9
  putting women first 79–80
  as a sex class 1, 3, 6, 7, 10–16, 74, 80
  and the sex–gender distinction 30
  shift from 'women' to 'gender' 85
women choosing women 145–78
  and gender-critical feminism 146
  housewives 155–9
  and other oppressed groups 164–5
  and radical feminism 145–6
  and separatism 151–2
  and trans-inclusionary feminism 147

women of colour 71, 78
  and feminist factionalisation 97
women *qua* women
  and the female sex class 74
  and feminism 6
  and gender-critical feminism 123
  inclusion of 62–4
  and poststructural feminism 98
  and radical feminism 145
  and second-wave feminism 181–2
  and sexual relations 7–8, 9
  as victims 77
women-only spaces 27–8, 63, 124, 125–6, 142
women's bodies 101–4
women's liberation 79, 178
  choosing women 147
  and equality and difference feminism 68
  and exclusion 93
  and gender inclusion 60, 63–4, 66, 67, 75
  and gender-critical feminism 130–1
  and second-wave feminism 112, 127
women's studies 82–3, 85
work
  enslaved Black women 152–3
  unpaid work and housewives 155–9
  women and work 152
workers
  and hierarchical relationships 180, 181
  rights of 157–9
working-class women 71, 78